MARVEL COMICS PROUDLY PRESENTS

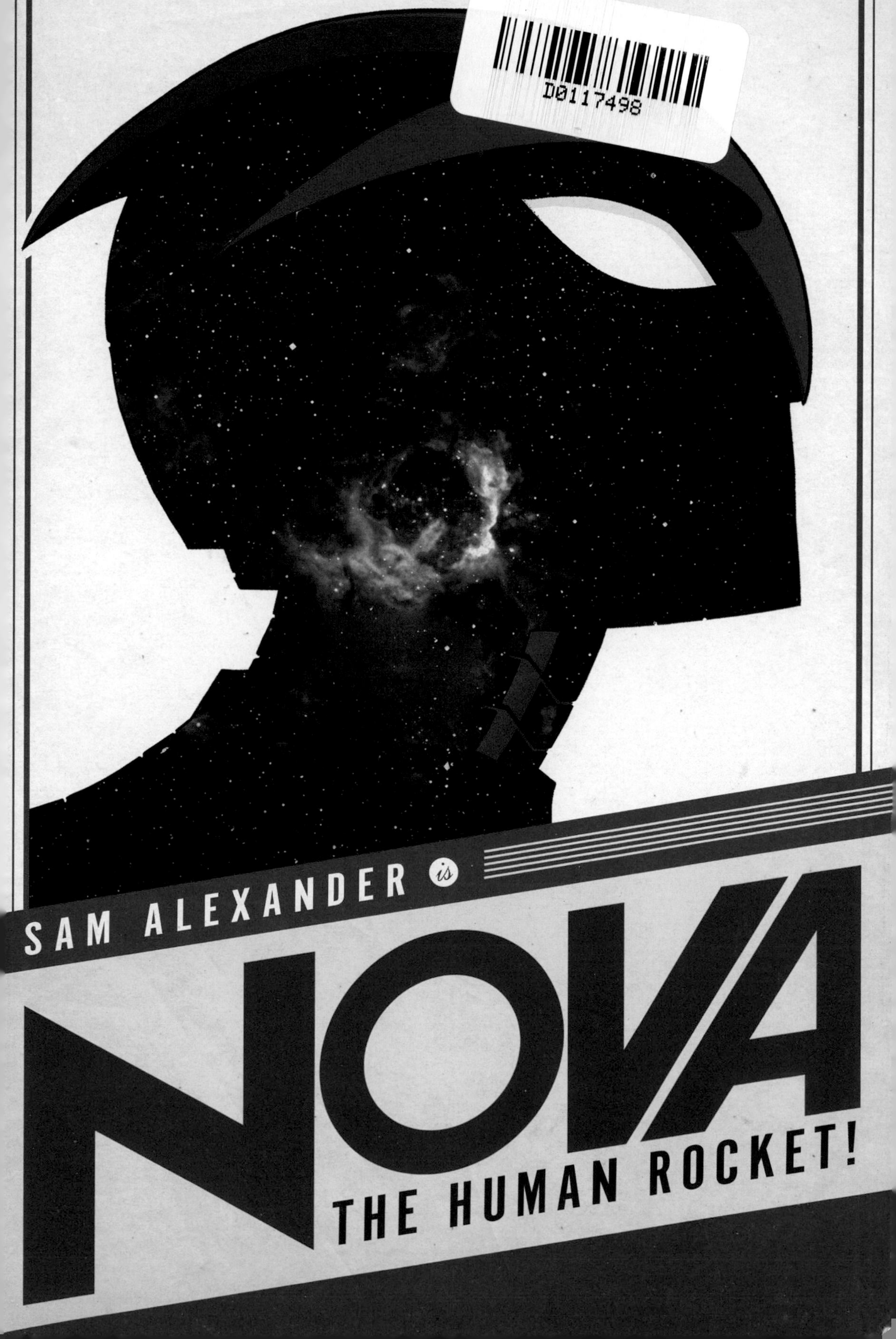

SAM ALEXANDER *is*

NOVA

THE HUMAN ROCKET!

ALEX STARBUCK
COLLECTION EDITOR

SARAH BRUNSTAD
ASSOCIATE EDITOR

JENNIFER GRÜNWALD & MARK D. BEAZLEY
EDITORS, SPECIAL PROJECTS

JEFF YOUNGQUIST
VP, PRODUCTION & SPECIAL PROJECTS

DAVID GABRIEL
SVP PRINT, SALES & MARKETING

ADAM DEL RE
BOOK DESIGNER

AXEL ALONSO
EDITOR IN CHIE

JOE QUESADA
CHIEF CREATIVE OFFICER

DAN BUCKLEY
PUBLISHER

ALAN FINE
EXECUTIVE PRODUCER

NOVA: THE HUMAN ROCKET VOL. 1 - BURN OUT. Contains material originally published in magazine form as NOVA #1-6. First printing 2016. ISBN# 978-0-7851-9650-1. Published by MARVEL WORLDWIDE, INC., a subsidiary of MARVEL ENTERTAINMENT, LLC. OFFICE OF PUBLICATION: 135 West 50th Street, New York, NY 10020. Copyright © 2016 MARVEL No similarity between any of the names, characters, persons, and/or institutions in this magazine with those of any living or dead person or institution is intended, and any such similarity which may exist is purely coincidental. **Printed in Canada.** ALAN FINE, President, Marvel Entertainment; DAN BUCKLEY, President, TV, Publishing & Brand Management; JOE QUESADA, Chief Creative Officer; TOM BREVOORT, SVP of Publishing; DAVID BOGART, SVP of Business Affairs & Operations, Publishing & Partnership; C.B. CEBULSKI, VP of Brand Management & Development, Asia; DAVID GABRIEL, SVP of Sales & Marketing, Publishing; JEFF YOUNGQUIST, VP of Production & Special Projects; DAN CARR, Executive Director of Publishing Technology; ALEX MORALES, Director of Publishing Operations; SUSAN CRESPI, Production Manager; STAN LEE, Chairman Emeritus. For information regarding advertising in Marvel Comics or on Marvel.com, please contact Vit DeBellis, Integrated Sales Manager, at vdebellis@marvel.com. For Marvel subscription inquiries, please call 888-511-5480. **Manufactured between 4/15/2016 and 5/23/2016 by SOLISCO PRINTERS, SCOTT, QC, CANADA.**

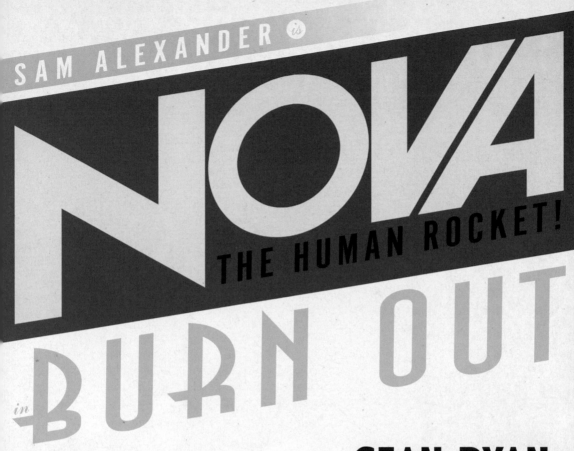

SAM ALEXANDER *is*

NOVA
THE HUMAN ROCKET!

in BURN OUT

SEAN RYAN
WRITER

CORY SMITH
WITH **SCOTT HANNA** (INKS, No. 5)
ARTISTS

DAVID CURIEL (Nos. 1-2, 4-6) &
ANDRES MOSSA (No. 3)
COLOR ARTISTS

COMICRAFT'S
ALBERT DESCHESNE
LETTERER

HUMBERTO RAMOS &
EDGAR DELGADO
COVER ART

WITHDRAWN

DEVIN LEWIS
EDITOR

NICK LOWE
SENIOR EDITOR

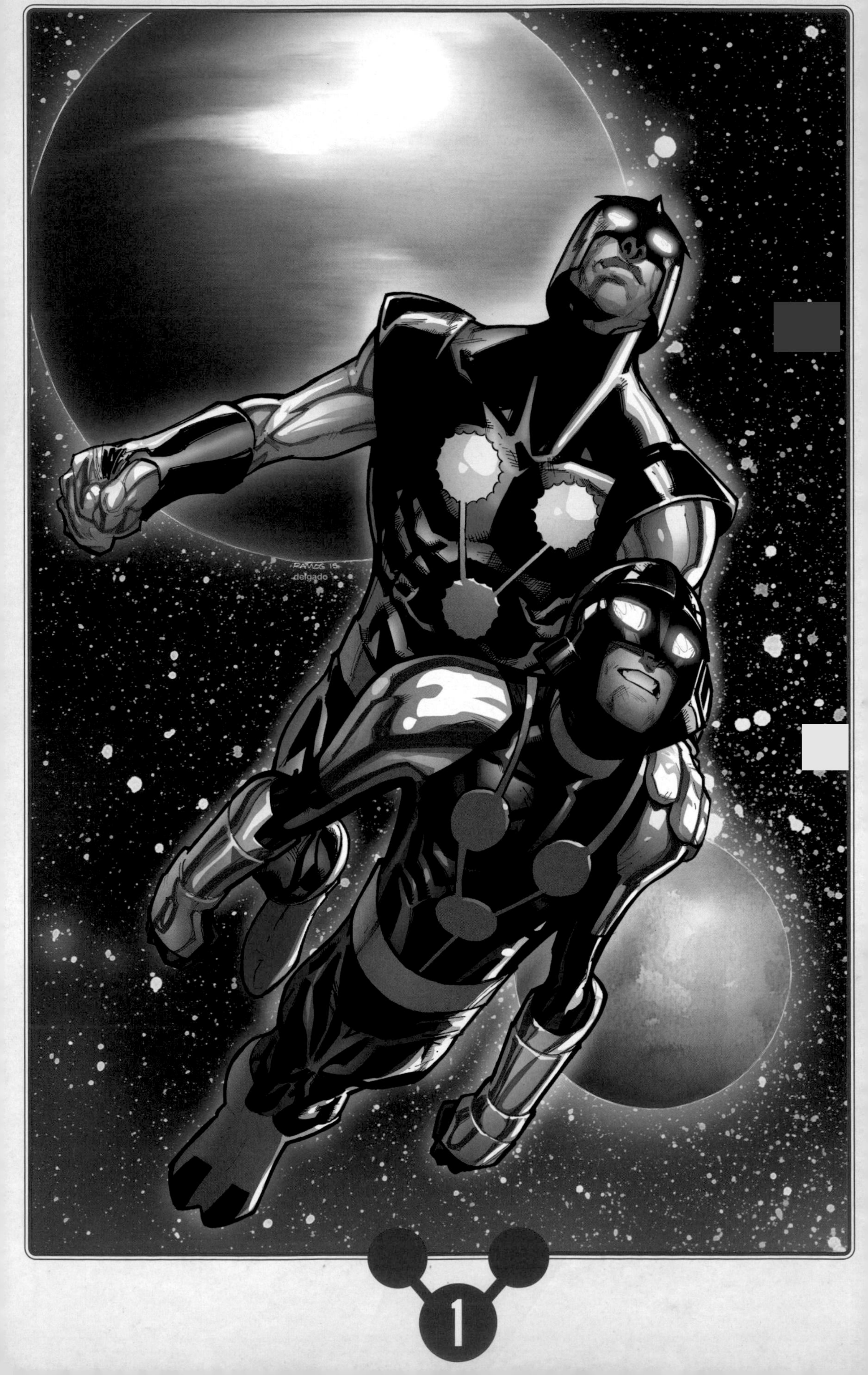
RAMOS 15
delgado

1

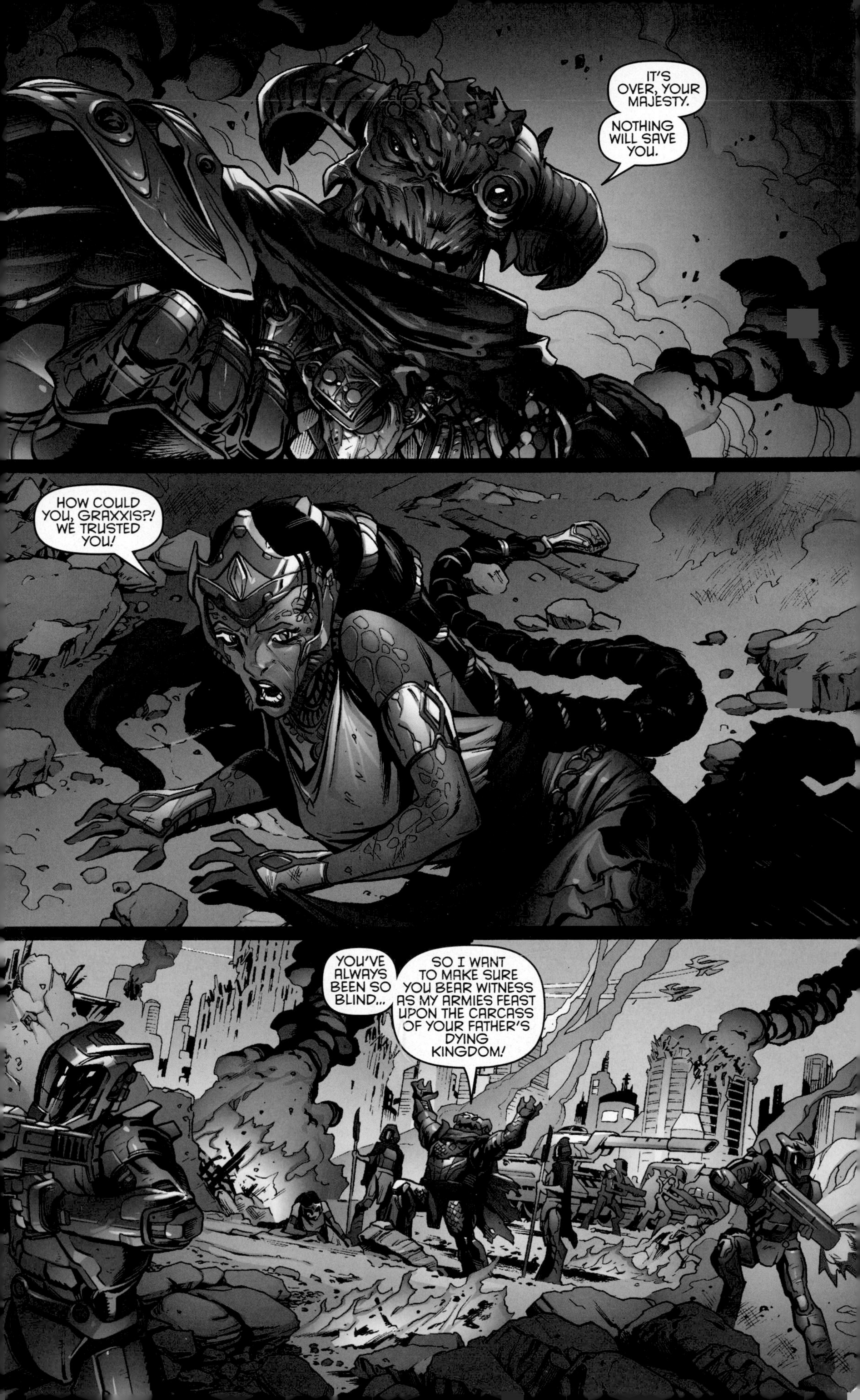
IT'S OVER, YOUR MAJESTY.
NOTHING WILL SAVE YOU.
HOW COULD YOU, GRAXXIS?! WE TRUSTED YOU!
YOU'VE ALWAYS BEEN SO BLIND...
SO I WANT TO MAKE SURE YOU BEAR WITNESS AS MY ARMIES FEAST UPON THE CARCASS OF YOUR FATHER'S DYING KINGDOM!

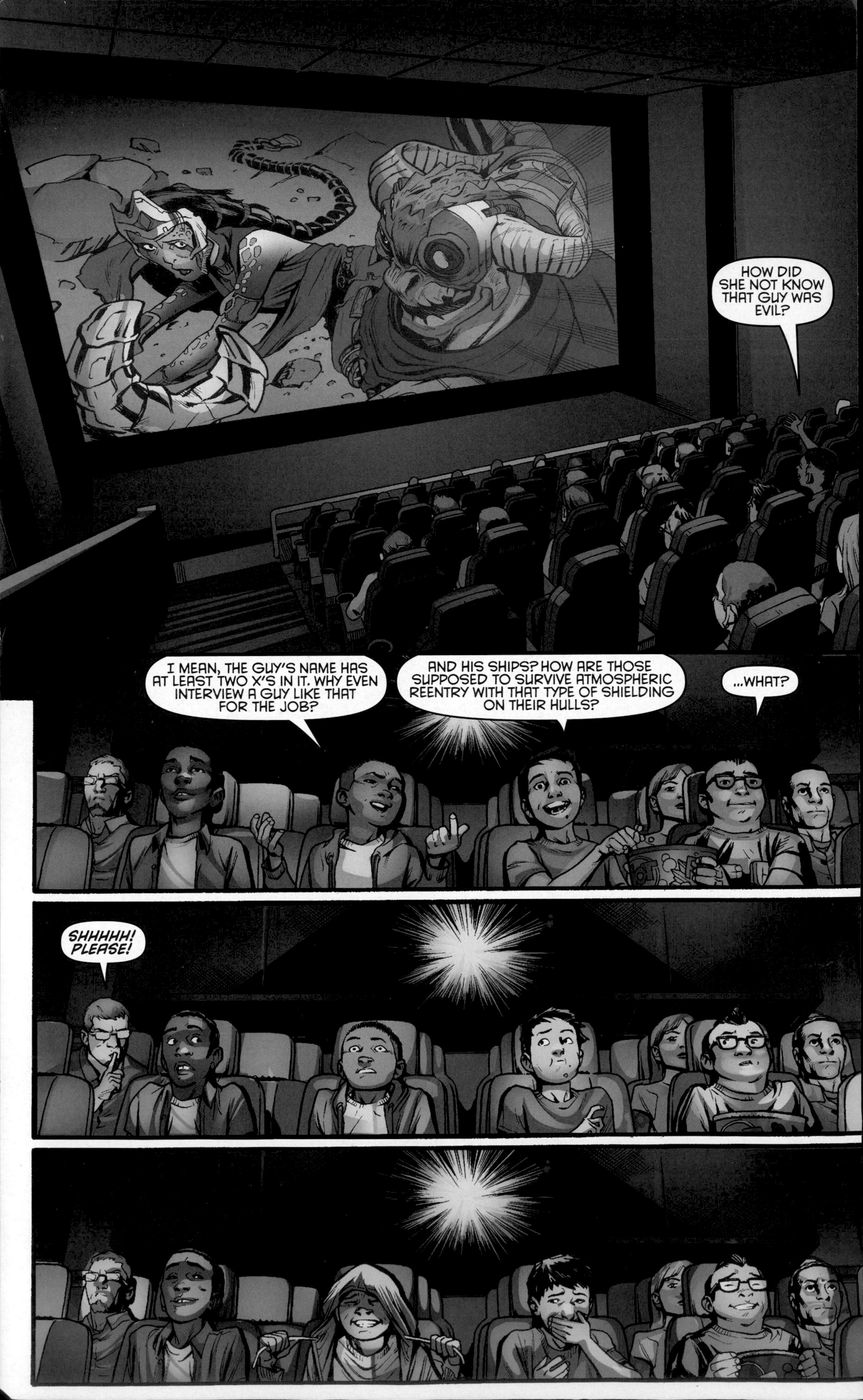
HOW DID SHE NOT KNOW THAT GUY WAS EVIL?
I MEAN, THE GUY'S NAME HAS AT LEAST TWO X'S IN IT. WHY EVEN INTERVIEW A GUY LIKE THAT FOR THE JOB?
AND HIS SHIPS? HOW ARE THOSE SUPPOSED TO SURVIVE ATMOSPHERIC REENTRY WITH THAT TYPE OF SHIELDING ON THEIR HULLS?
...WHAT?
SHHHHH! PLEASE!

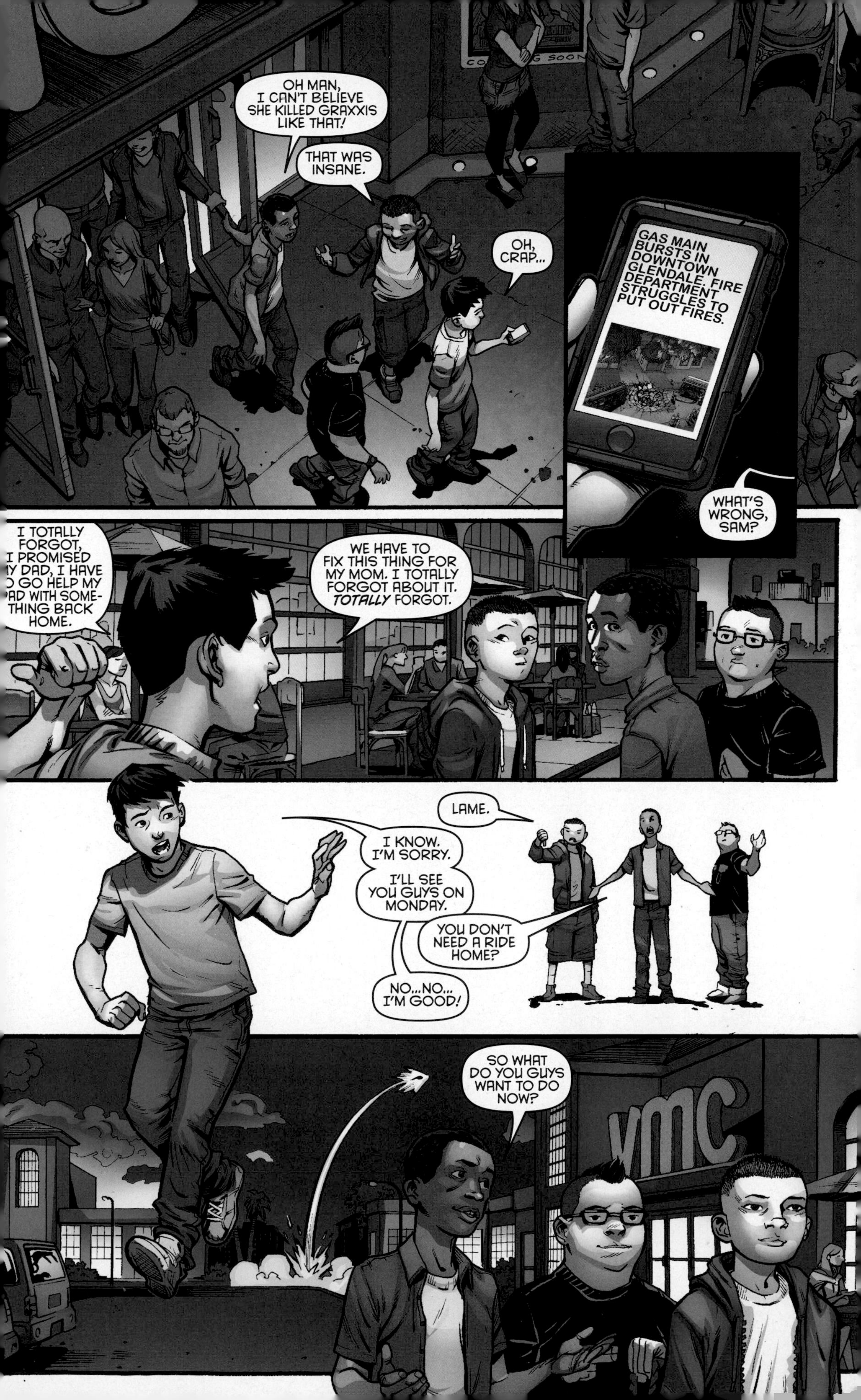
COMING SOON
OH MAN, I CAN'T BELIEVE SHE KILLED GRAXXIS LIKE THAT!
THAT WAS INSANE.
OH, CRAP...
GAS MAIN BURSTS IN DOWNTOWN GLENDALE. FIRE DEPARTMENT STRUGGLES TO PUT OUT FIRES.
WHAT'S WRONG, SAM?
I TOTALLY FORGOT, I PROMISED MY DAD, I HAVE TO GO HELP MY DAD WITH SOMETHING BACK HOME.
WE HAVE TO FIX THIS THING FOR MY MOM. I TOTALLY FORGOT ABOUT IT. *TOTALLY* FORGOT.
LAME.
I KNOW. I'M SORRY.
I'LL SEE YOU GUYS ON MONDAY.
YOU DON'T NEED A RIDE HOME?
NO...NO... I'M GOOD!
SO WHAT DO YOU GUYS WANT TO DO NOW?
VMC

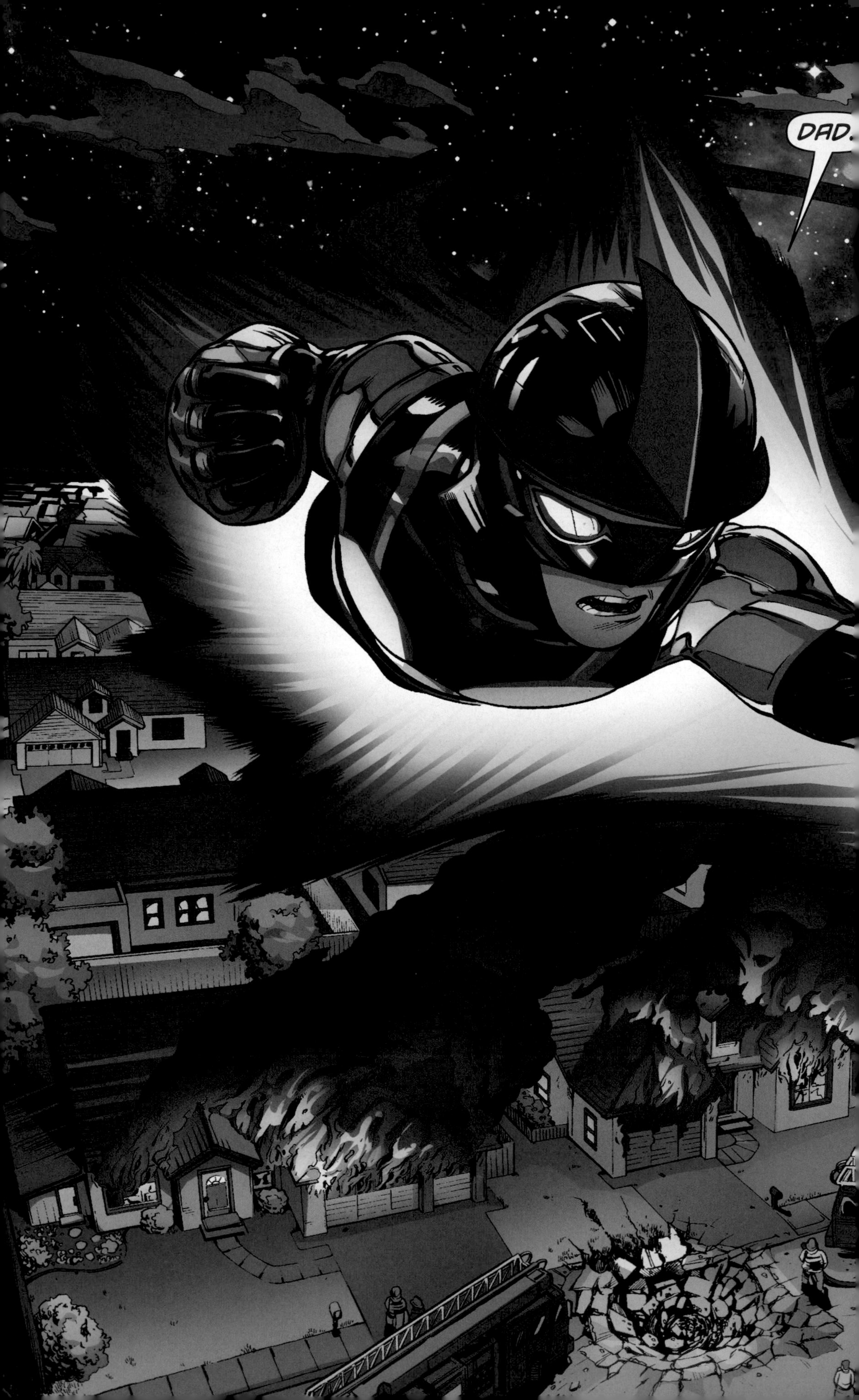
DAD.

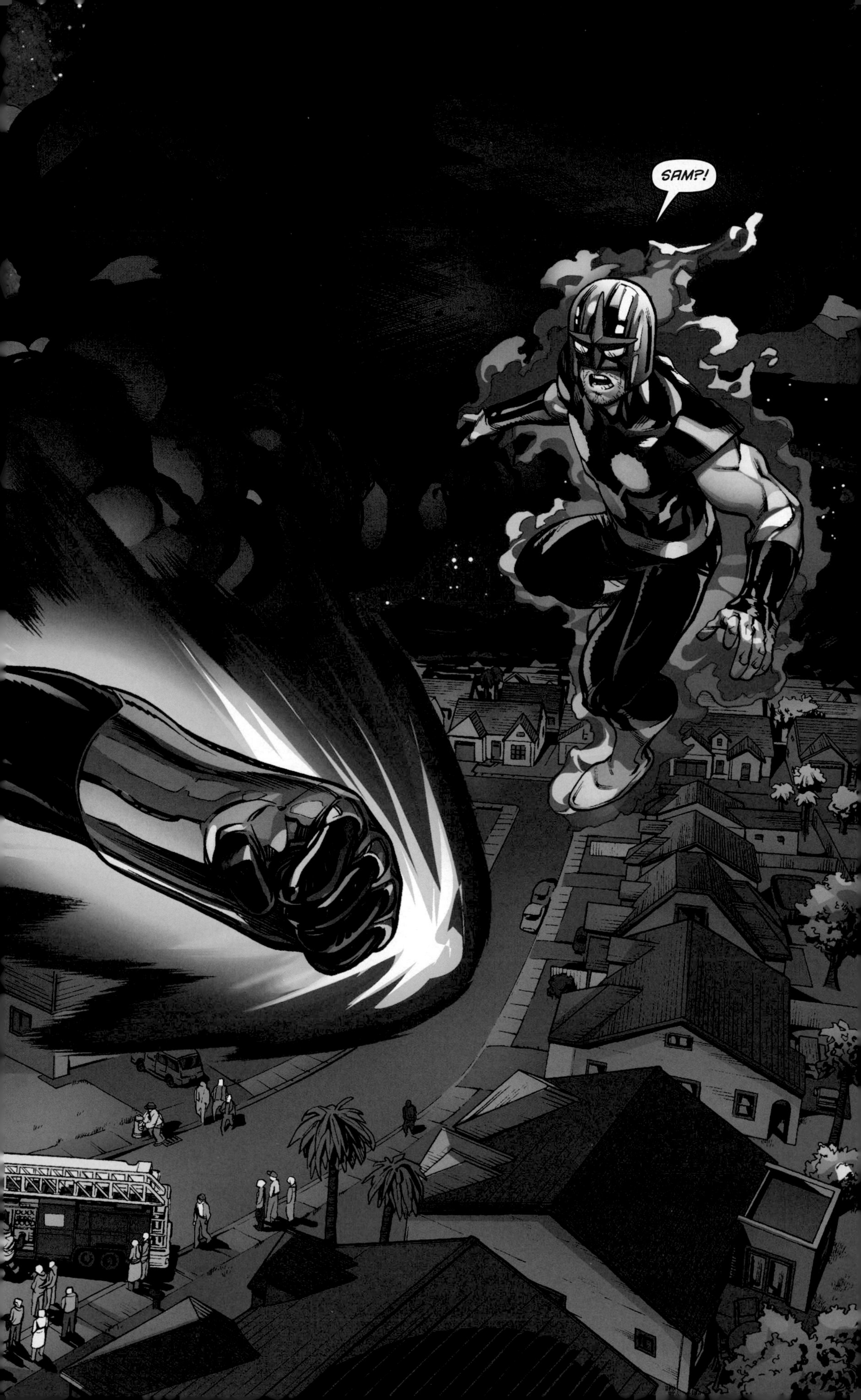
SAM?!

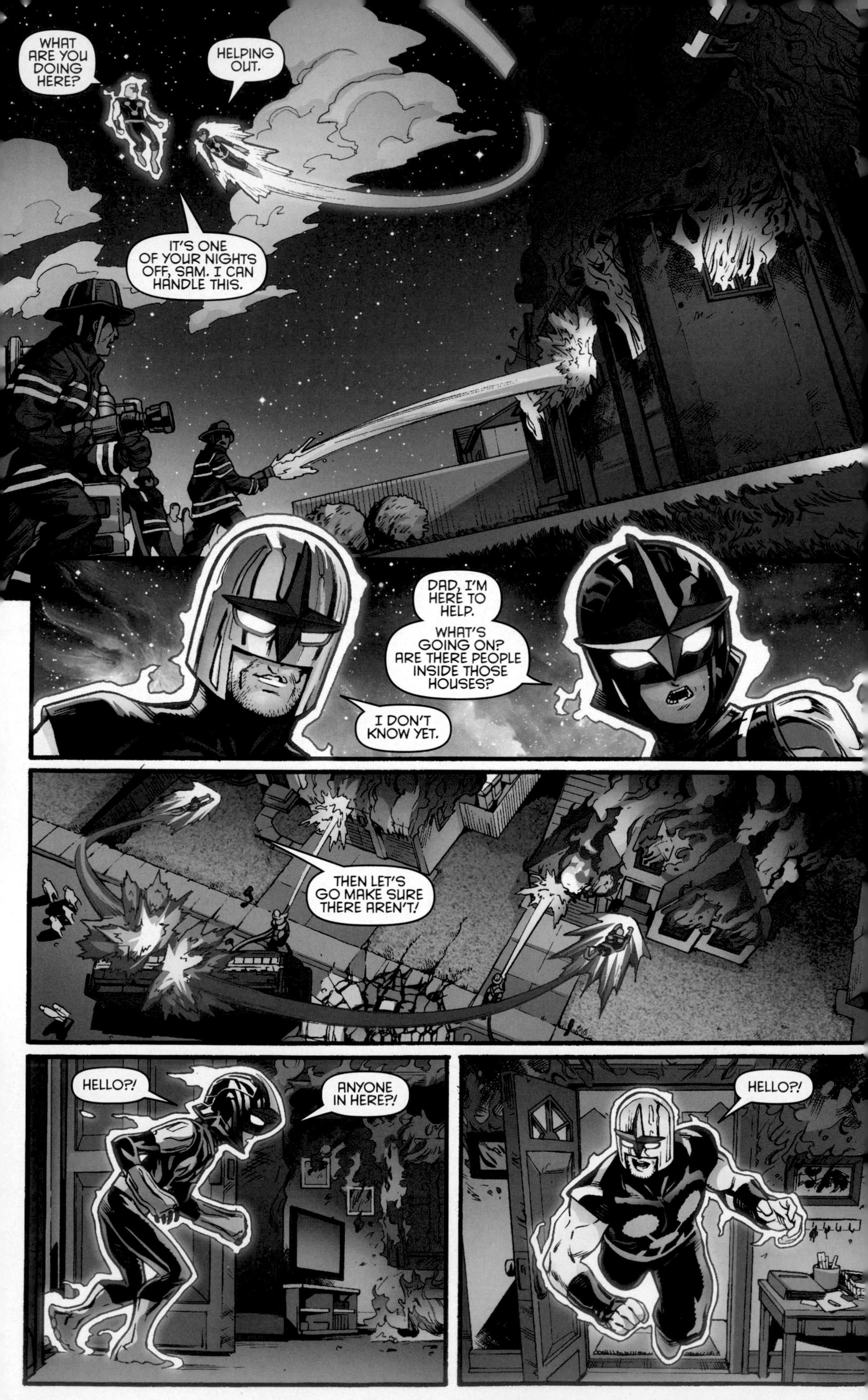
WHAT ARE YOU DOING HERE?
HELPING OUT.
IT'S ONE OF YOUR NIGHTS OFF, SAM. I CAN HANDLE THIS.
DAD, I'M HERE TO HELP.
WHAT'S GOING ON? ARE THERE PEOPLE INSIDE THOSE HOUSES?
I DON'T KNOW YET.
THEN LET'S GO MAKE SURE THERE AREN'T!
HELLO?!
ANYONE IN HERE?!
HELLO?!

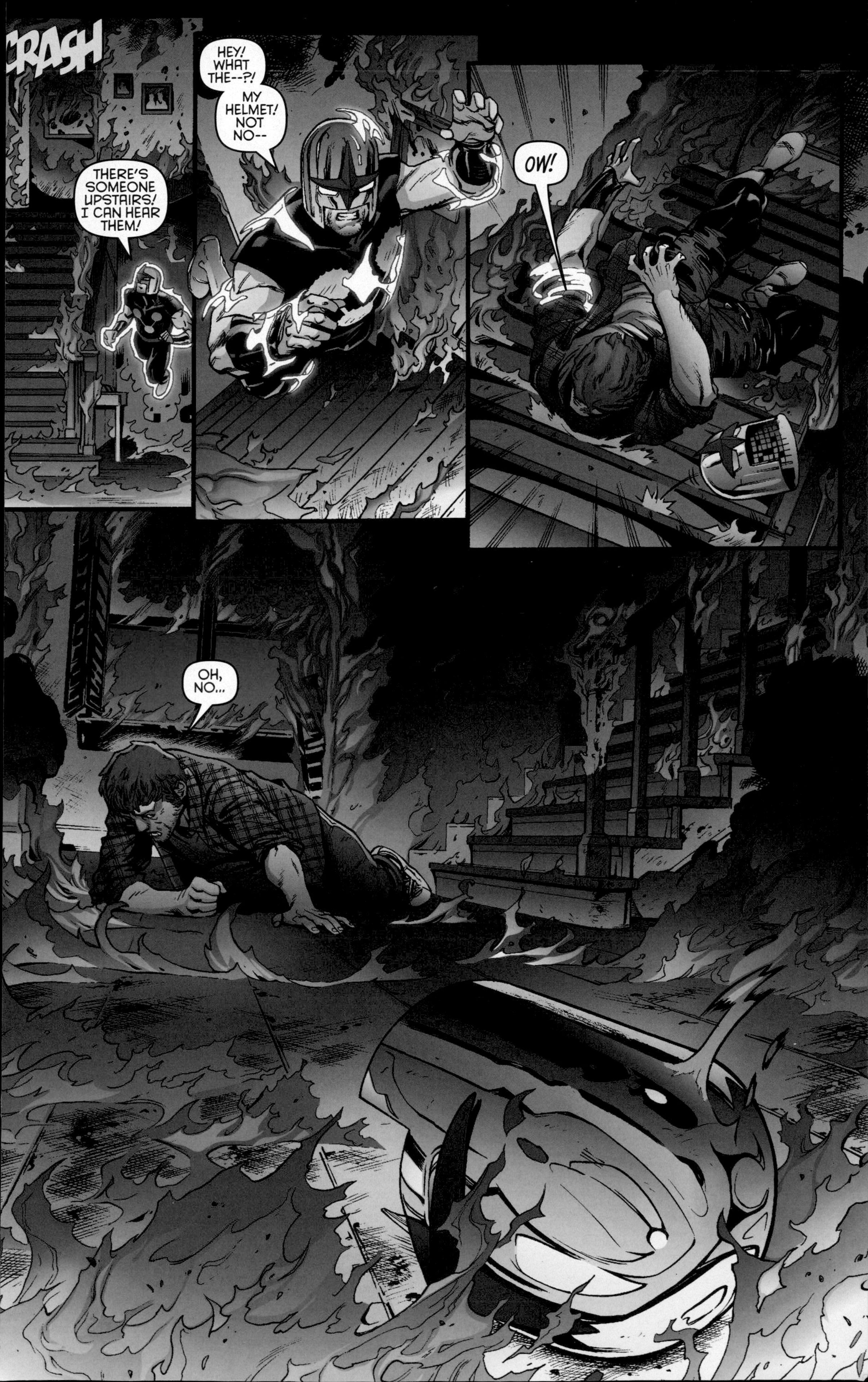
CRASH
THERE'S SOMEONE UPSTAIRS! I CAN HEAR THEM!
HEY! WHAT THE--?!
MY HELMET! NOT NO--
OW!
OH, NO...

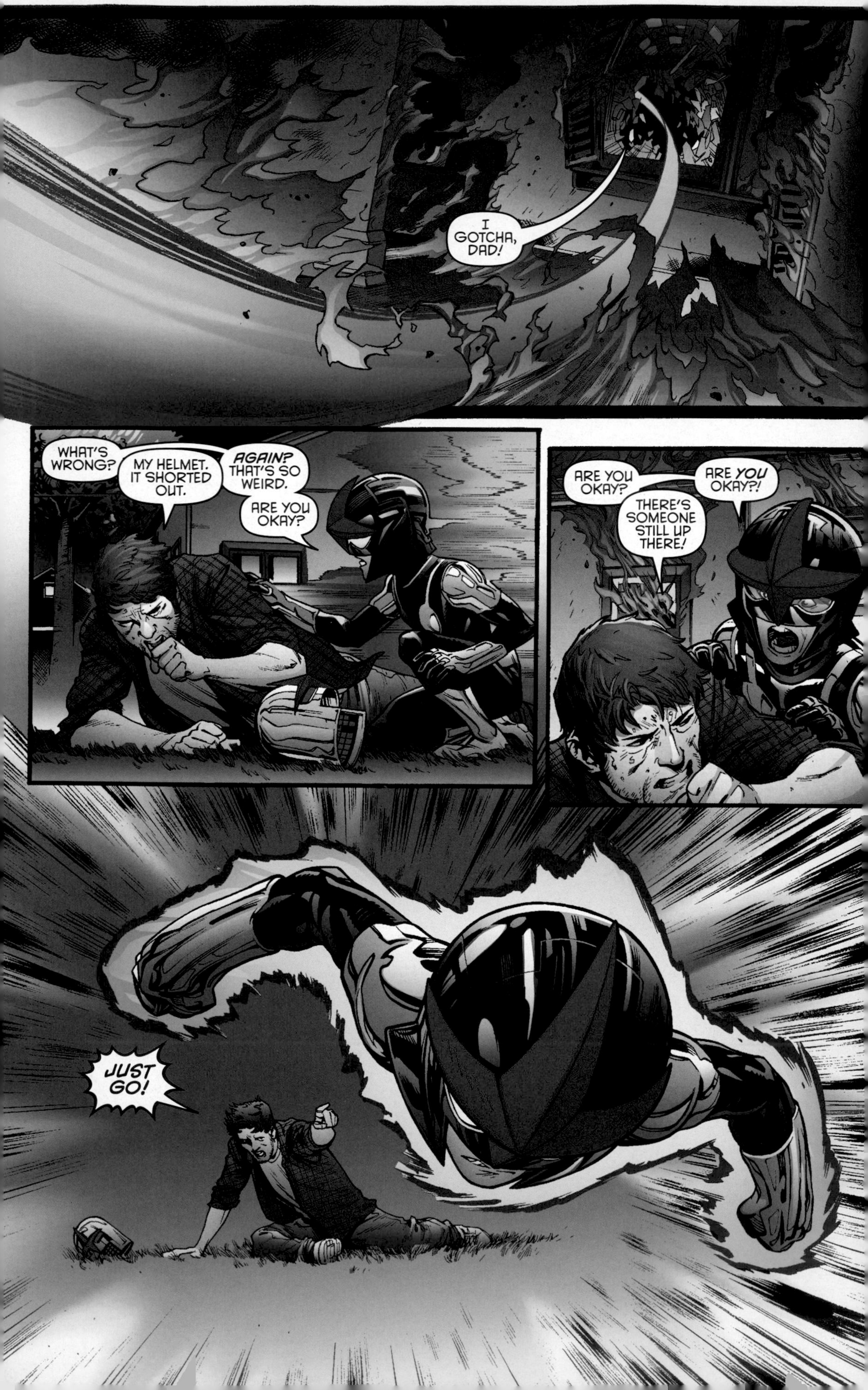
I GOTCHA, DAD!
WHAT'S WRONG?
MY HELMET. IT SHORTED OUT.
AGAIN? THAT'S SO WEIRD.
ARE YOU OKAY?
ARE YOU OKAY?
ARE YOU OKAY?!
THERE'S SOMEONE STILL UP THERE!
JUST GO!

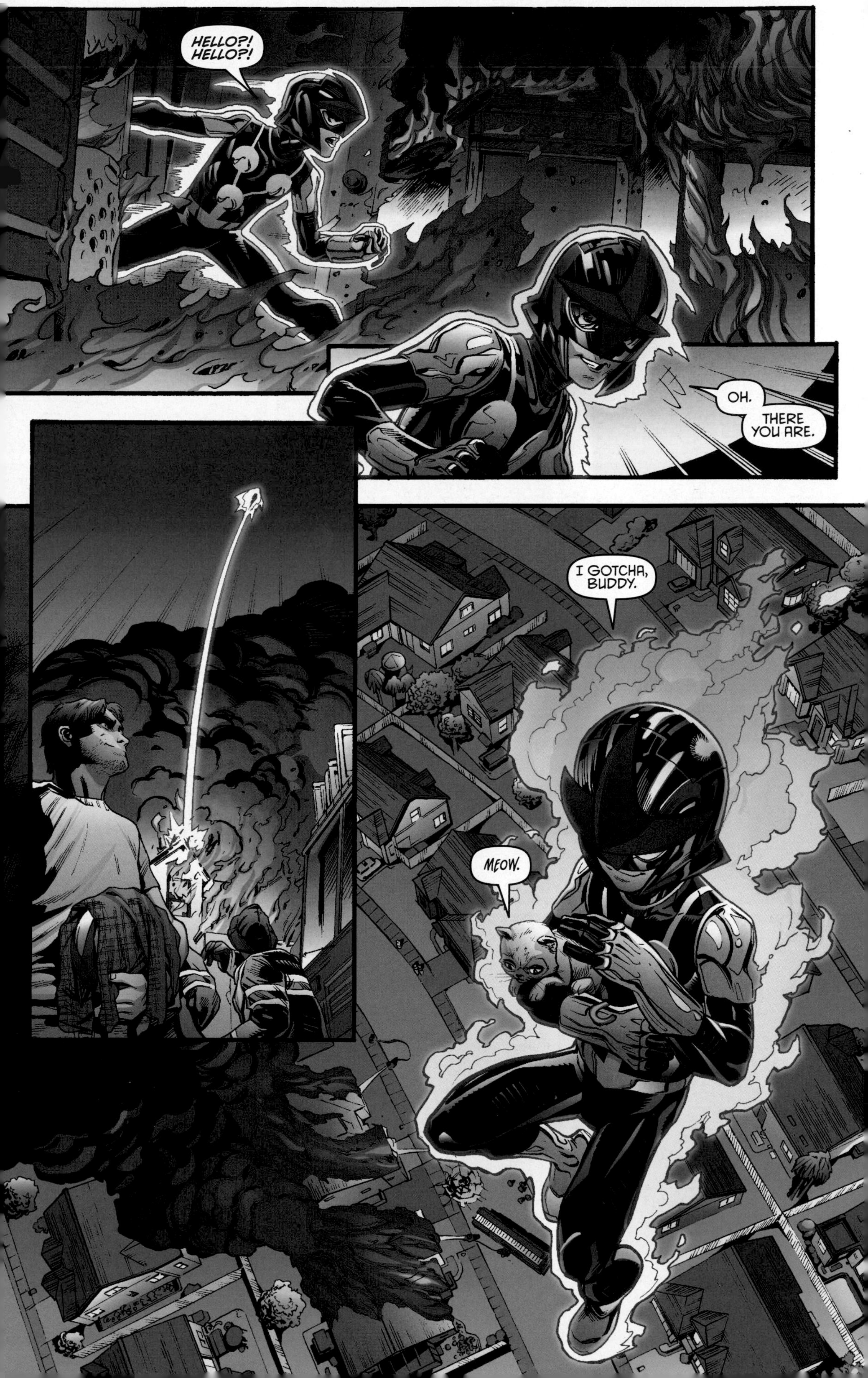
HELLO?! HELLO?!
OH.
THERE YOU ARE.
I GOTCHA, BUDDY.
MEOW.

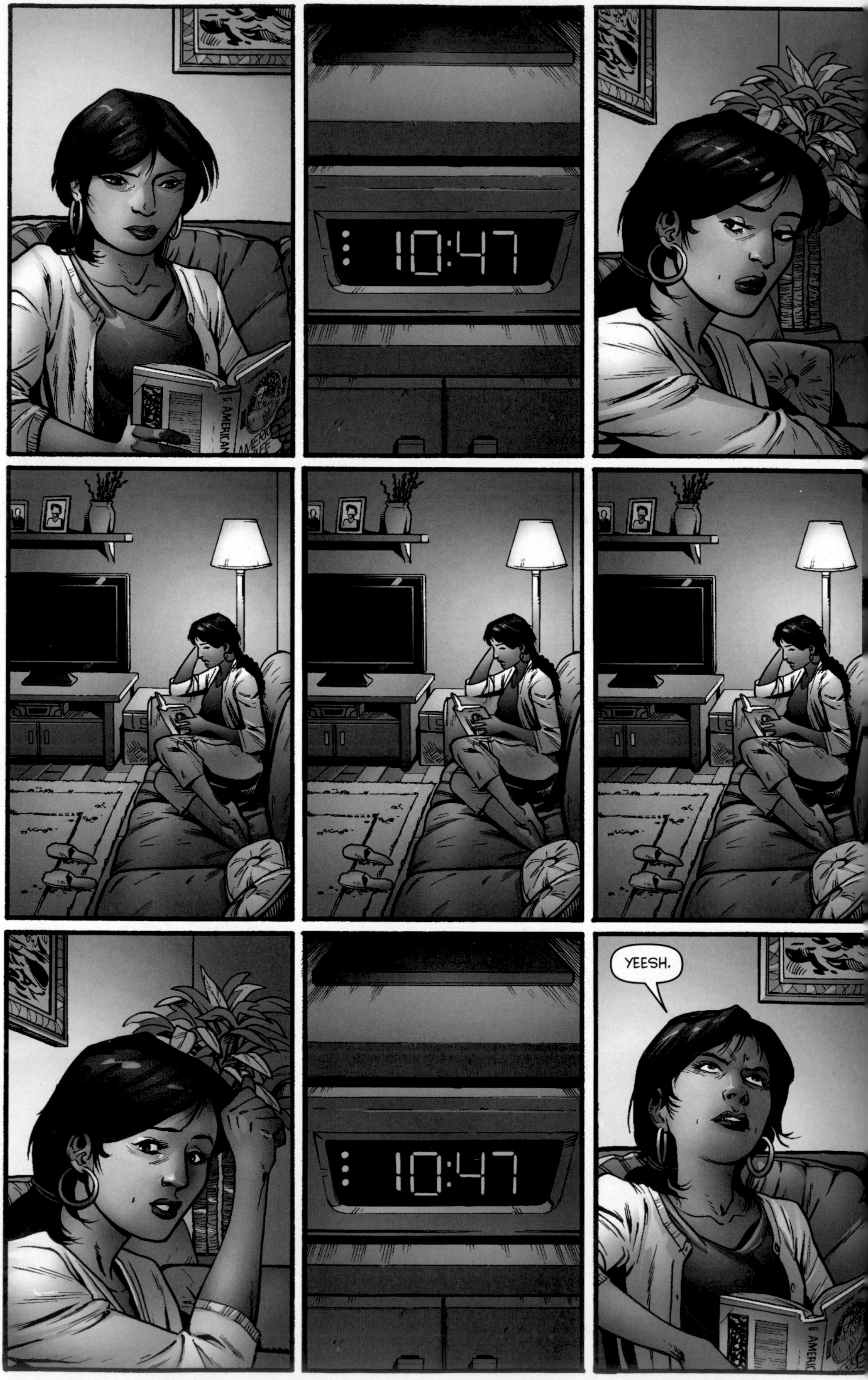
AMERICAN
10:47
10:47
YEESH.

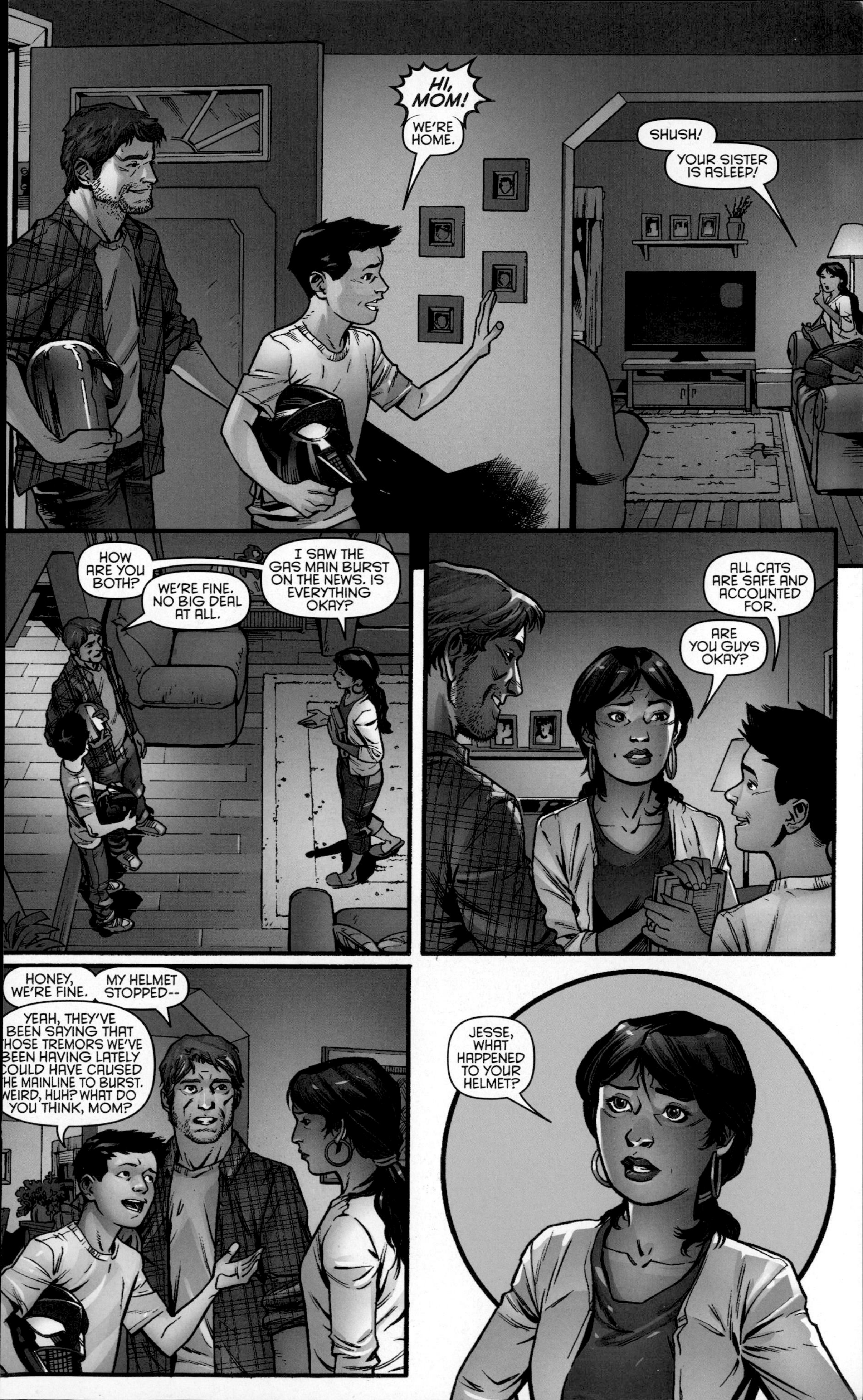
HI, MOM!
WE'RE HOME.
SHUSH!
YOUR SISTER IS ASLEEP!
HOW ARE YOU BOTH?
I SAW THE GAS MAIN BURST ON THE NEWS. IS EVERYTHING OKAY?
WE'RE FINE. NO BIG DEAL AT ALL.
ALL CATS ARE SAFE AND ACCOUNTED FOR.
ARE YOU GUYS OKAY?
HONEY, WE'RE FINE.
MY HELMET STOPPED--
YEAH, THEY'VE BEEN SAYING THAT THOSE TREMORS WE'VE BEEN HAVING LATELY COULD HAVE CAUSED THE MAINLINE TO BURST. WEIRD, HUH? WHAT DO YOU THINK, MOM?
JESSE, WHAT HAPPENED TO YOUR HELMET?

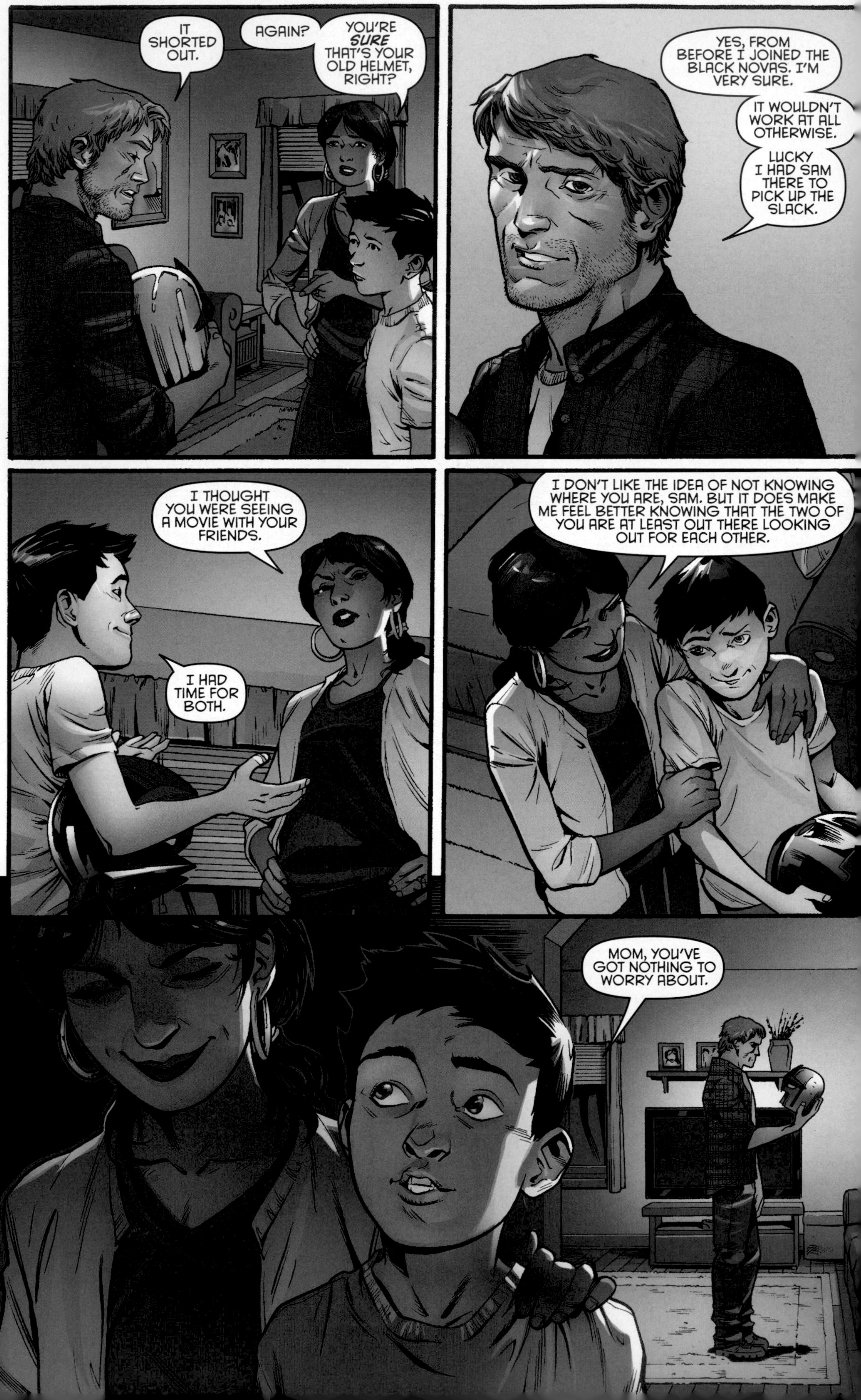
IT SHORTED OUT.
AGAIN?
YOU'RE SURE THAT'S YOUR OLD HELMET, RIGHT?
YES, FROM BEFORE I JOINED THE BLACK NOVAS. I'M VERY SURE.
IT WOULDN'T WORK AT ALL OTHERWISE.
LUCKY I HAD SAM THERE TO PICK UP THE SLACK.
I THOUGHT YOU WERE SEEING A MOVIE WITH YOUR FRIENDS.
I HAD TIME FOR BOTH.
I DON'T LIKE THE IDEA OF NOT KNOWING WHERE YOU ARE, SAM. BUT IT DOES MAKE ME FEEL BETTER KNOWING THAT THE TWO OF YOU ARE AT LEAST OUT THERE LOOKING OUT FOR EACH OTHER.
MOM, YOU'VE GOT NOTHING TO WORRY ABOUT.

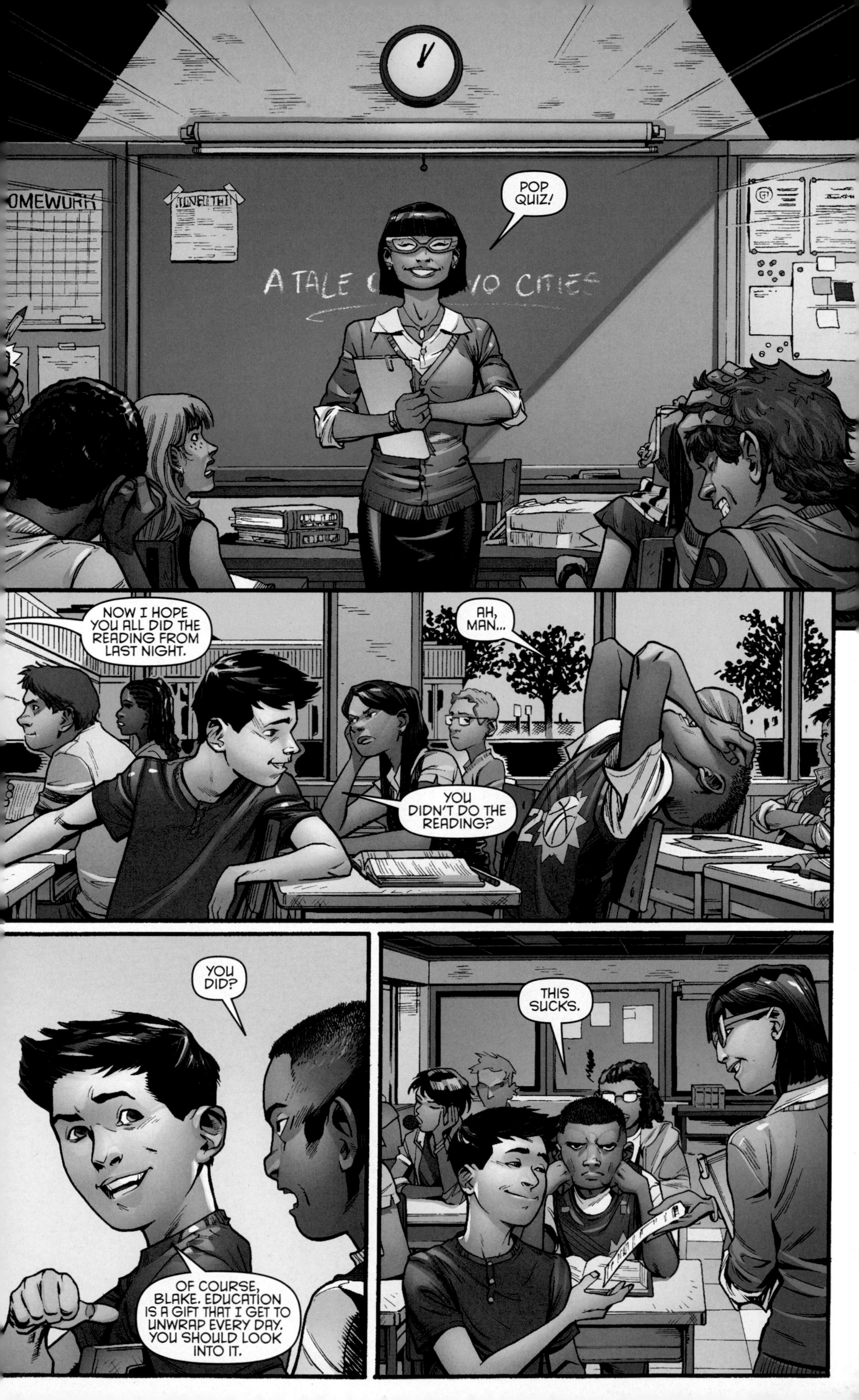
A TALE O WO CITIES
POP QUIZ!
NOW I HOPE YOU ALL DID THE READING FROM LAST NIGHT.
AH, MAN...
YOU DIDN'T DO THE READING?
YOU DID?
OF COURSE, BLAKE. EDUCATION IS A GIFT THAT I GET TO UNWRAP EVERY DAY. YOU SHOULD LOOK INTO IT.
THIS SUCKS.

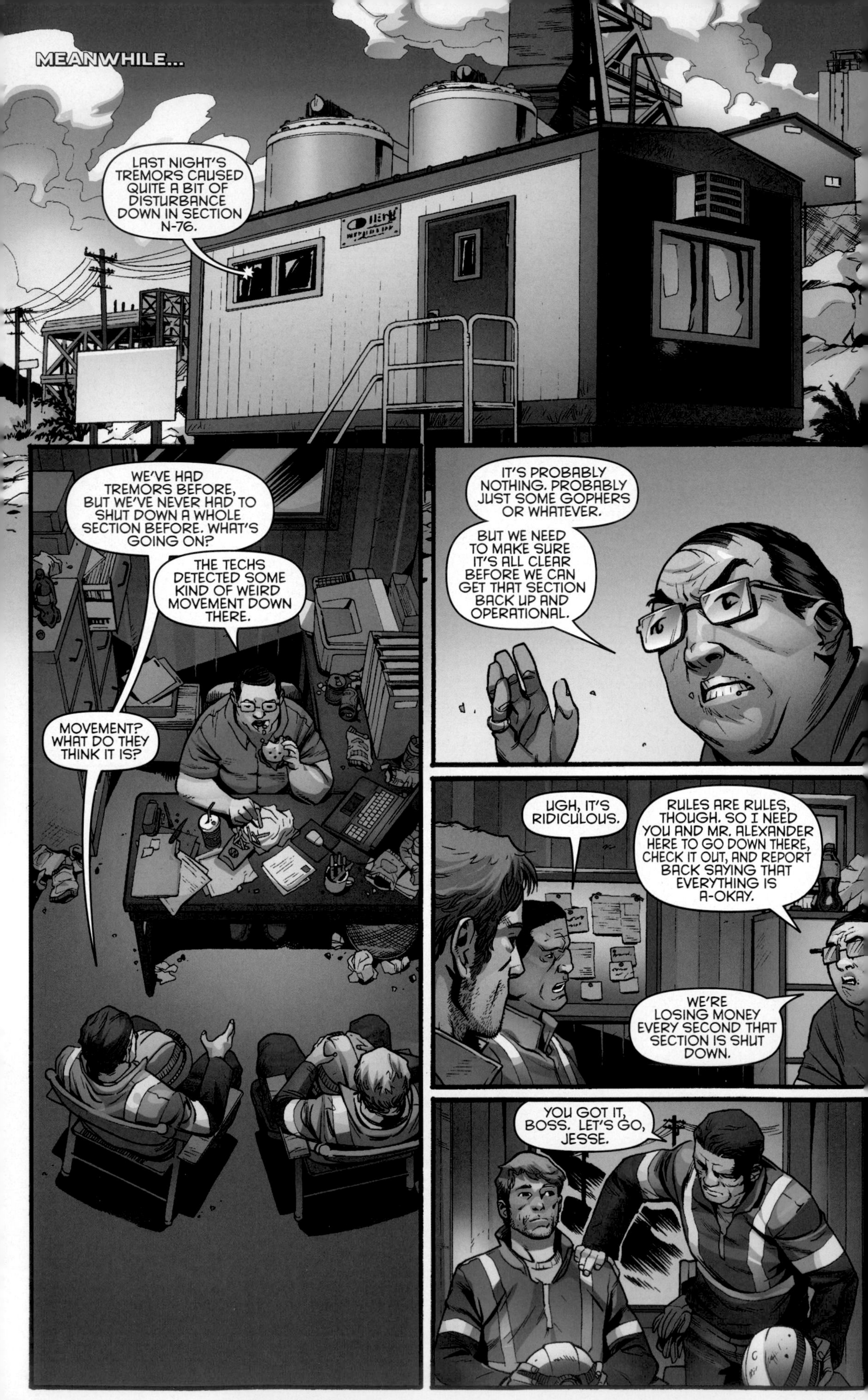
MEANWHILE...
LAST NIGHT'S TREMORS CAUSED QUITE A BIT OF DISTURBANCE DOWN IN SECTION N-76.
WE'VE HAD TREMORS BEFORE, BUT WE'VE NEVER HAD TO SHUT DOWN A WHOLE SECTION BEFORE. WHAT'S GOING ON?
THE TECHS DETECTED SOME KIND OF WEIRD MOVEMENT DOWN THERE.
MOVEMENT? WHAT DO THEY THINK IT IS?
IT'S PROBABLY NOTHING. PROBABLY JUST SOME GOPHERS OR WHATEVER.
BUT WE NEED TO MAKE SURE IT'S ALL CLEAR BEFORE WE CAN GET THAT SECTION BACK UP AND OPERATIONAL.
UGH, IT'S RIDICULOUS.
RULES ARE RULES, THOUGH. SO I NEED YOU AND MR. ALEXANDER HERE TO GO DOWN THERE, CHECK IT OUT, AND REPORT BACK SAYING THAT EVERYTHING IS A-OKAY.
WE'RE LOSING MONEY EVERY SECOND THAT SECTION IS SHUT DOWN.
YOU GOT IT, BOSS. LET'S GO, JESSE.

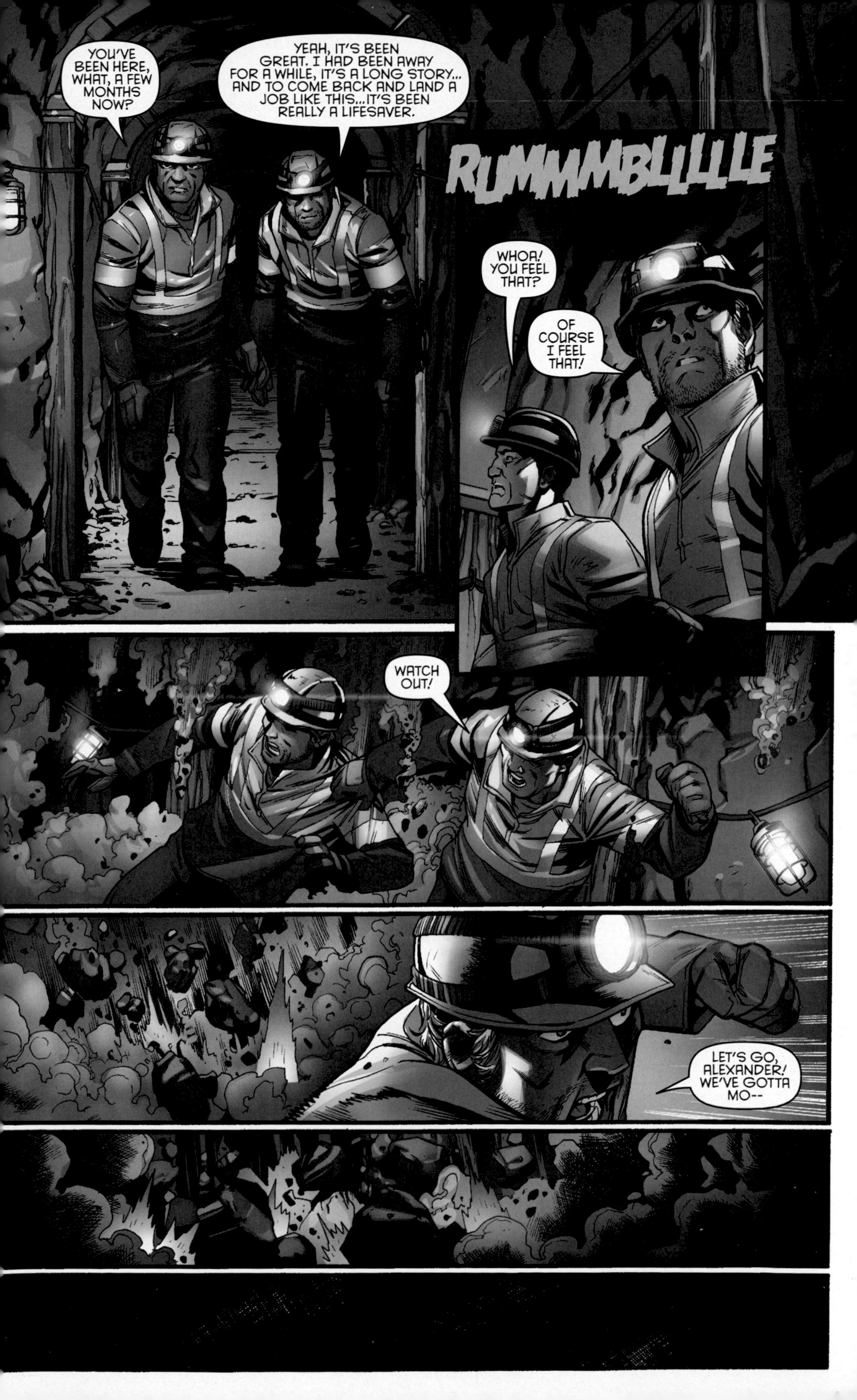
YOU'VE BEEN HERE, WHAT, A FEW MONTHS NOW?
YEAH, IT'S BEEN GREAT. I HAD BEEN AWAY FOR A WHILE, IT'S A LONG STORY... AND TO COME BACK AND LAND A JOB LIKE THIS...IT'S BEEN REALLY A LIFESAVER.
RUMMMBLLLLLE
WHOA! YOU FEEL THAT?
OF COURSE I FEEL THAT!
WATCH OUT!
LET'S GO, ALEXANDER! WE'VE GOTTA MO--

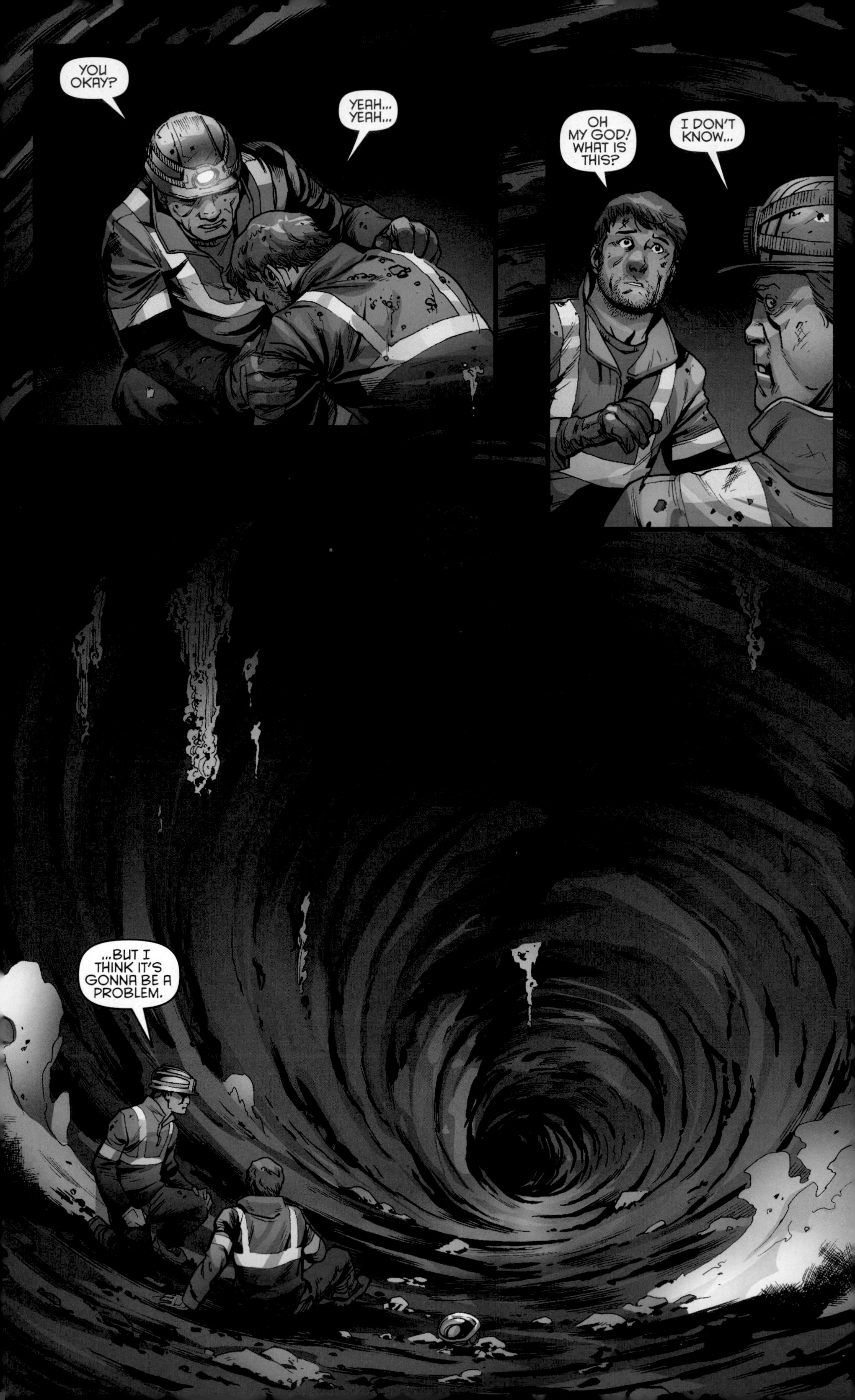
YOU OKAY?
YEAH... YEAH...
OH MY GOD! WHAT IS THIS?
I DON'T KNOW...
...BUT I THINK IT'S GONNA BE A PROBLEM.

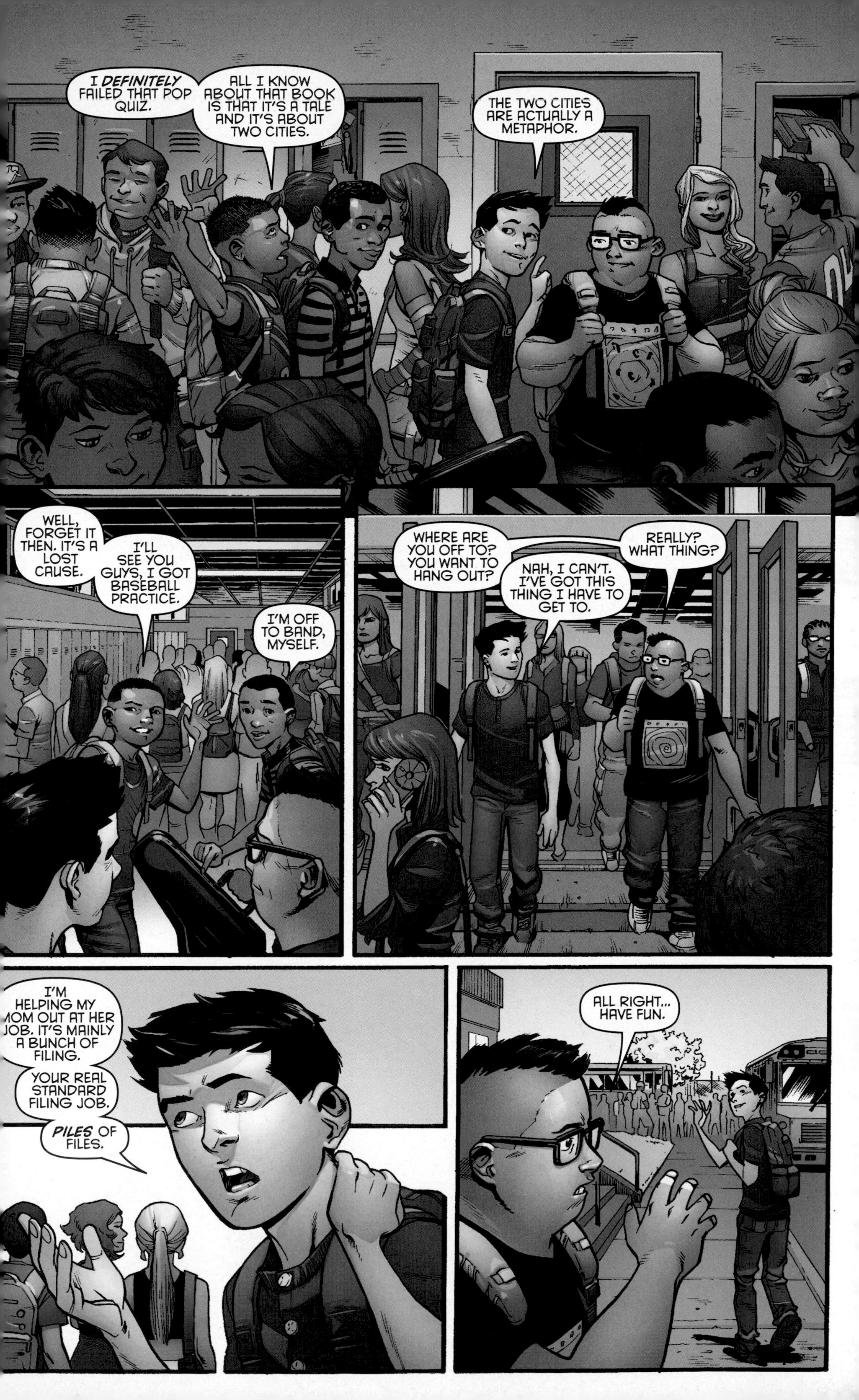
I DEFINITELY FAILED THAT POP QUIZ.
ALL I KNOW ABOUT THAT BOOK IS THAT IT'S A TALE AND IT'S ABOUT TWO CITIES.
THE TWO CITIES ARE ACTUALLY A METAPHOR.
WELL, FORGET IT THEN. IT'S A LOST CAUSE.
I'LL SEE YOU GUYS, I GOT BASEBALL PRACTICE.
I'M OFF TO BAND, MYSELF.
WHERE ARE YOU OFF TO? YOU WANT TO HANG OUT?
NAH, I CAN'T. I'VE GOT THIS THING I HAVE TO GET TO.
REALLY? WHAT THING?
I'M HELPING MY MOM OUT AT HER JOB. IT'S MAINLY A BUNCH OF FILING.
YOUR REAL STANDARD FILING JOB.
PILES OF FILES.
ALL RIGHT... HAVE FUN.

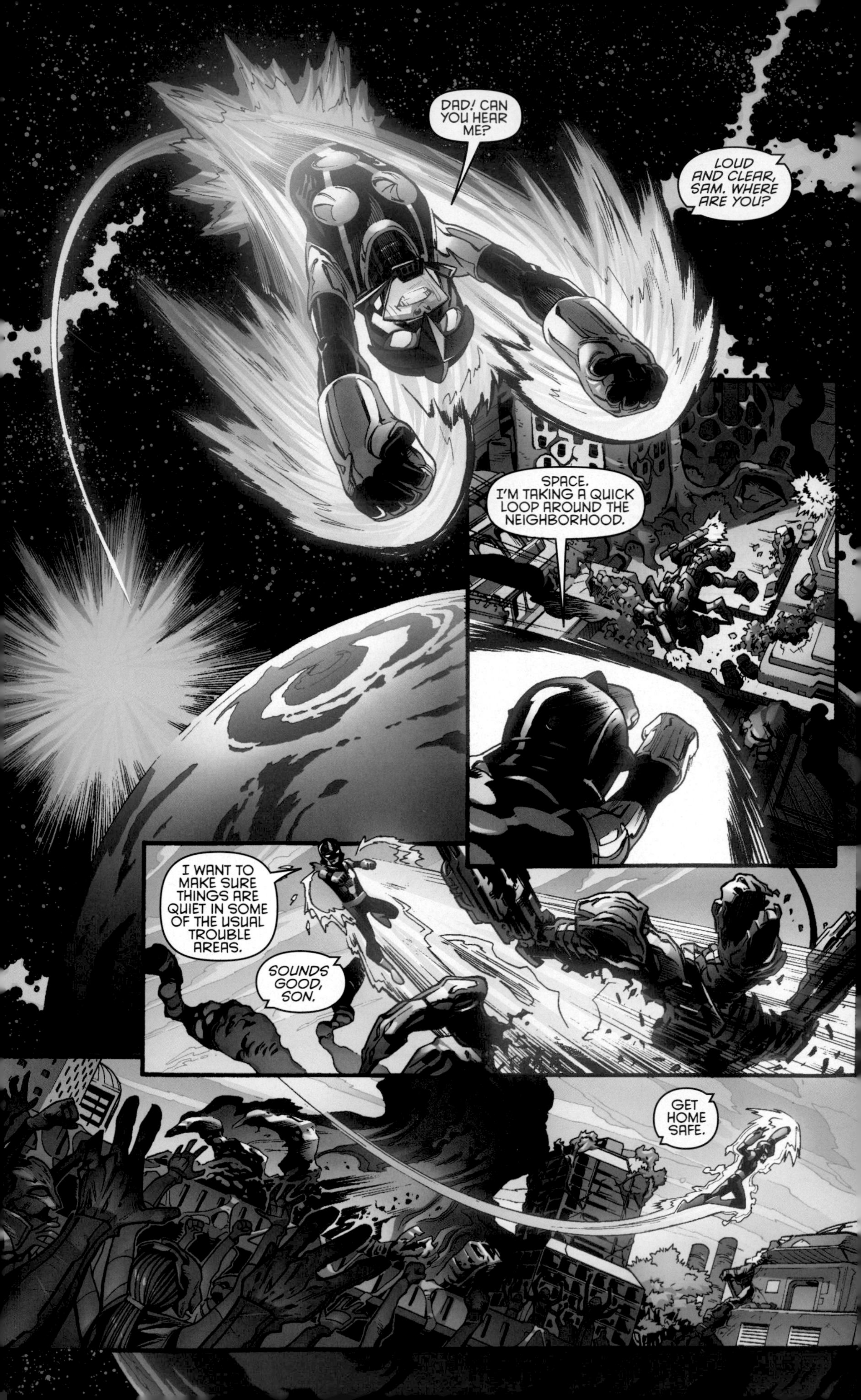
DAD! CAN YOU HEAR ME?
LOUD AND CLEAR, SAM. WHERE ARE YOU?
SPACE. I'M TAKING A QUICK LOOP AROUND THE NEIGHBORHOOD.
I WANT TO MAKE SURE THINGS ARE QUIET IN SOME OF THE USUAL TROUBLE AREAS.
SOUNDS GOOD, SON.
GET HOME SAFE.

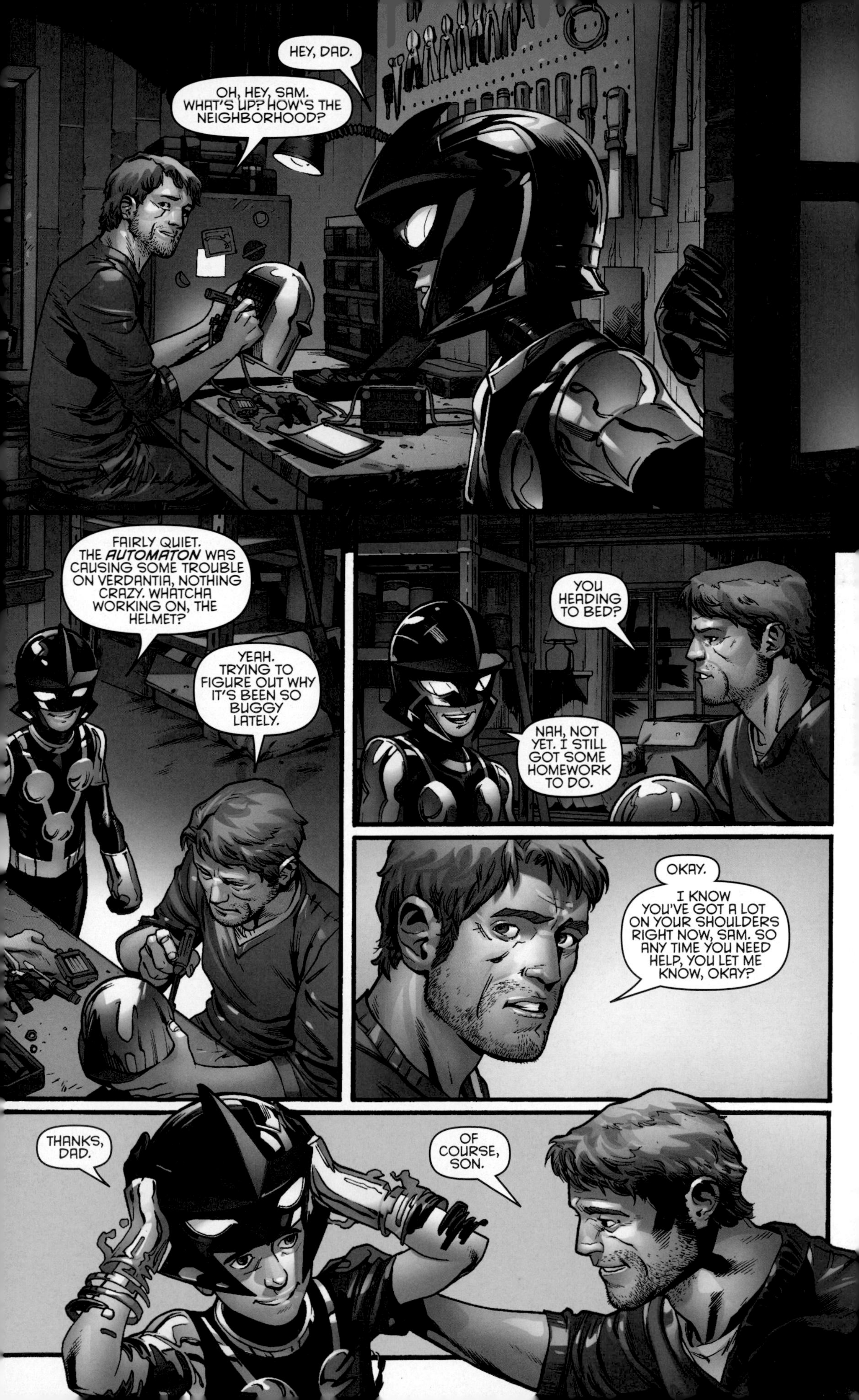
HEY, DAD.
OH, HEY, SAM. WHAT'S UP? HOW'S THE NEIGHBORHOOD?
FAIRLY QUIET. THE *AUTOMATON* WAS CAUSING SOME TROUBLE ON VERDANTIA, NOTHING CRAZY. WHATCHA WORKING ON, THE HELMET?
YEAH. TRYING TO FIGURE OUT WHY IT'S BEEN SO BUGGY LATELY.
YOU HEADING TO BED?
NAH, NOT YET. I STILL GOT SOME HOMEWORK TO DO.
OKAY.
I KNOW YOU'VE GOT A LOT ON YOUR SHOULDERS RIGHT NOW, SAM. SO ANY TIME YOU NEED HELP, YOU LET ME KNOW, OKAY?
THANKS, DAD.
OF COURSE, SON.

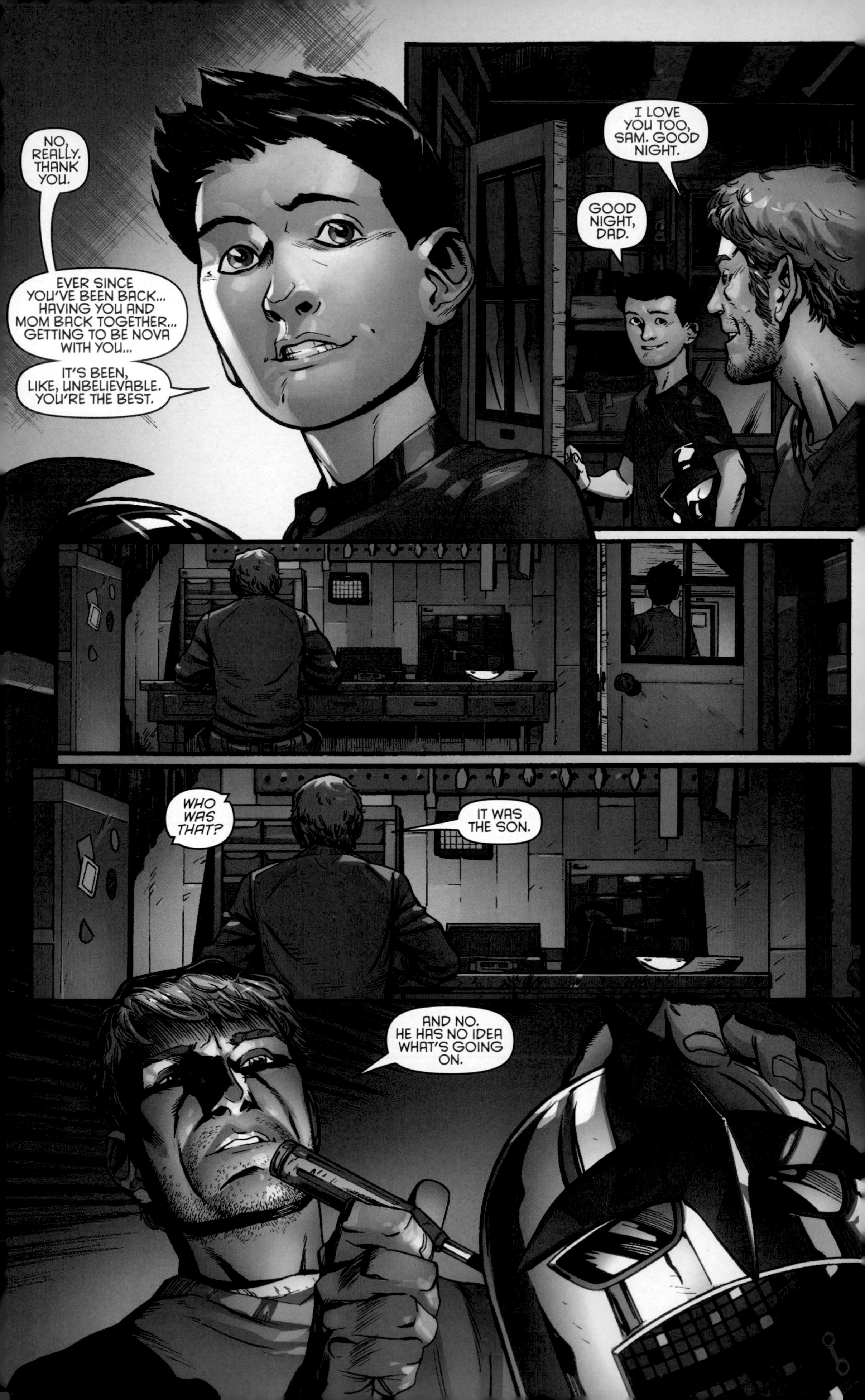
NO, REALLY. THANK YOU.
EVER SINCE YOU'VE BEEN BACK... HAVING YOU AND MOM BACK TOGETHER... GETTING TO BE NOVA WITH YOU...
IT'S BEEN, LIKE, UNBELIEVABLE. YOU'RE THE BEST.
I LOVE YOU TOO, SAM. GOOD NIGHT.
GOOD NIGHT, DAD.
WHO WAS THAT?
IT WAS THE SON.
AND NO. HE HAS NO IDEA WHAT'S GOING ON.

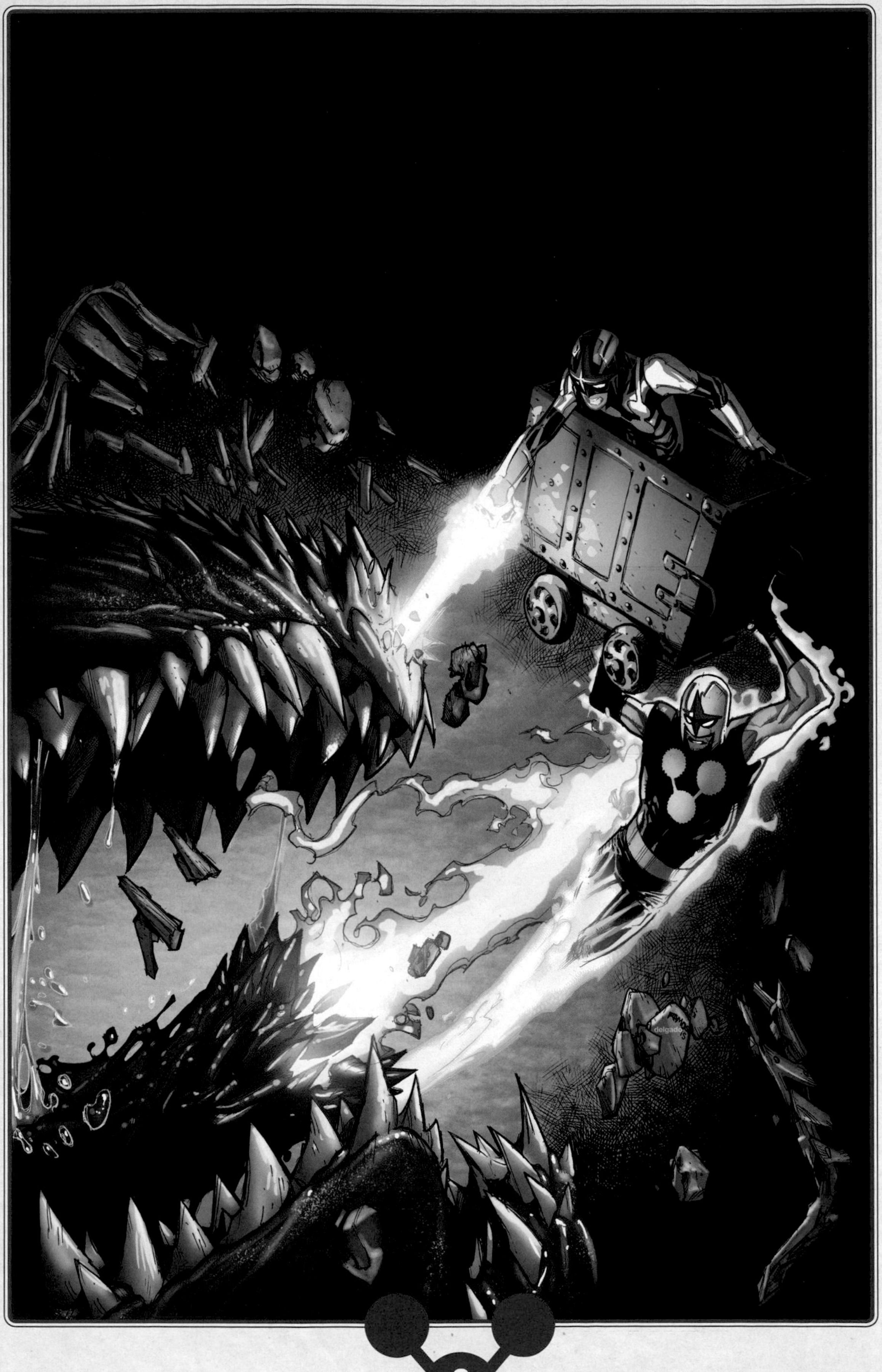

2

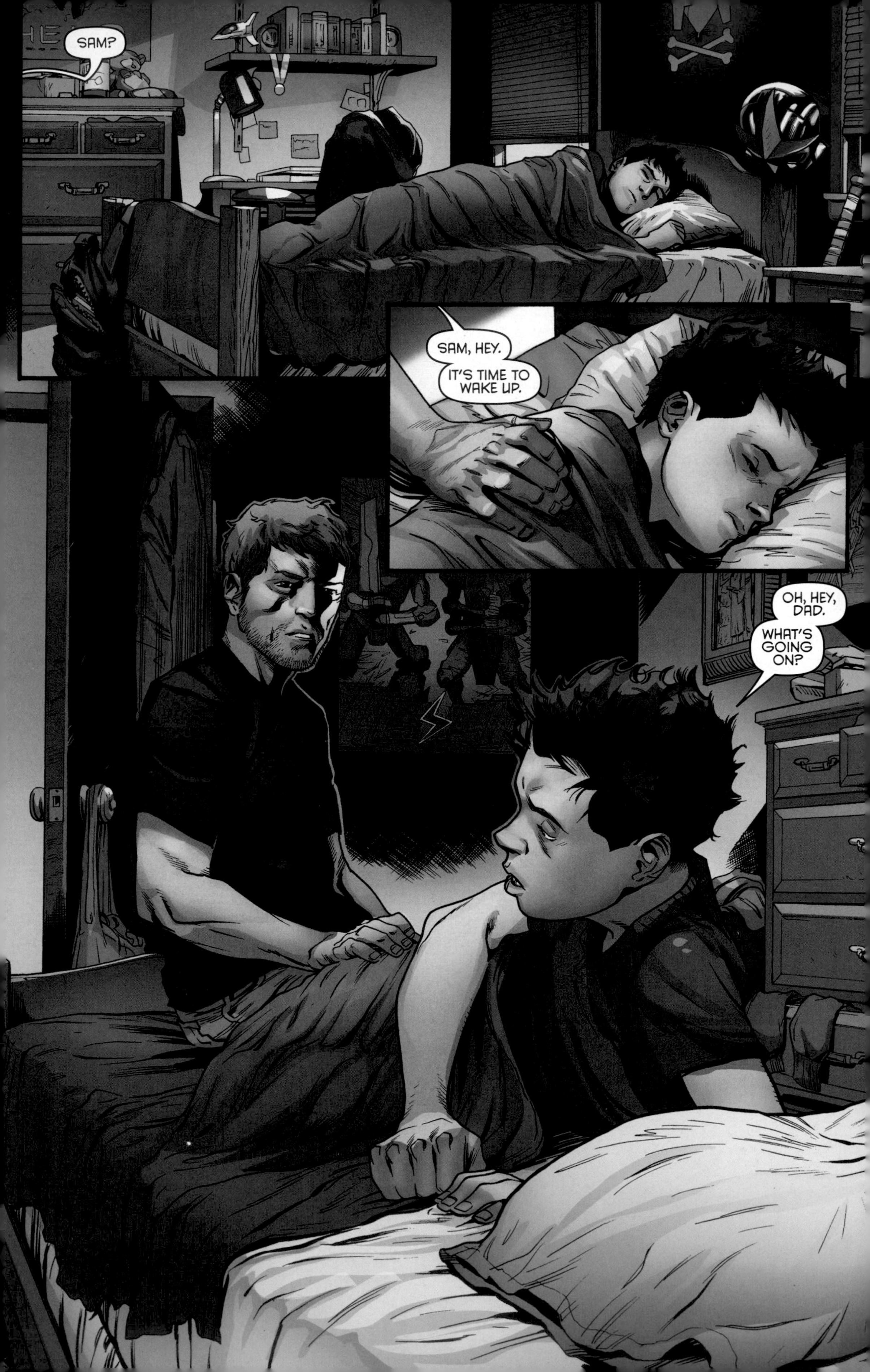
SAM?
SAM, HEY.
IT'S TIME TO WAKE UP.
OH, HEY, DAD.
WHAT'S GOING ON?

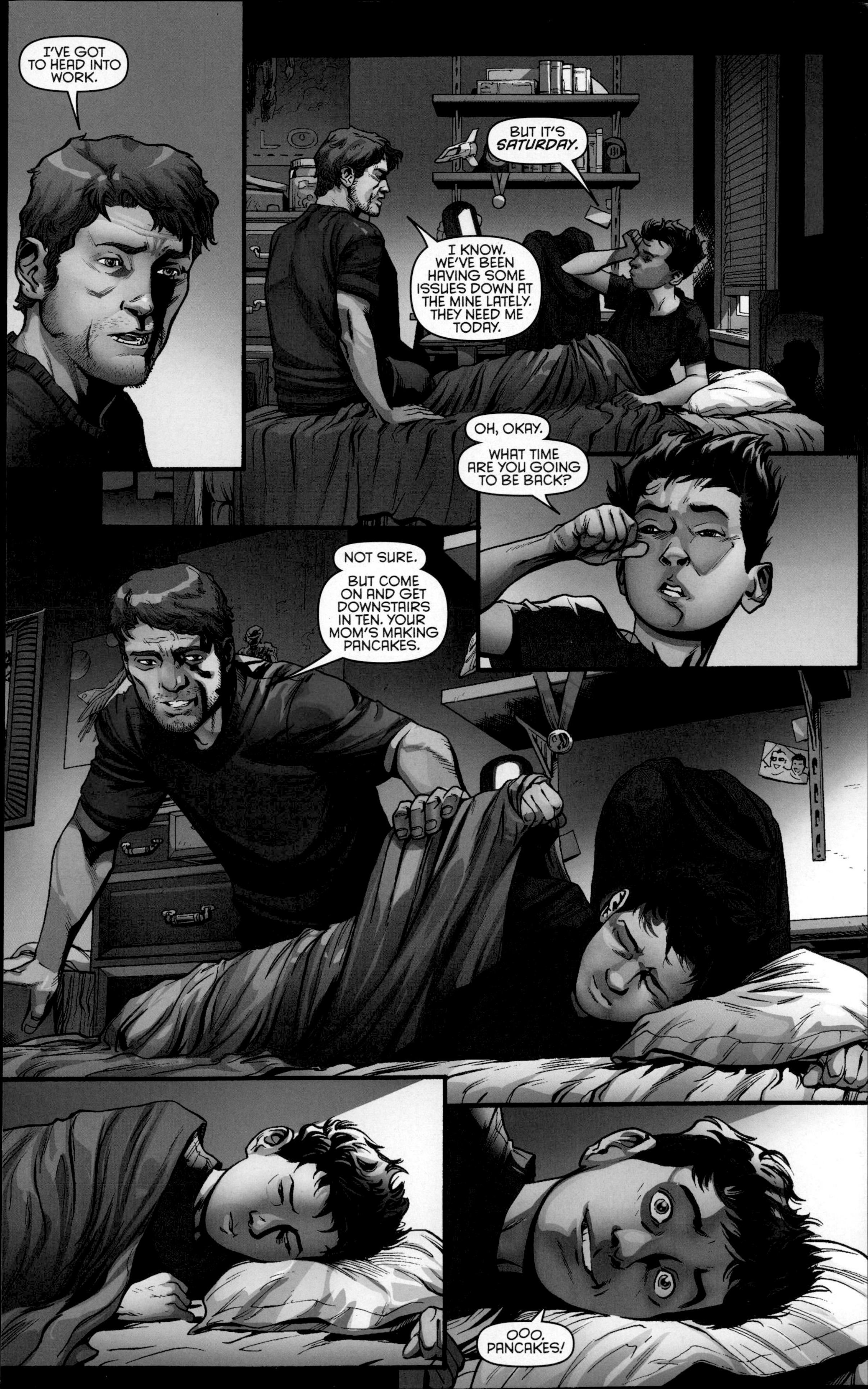
I'VE GOT TO HEAD INTO WORK.
BUT IT'S SATURDAY.
I KNOW. WE'VE BEEN HAVING SOME ISSUES DOWN AT THE MINE LATELY. THEY NEED ME TODAY.
OH, OKAY.
WHAT TIME ARE YOU GOING TO BE BACK?
NOT SURE.
BUT COME ON AND GET DOWNSTAIRS IN TEN. YOUR MOM'S MAKING PANCAKES.
OOO. PANCAKES!

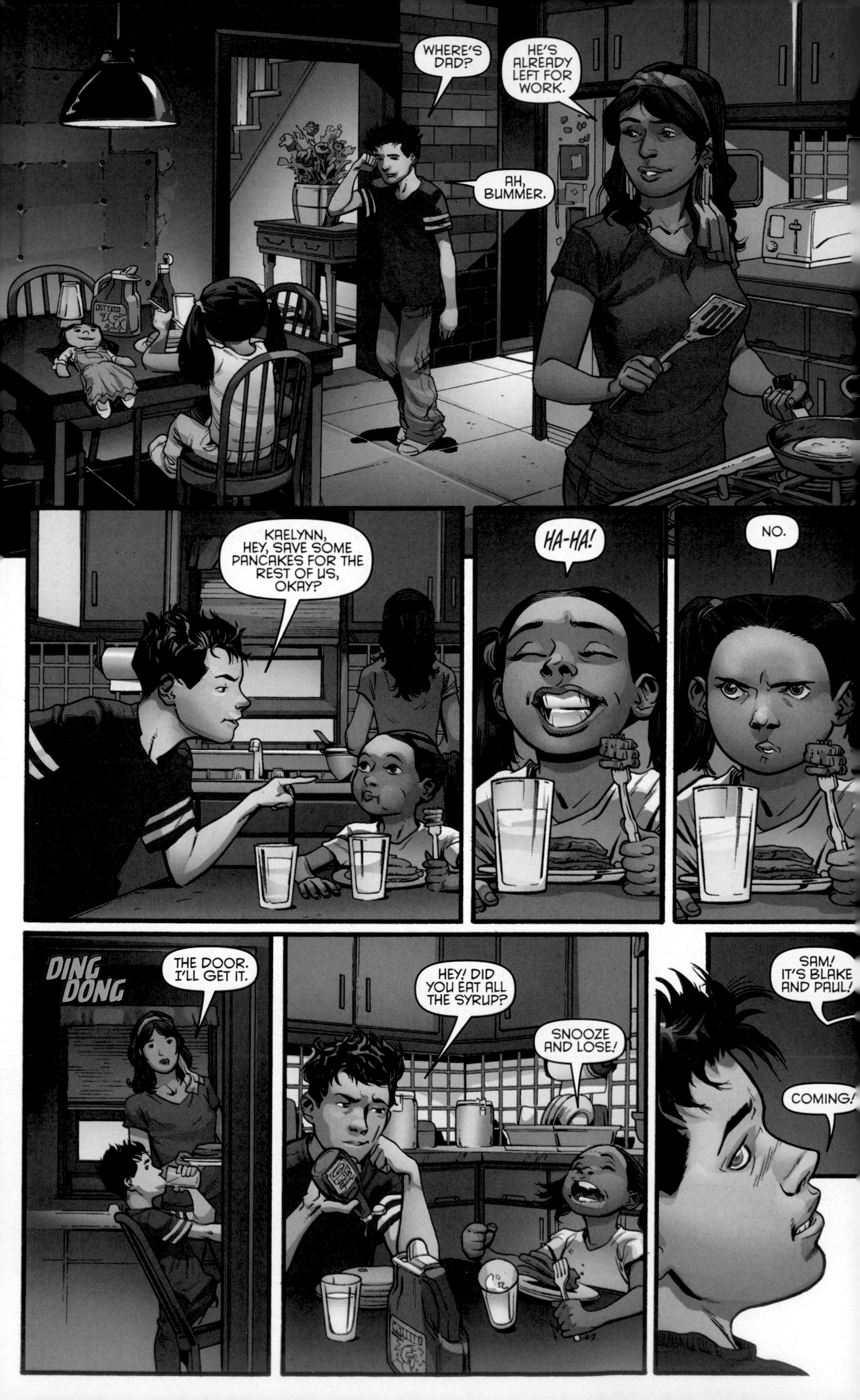

WHERE'S DAD?
HE'S ALREADY LEFT FOR WORK.
AH, BUMMER.
KAELYNN, HEY, SAVE SOME PANCAKES FOR THE REST OF US, OKAY?
HA-HA!
NO.
DING DONG
THE DOOR. I'LL GET IT.
HEY! DID YOU EAT ALL THE SYRUP?
SNOOZE AND LOSE!
SAM! IT'S BLAKE AND PAUL!
COMING!

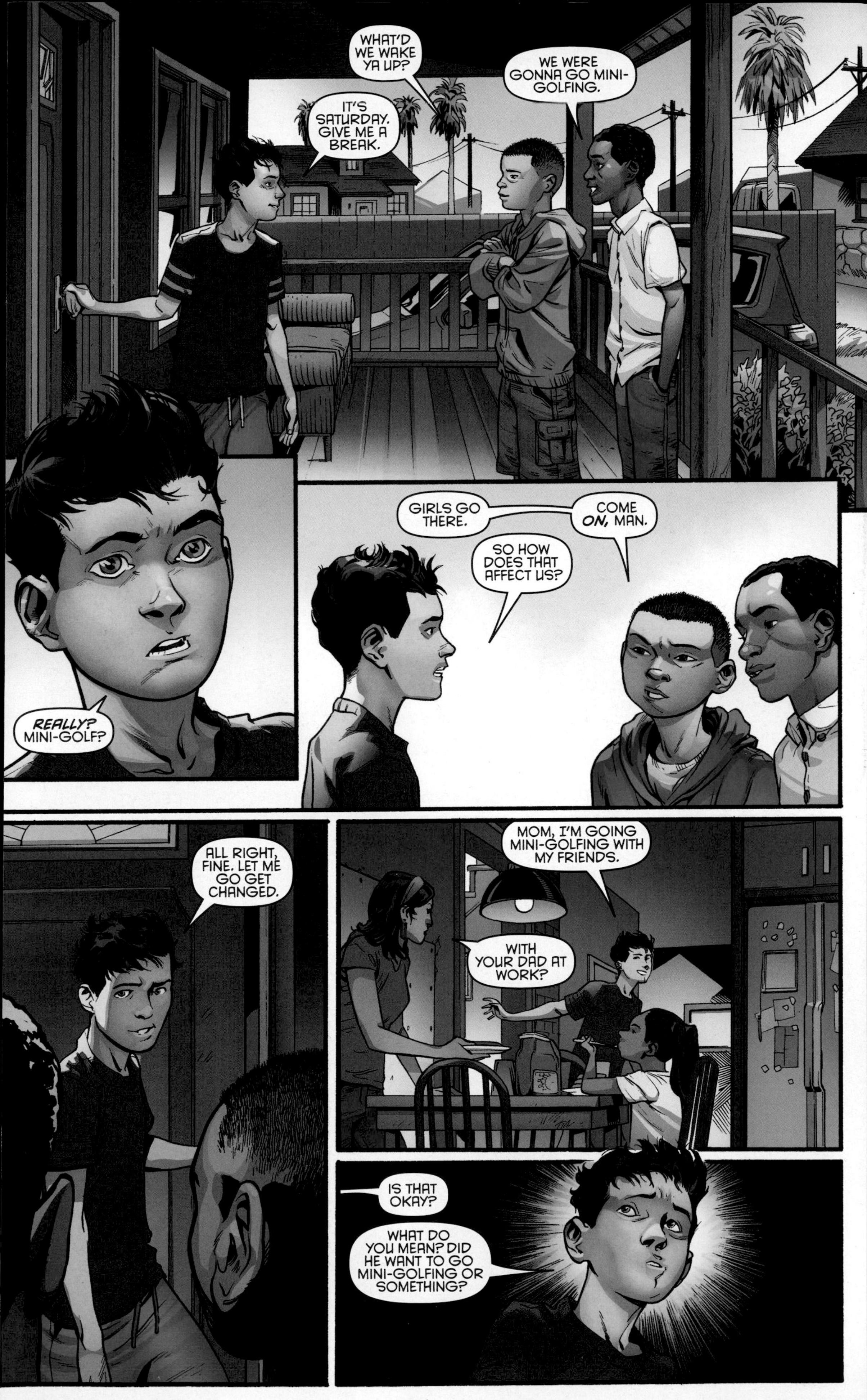

WHAT'D WE WAKE YA UP?
IT'S SATURDAY. GIVE ME A BREAK.
WE WERE GONNA GO MINI-GOLFING.
REALLY? MINI-GOLF?
GIRLS GO THERE.
SO HOW DOES THAT AFFECT US?
COME ON, MAN.
ALL RIGHT, FINE. LET ME GO GET CHANGED.
MOM, I'M GOING MINI-GOLFING WITH MY FRIENDS.
WITH YOUR DAD AT WORK?
IS THAT OKAY?
WHAT DO YOU MEAN? DID HE WANT TO GO MINI-GOLFING OR SOMETHING?

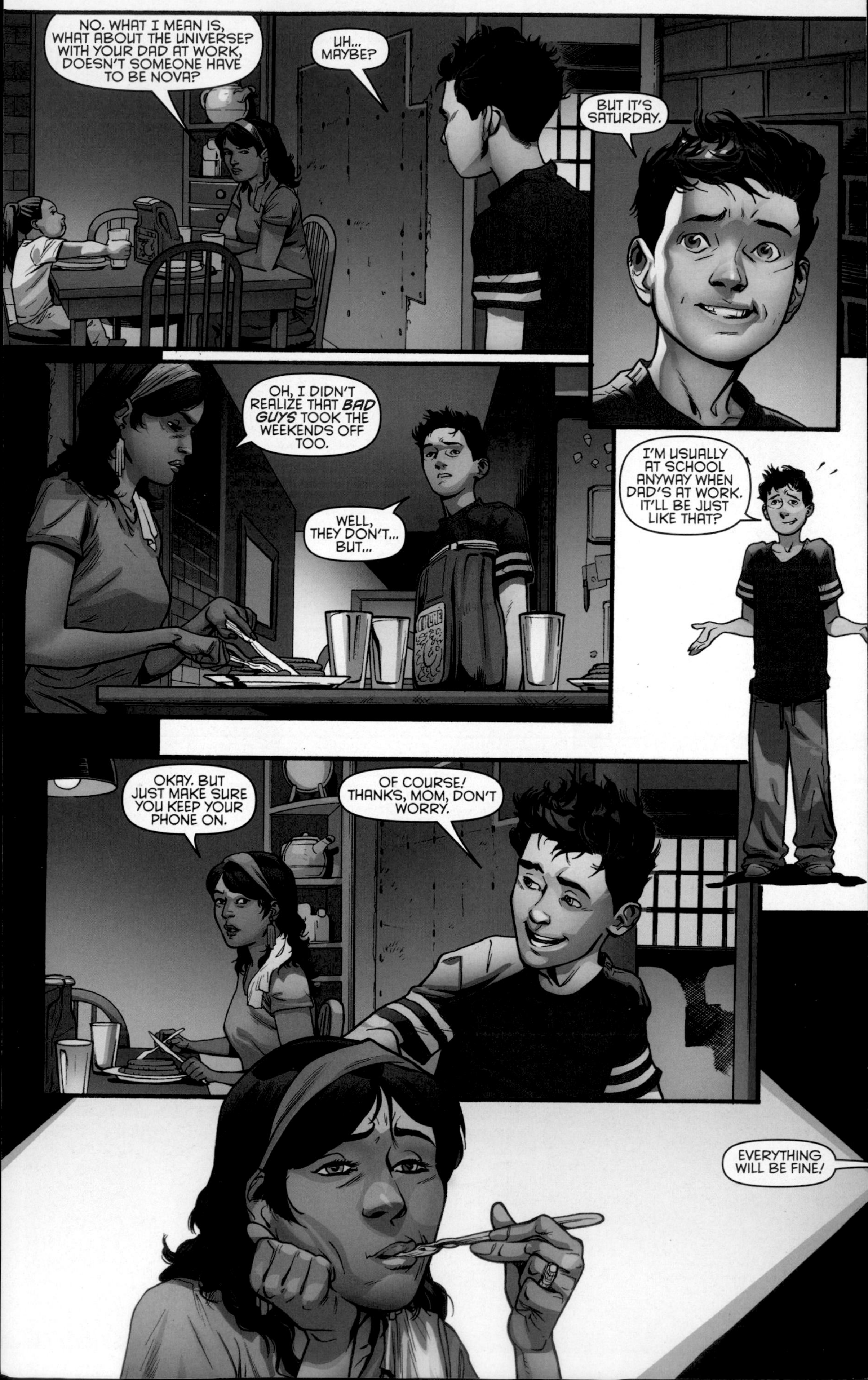
NO. WHAT I MEAN IS, WHAT ABOUT THE UNIVERSE? WITH YOUR DAD AT WORK, DOESN'T SOMEONE HAVE TO BE NOVA?
UH... MAYBE?
BUT IT'S SATURDAY.
OH, I DIDN'T REALIZE THAT BAD GUYS TOOK THE WEEKENDS OFF TOO.
WELL, THEY DON'T... BUT...
I'M USUALLY AT SCHOOL ANYWAY WHEN DAD'S AT WORK. IT'LL BE JUST LIKE THAT?
OKAY. BUT JUST MAKE SURE YOU KEEP YOUR PHONE ON.
OF COURSE! THANKS, MOM, DON'T WORRY.
EVERYTHING WILL BE FINE!

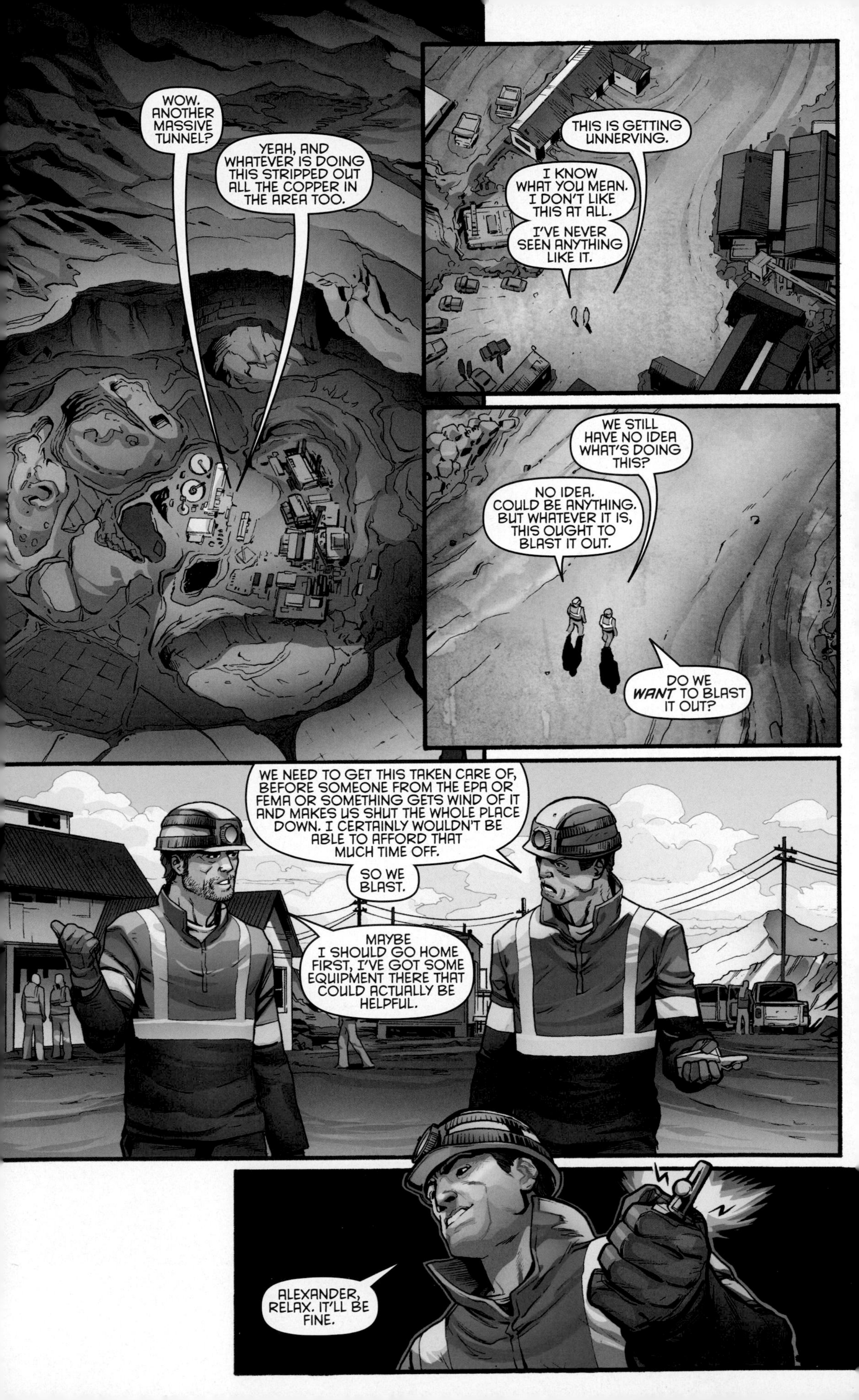
WOW. ANOTHER MASSIVE TUNNEL?
YEAH, AND WHATEVER IS DOING THIS STRIPPED OUT ALL THE COPPER IN THE AREA TOO.
THIS IS GETTING UNNERVING.
I KNOW WHAT YOU MEAN. I DON'T LIKE THIS AT ALL.
I'VE NEVER SEEN ANYTHING LIKE IT.
WE STILL HAVE NO IDEA WHAT'S DOING THIS?
NO IDEA. COULD BE ANYTHING. BUT WHATEVER IT IS, THIS OUGHT TO BLAST IT OUT.
DO WE *WANT* TO BLAST IT OUT?
WE NEED TO GET THIS TAKEN CARE OF, BEFORE SOMEONE FROM THE EPA OR FEMA OR SOMETHING GETS WIND OF IT AND MAKES US SHUT THE WHOLE PLACE DOWN. I CERTAINLY WOULDN'T BE ABLE TO AFFORD THAT MUCH TIME OFF.
SO WE BLAST.
MAYBE I SHOULD GO HOME FIRST, I'VE GOT SOME EQUIPMENT THERE THAT COULD ACTUALLY BE HELPFUL.
ALEXANDER, RELAX. IT'LL BE FINE.

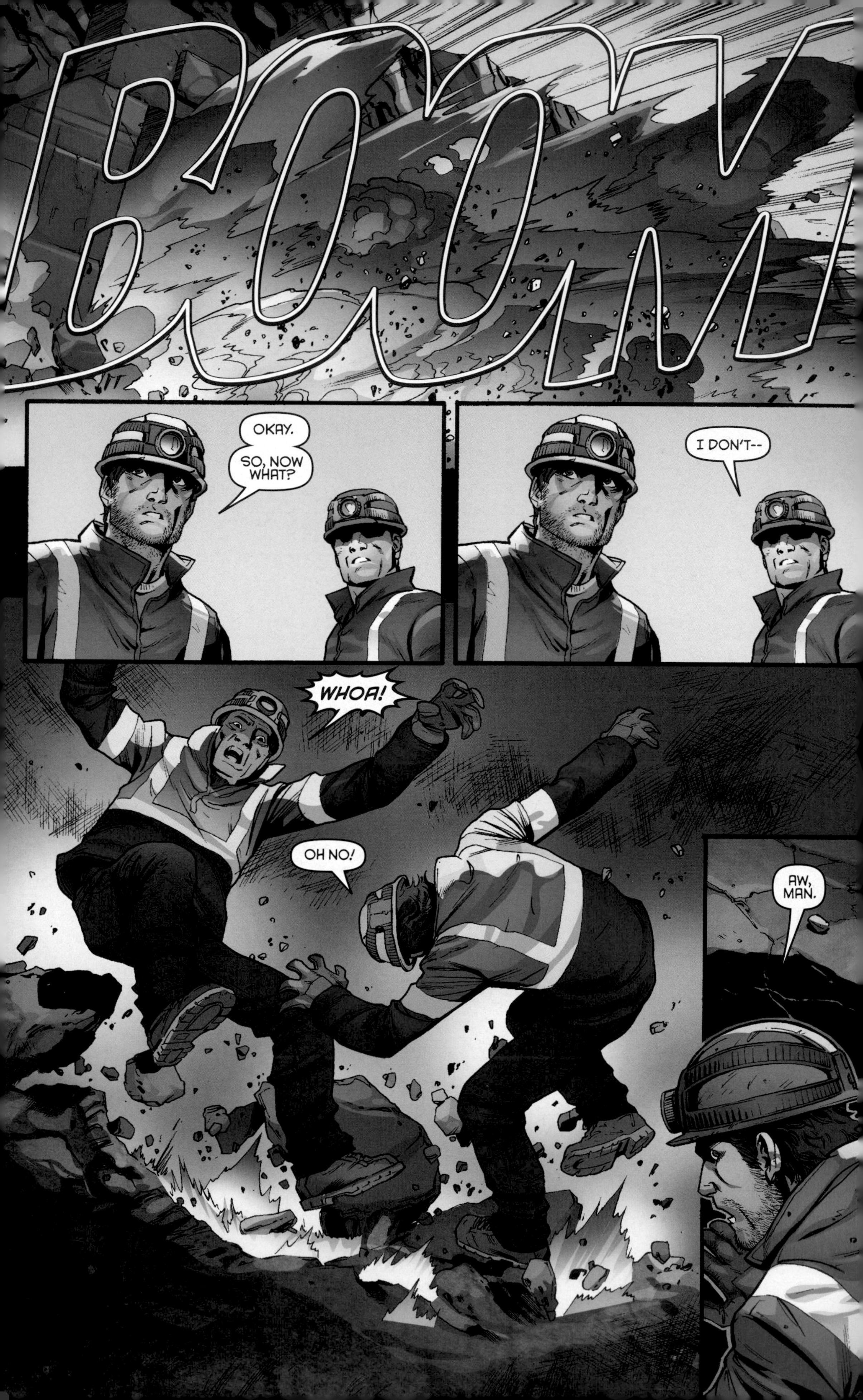
BOOM
OKAY.
SO, NOW WHAT?
I DON'T--
WHOA!
OH NO!
AW, MAN.

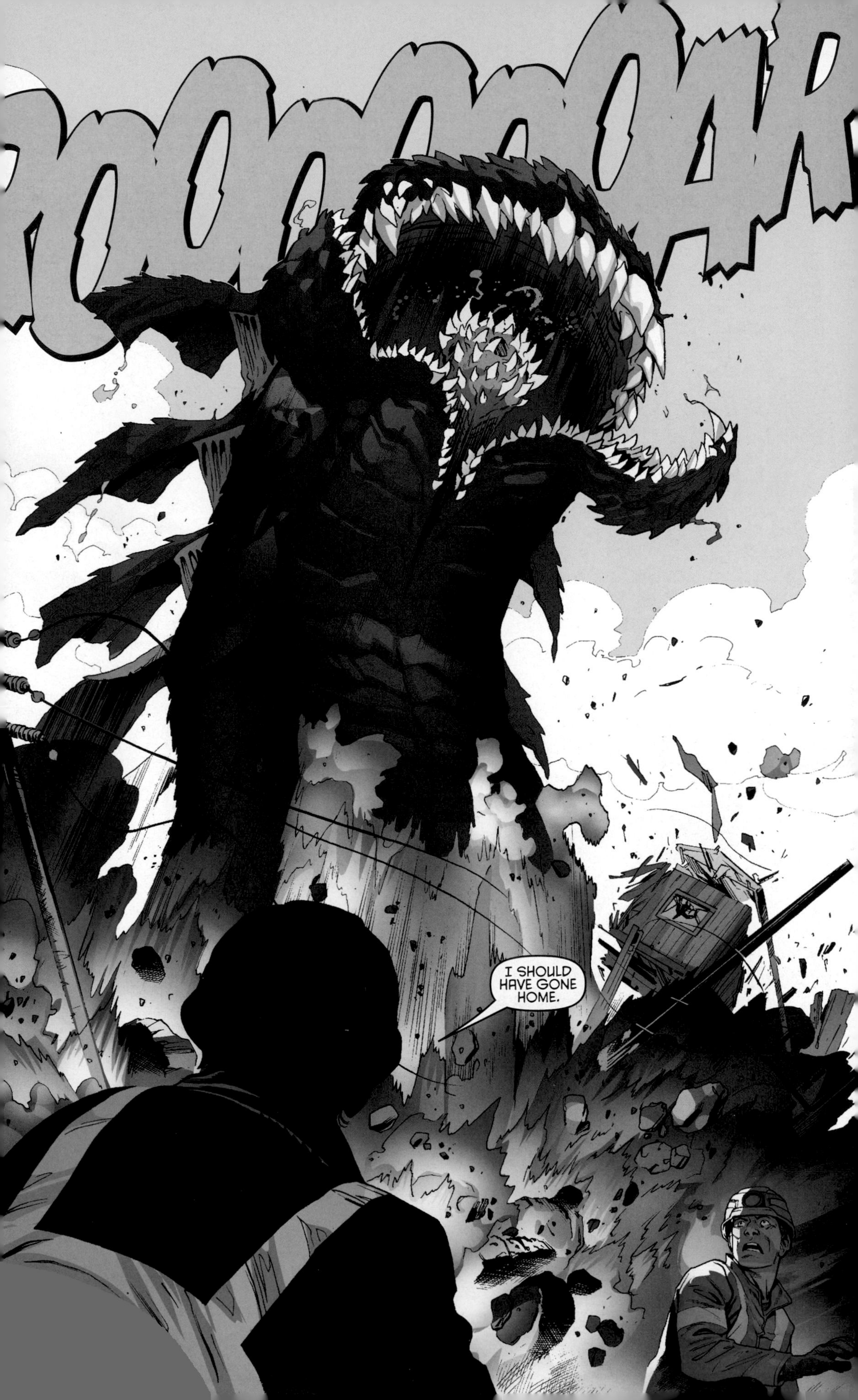
ROOOOOOOAR
I SHOULD HAVE GONE HOME.

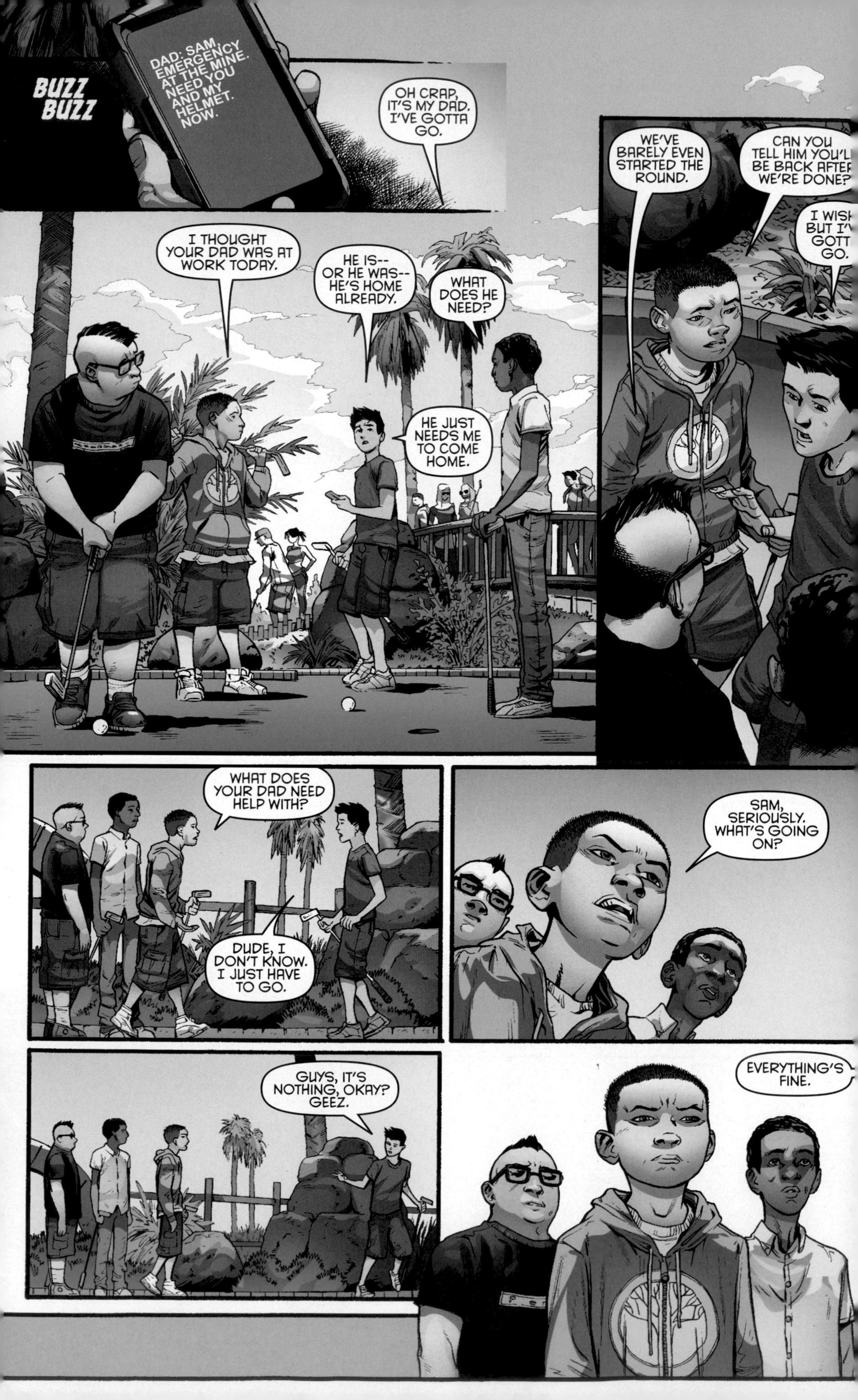
BUZZ BUZZ
DAD: SAM, EMERGENCY AT THE MINE. NEED YOU AND MY HELMET. NOW.
OH CRAP, IT'S MY DAD. I'VE GOTTA GO.
I THOUGHT YOUR DAD WAS AT WORK TODAY.
HE IS-- OR HE WAS-- HE'S HOME ALREADY.
WHAT DOES HE NEED?
HE JUST NEEDS ME TO COME HOME.
WE'VE BARELY EVEN STARTED THE ROUND.
CAN YOU TELL HIM YOU'L BE BACK AFTEF WE'RE DONE?
I WISH BUT I' GOTT GO.
WHAT DOES YOUR DAD NEED HELP WITH?
DUDE, I DON'T KNOW. I JUST HAVE TO GO.
SAM, SERIOUSLY. WHAT'S GOING ON?
GUYS, IT'S NOTHING, OKAY? GEEZ.
EVERYTHING'S FINE.

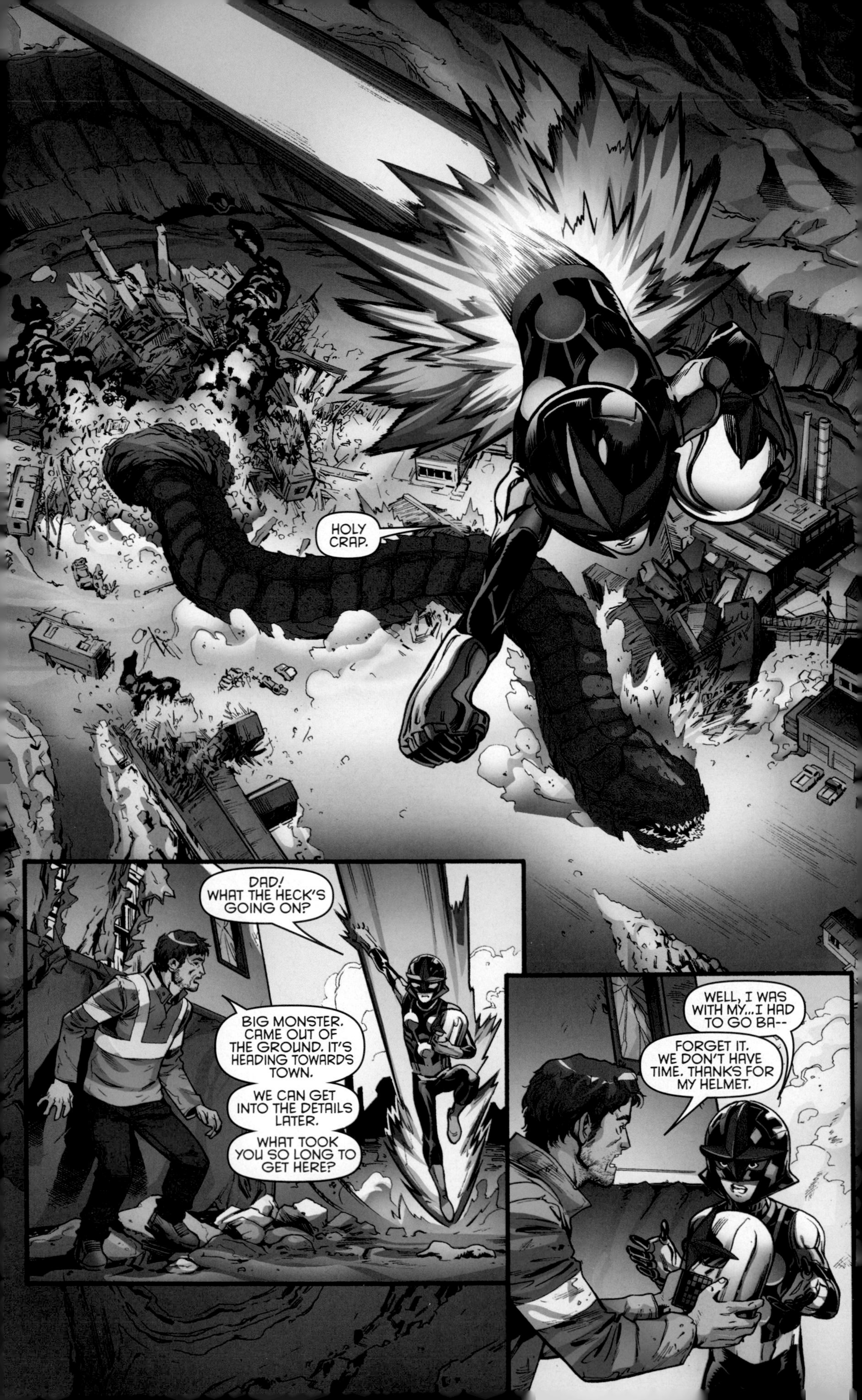
HOLY CRAP.
DAD! WHAT THE HECK'S GOING ON?
BIG MONSTER. CAME OUT OF THE GROUND. IT'S HEADING TOWARDS TOWN.
WE CAN GET INTO THE DETAILS LATER.
WHAT TOOK YOU SO LONG TO GET HERE?
WELL, I WAS WITH MY...I HAD TO GO BA--
FORGET IT. WE DON'T HAVE TIME. THANKS FOR MY HELMET.

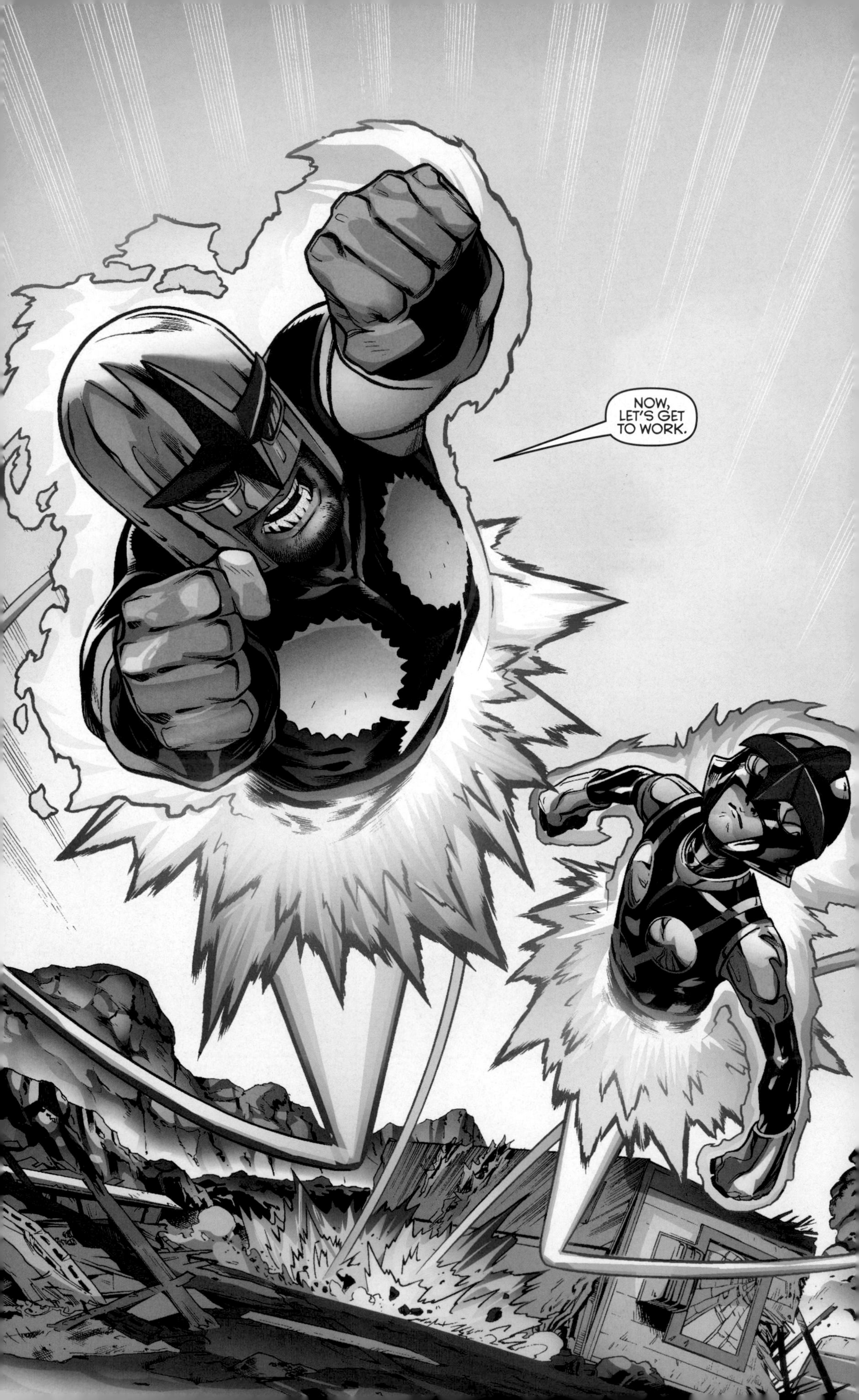
NOW, LET'S GET TO WORK.

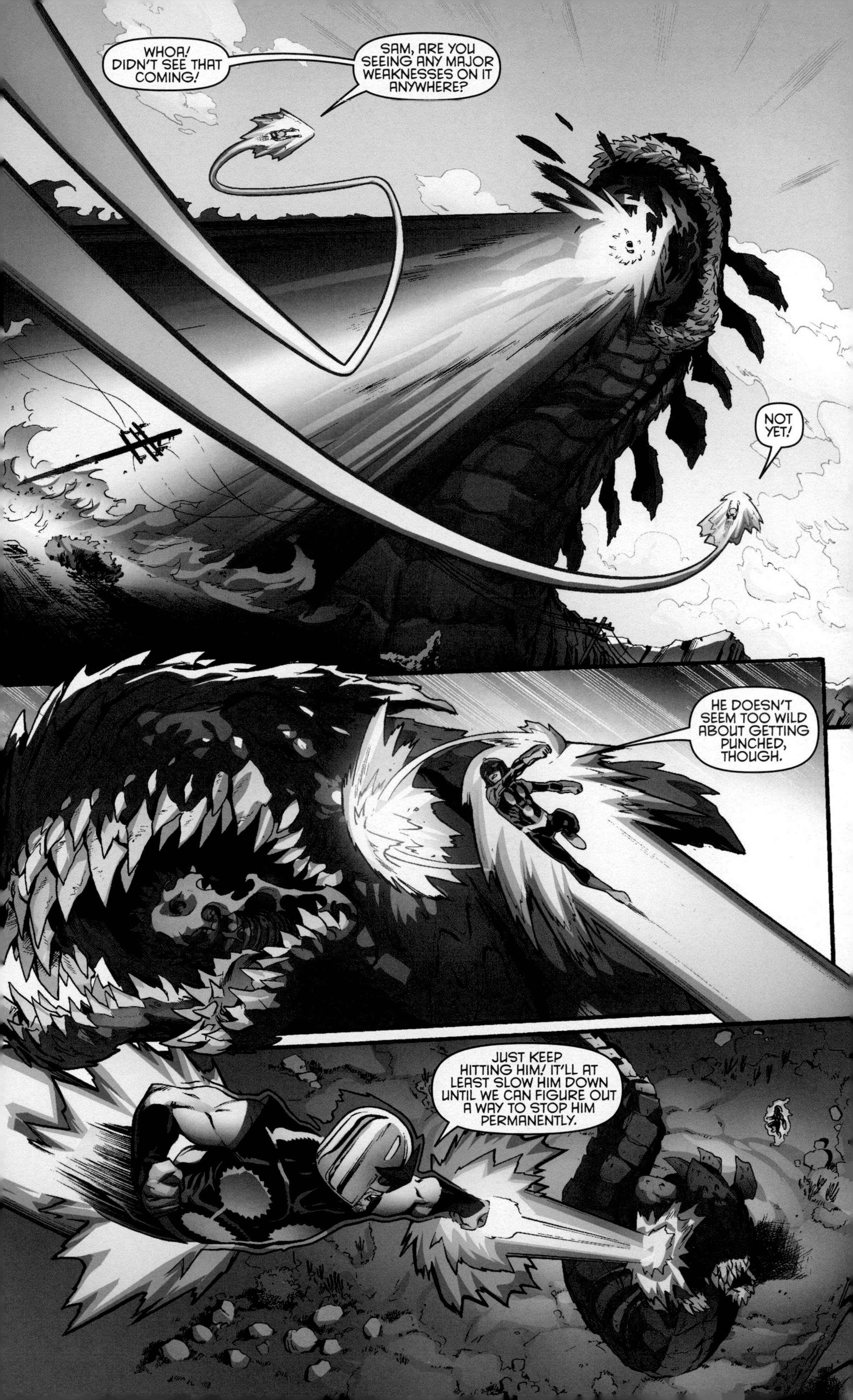
WHOA! DIDN'T SEE THAT COMING!
SAM, ARE YOU SEEING ANY MAJOR WEAKNESSES ON IT ANYWHERE?
NOT YET!
HE DOESN'T SEEM TOO WILD ABOUT GETTING PUNCHED, THOUGH.
JUST KEEP HITTING HIM! IT'LL AT LEAST SLOW HIM DOWN UNTIL WE CAN FIGURE OUT A WAY TO STOP HIM PERMANENTLY.

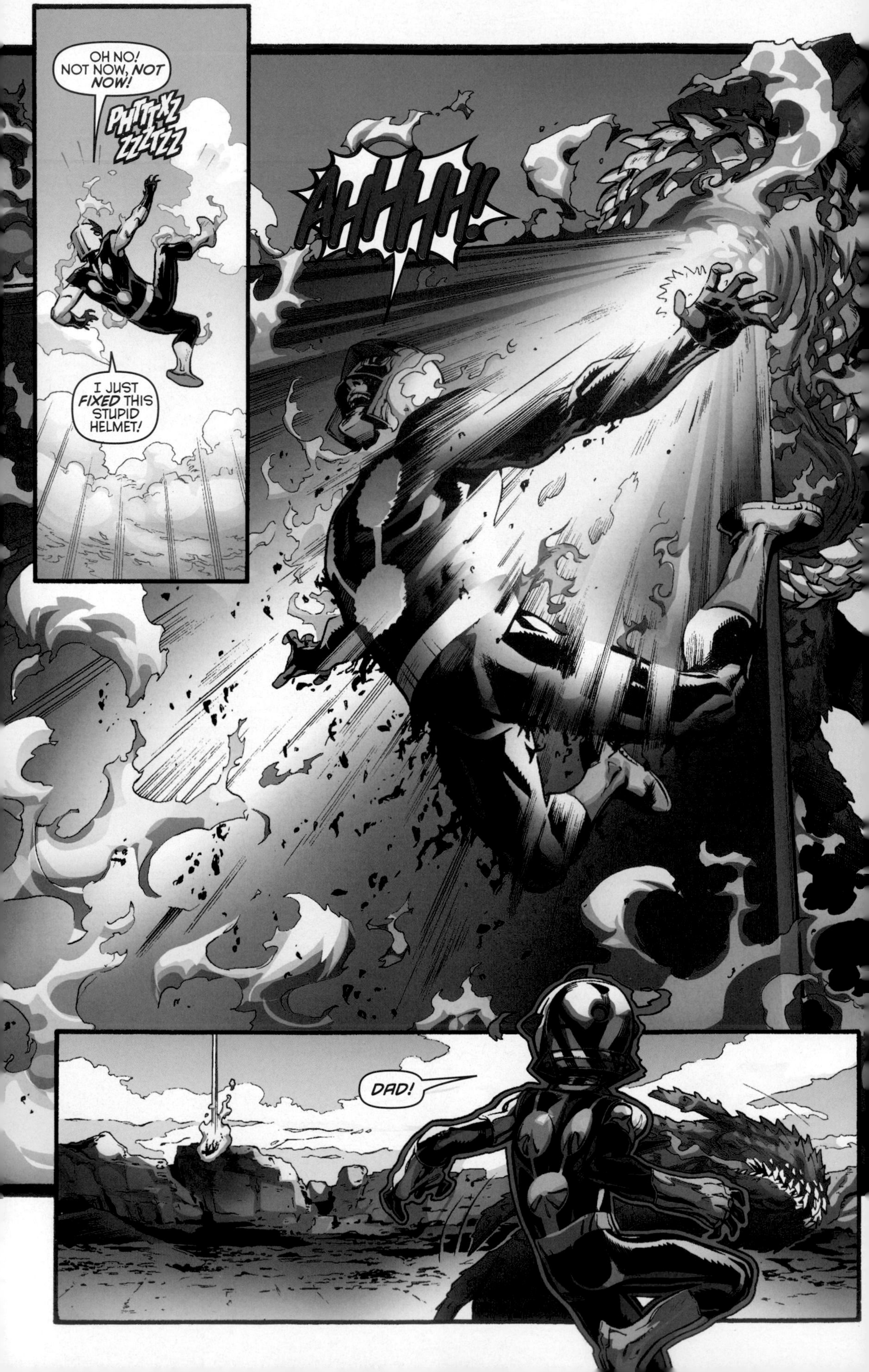
OH NO! NOT NOW, *NOT NOW!*
PHTTTXZ ZZZTZZ
I JUST *FIXED* THIS STUPID HELMET!
AHHHH!
DAD!

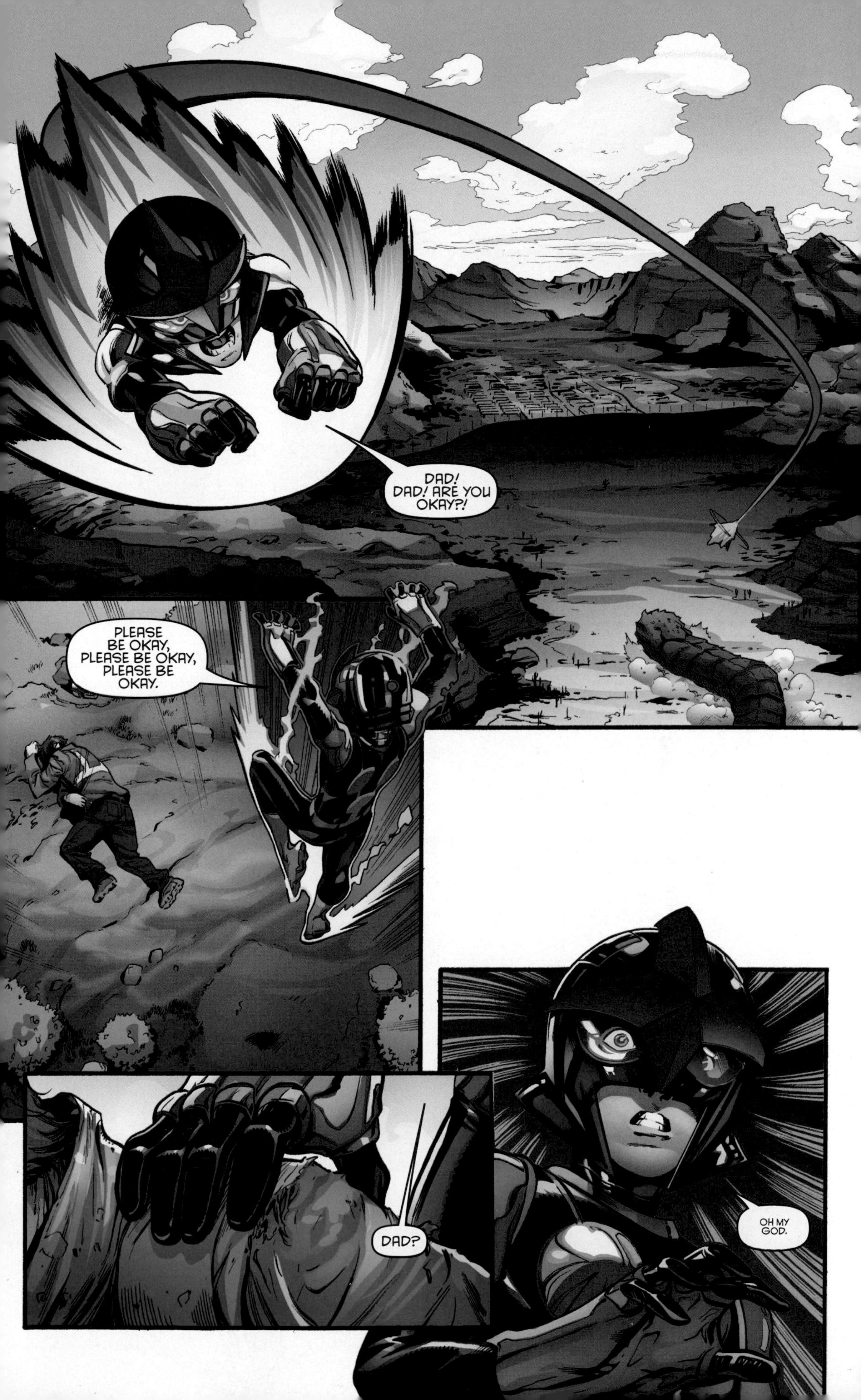
DAD! DAD! ARE YOU OKAY?!
PLEASE BE OKAY, PLEASE BE OKAY, PLEASE BE OKAY.
OH MY GOD.
DAD?

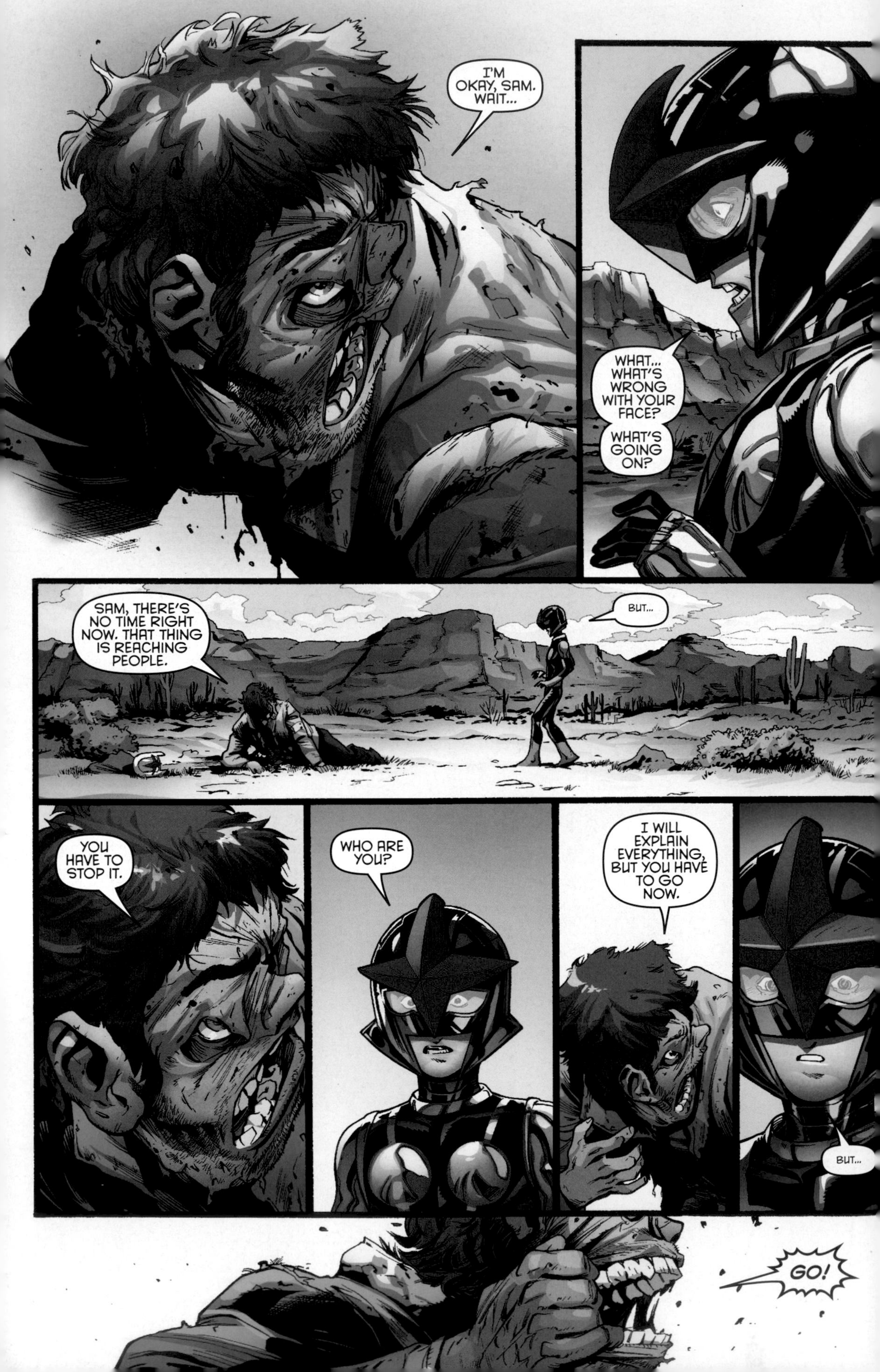

I'M OKAY, SAM. WAIT...
WHAT... WHAT'S WRONG WITH YOUR FACE?
WHAT'S GOING ON?
SAM, THERE'S NO TIME RIGHT NOW. THAT THING IS REACHING PEOPLE.
BUT...
YOU HAVE TO STOP IT.
WHO ARE YOU?
I WILL EXPLAIN EVERYTHING, BUT YOU HAVE TO GO NOW.
BUT...
GO!

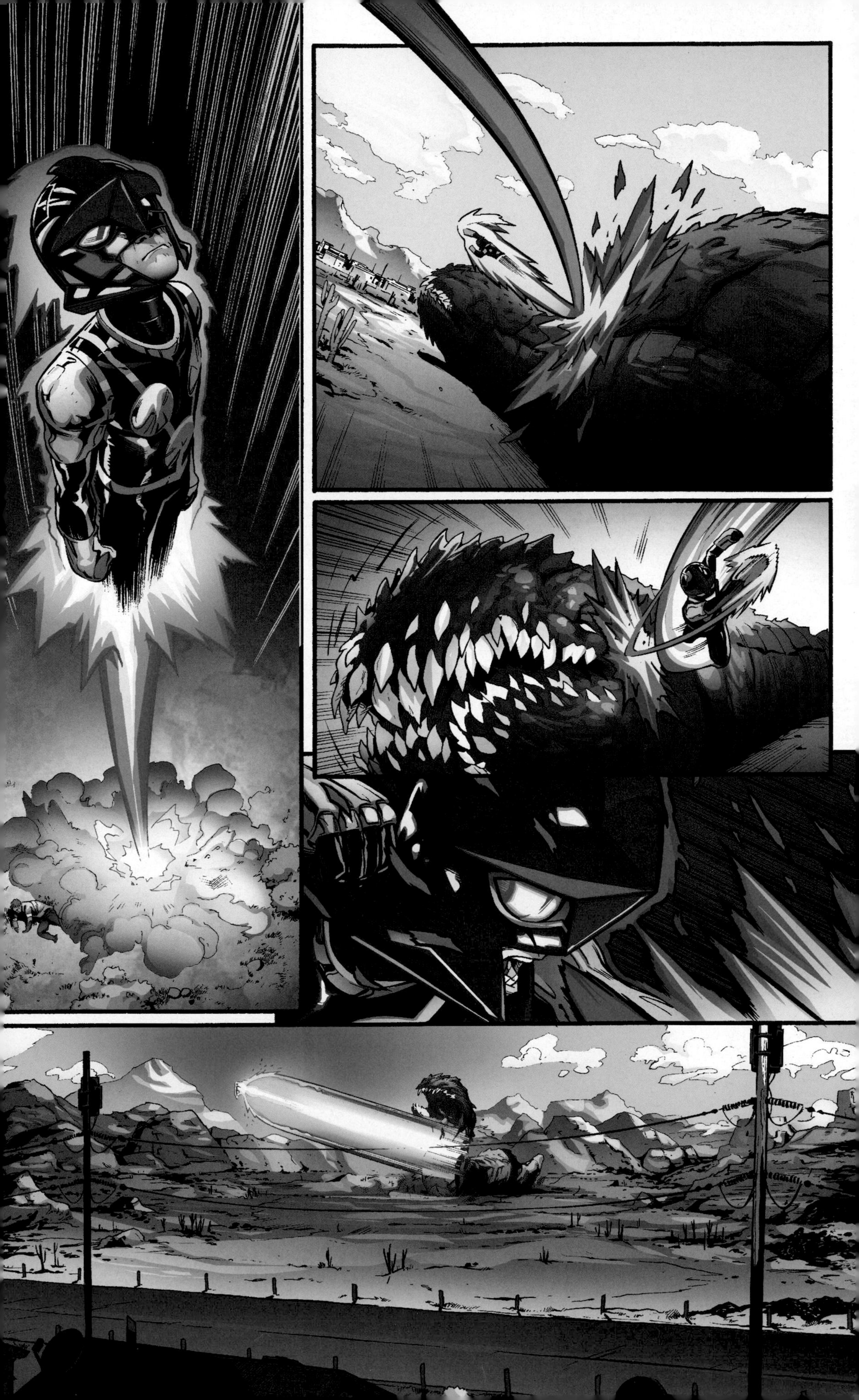

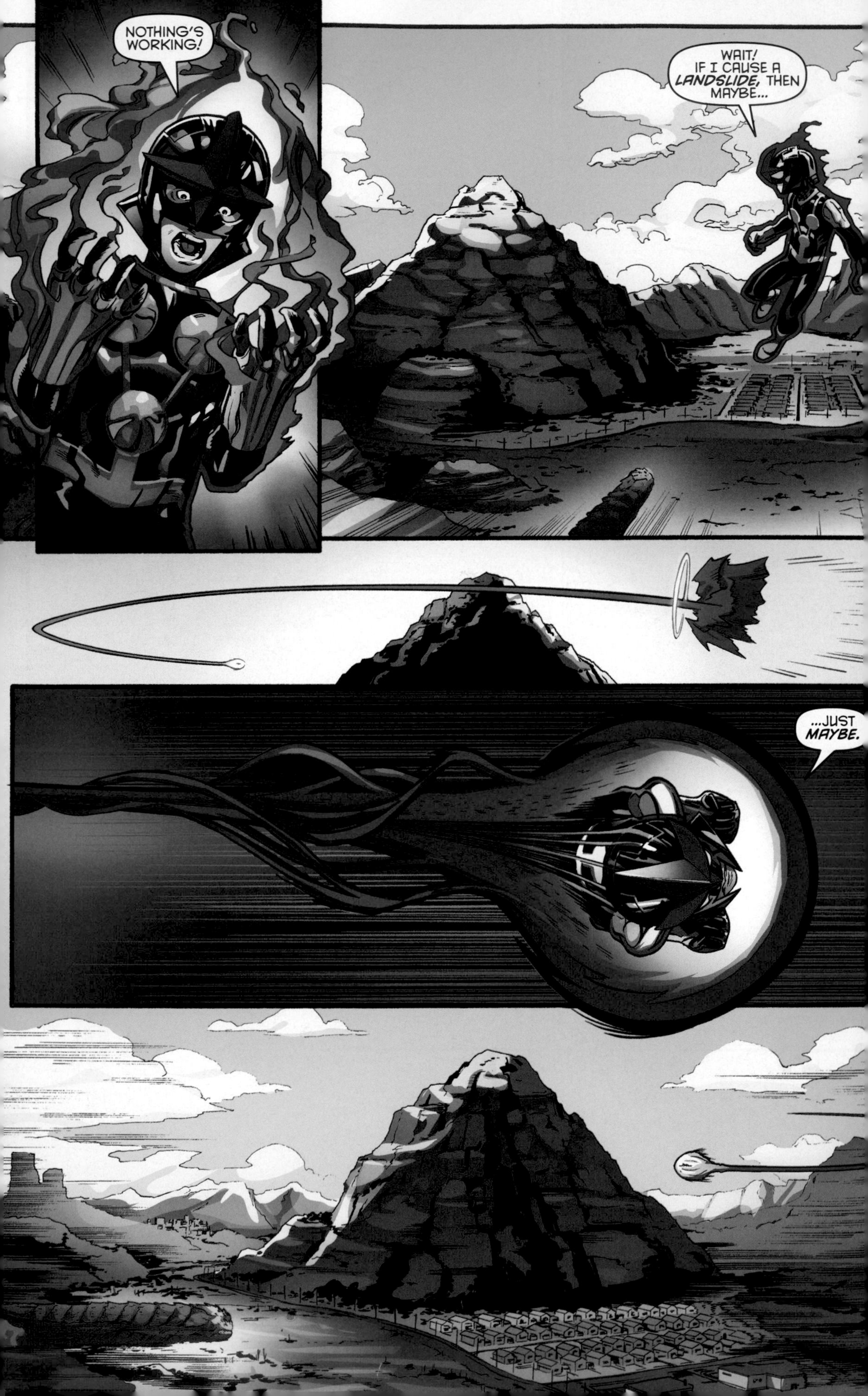
NOTHING'S WORKING!
WAIT! IF I CAUSE A LANDSLIDE, THEN MAYBE...
...JUST MAYBE.

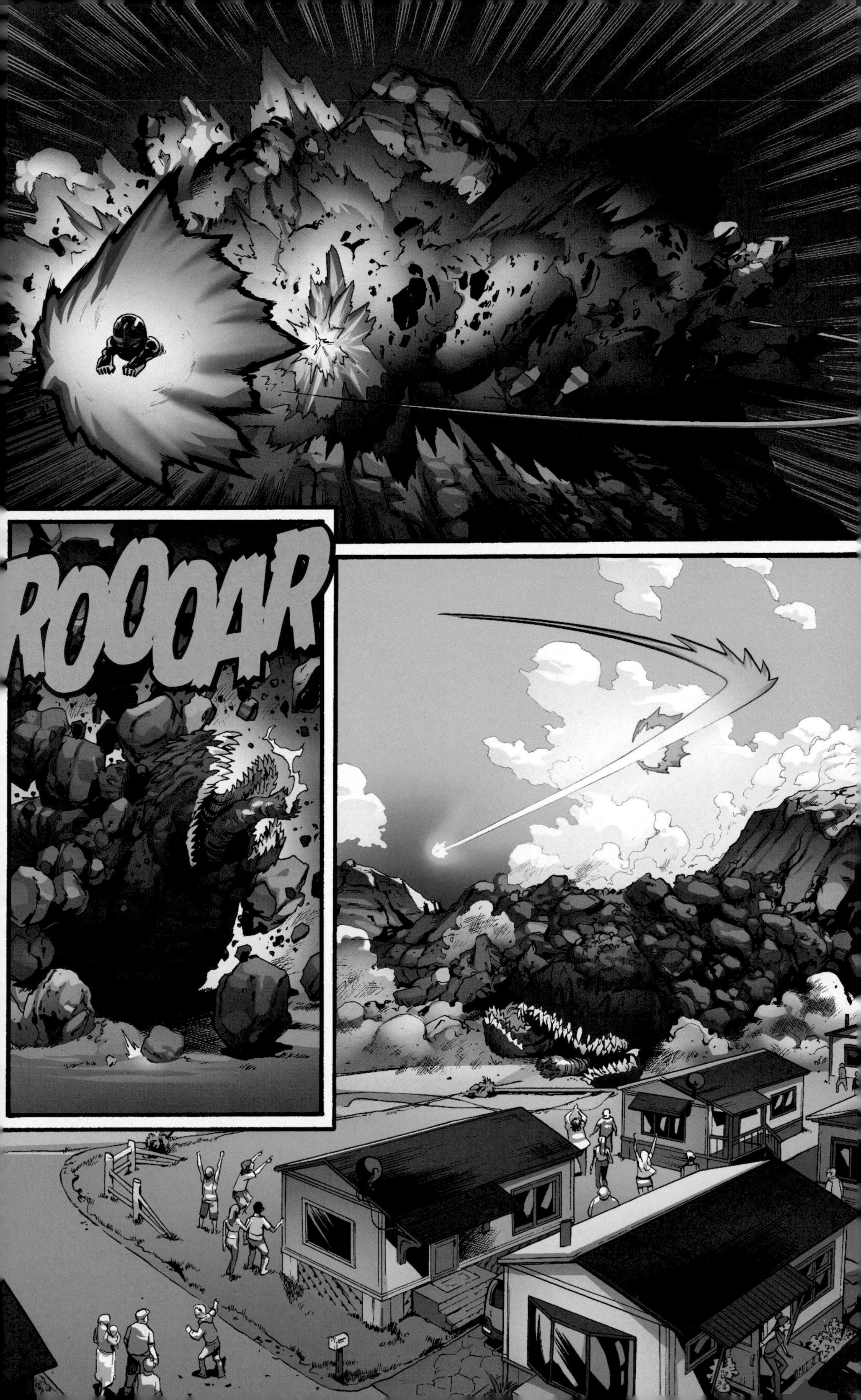
ROOOAR

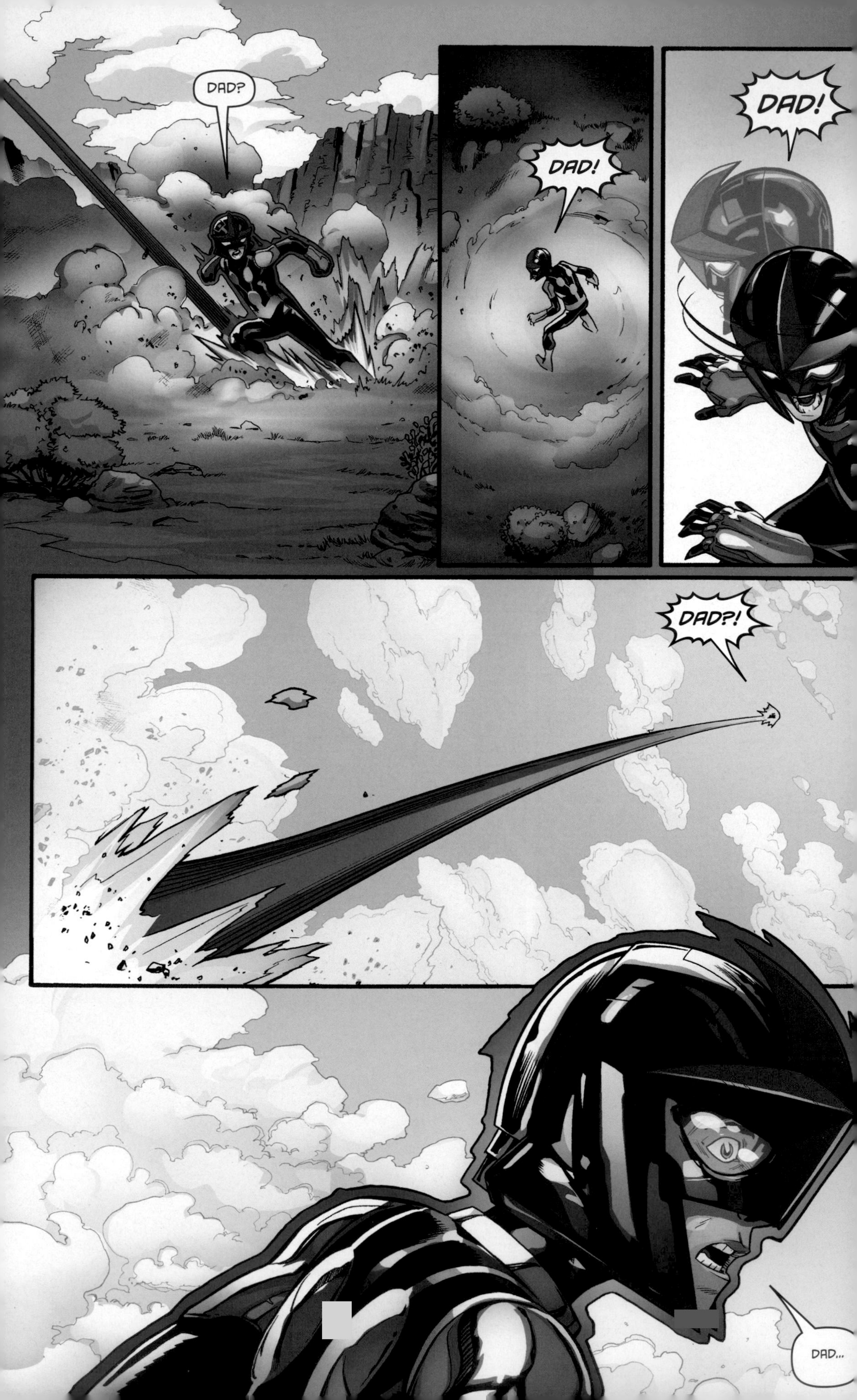
DAD?
DAD!
DAD!
DAD?!
DAD...

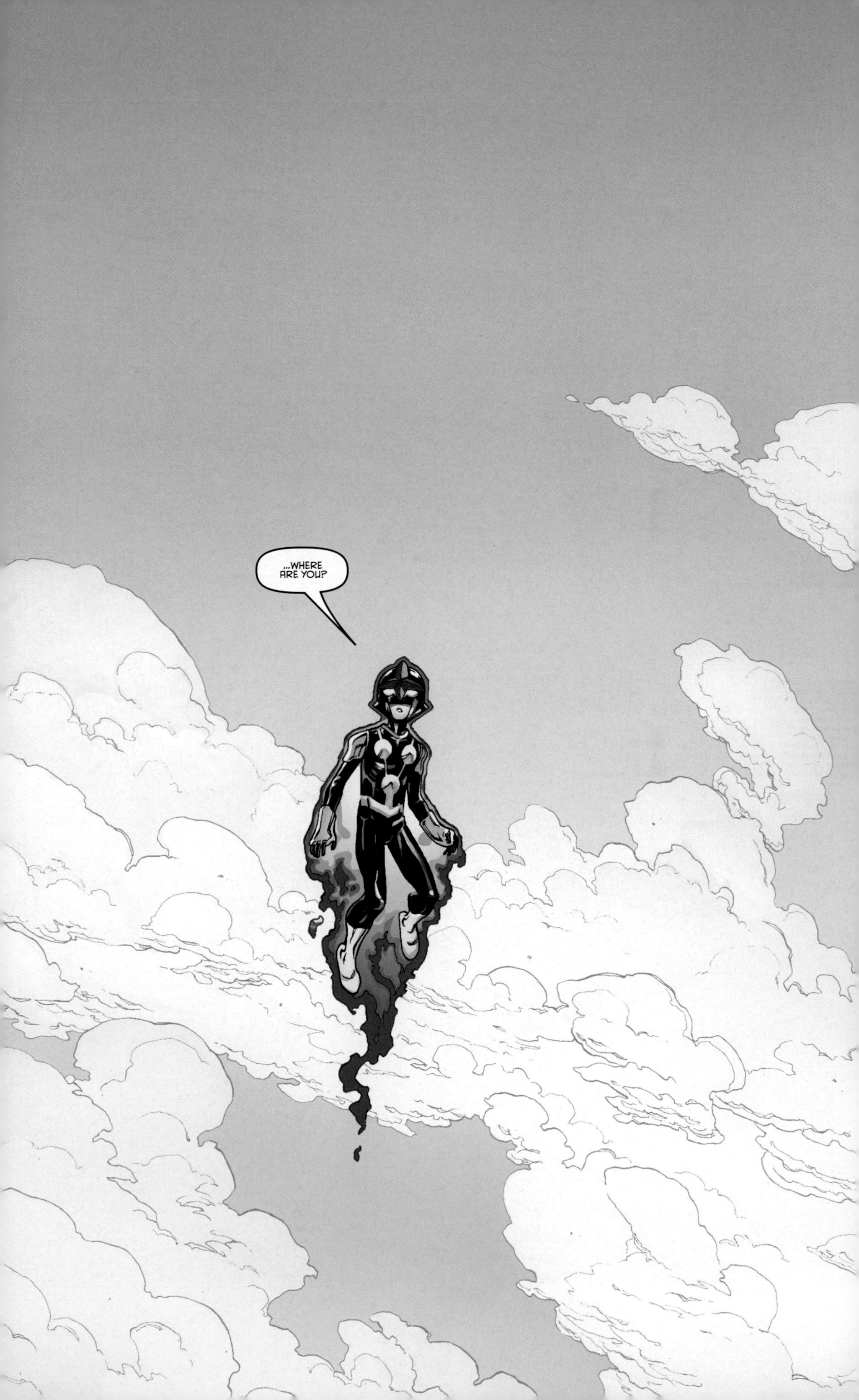
...WHERE ARE YOU?

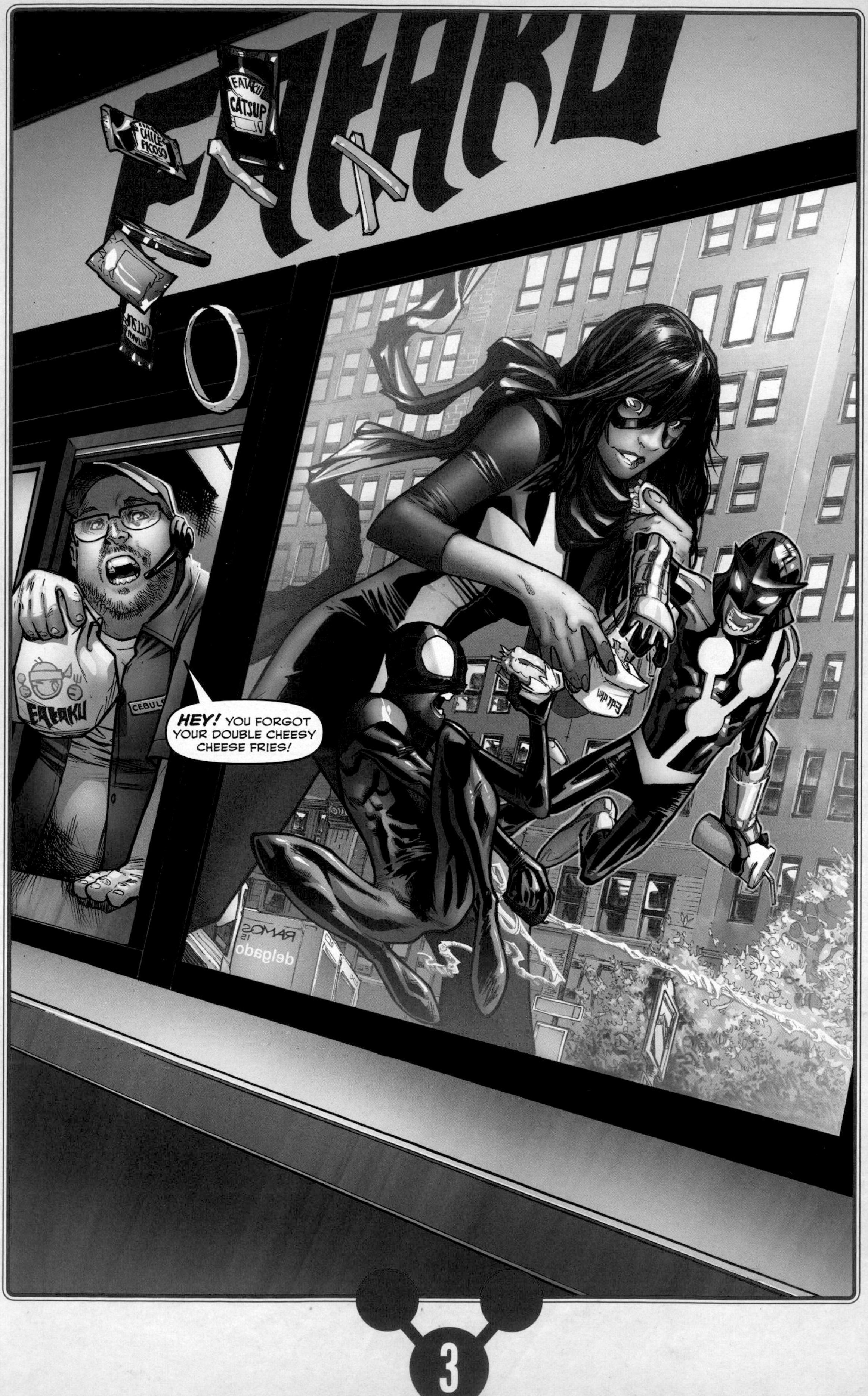
EATAKU
CATSUP
CHILE PICOSO
EATAKU
CEBULS
HEY! YOU FORGOT YOUR DOUBLE CHEESY CHEESE FRIES!
RAMOS
delgado

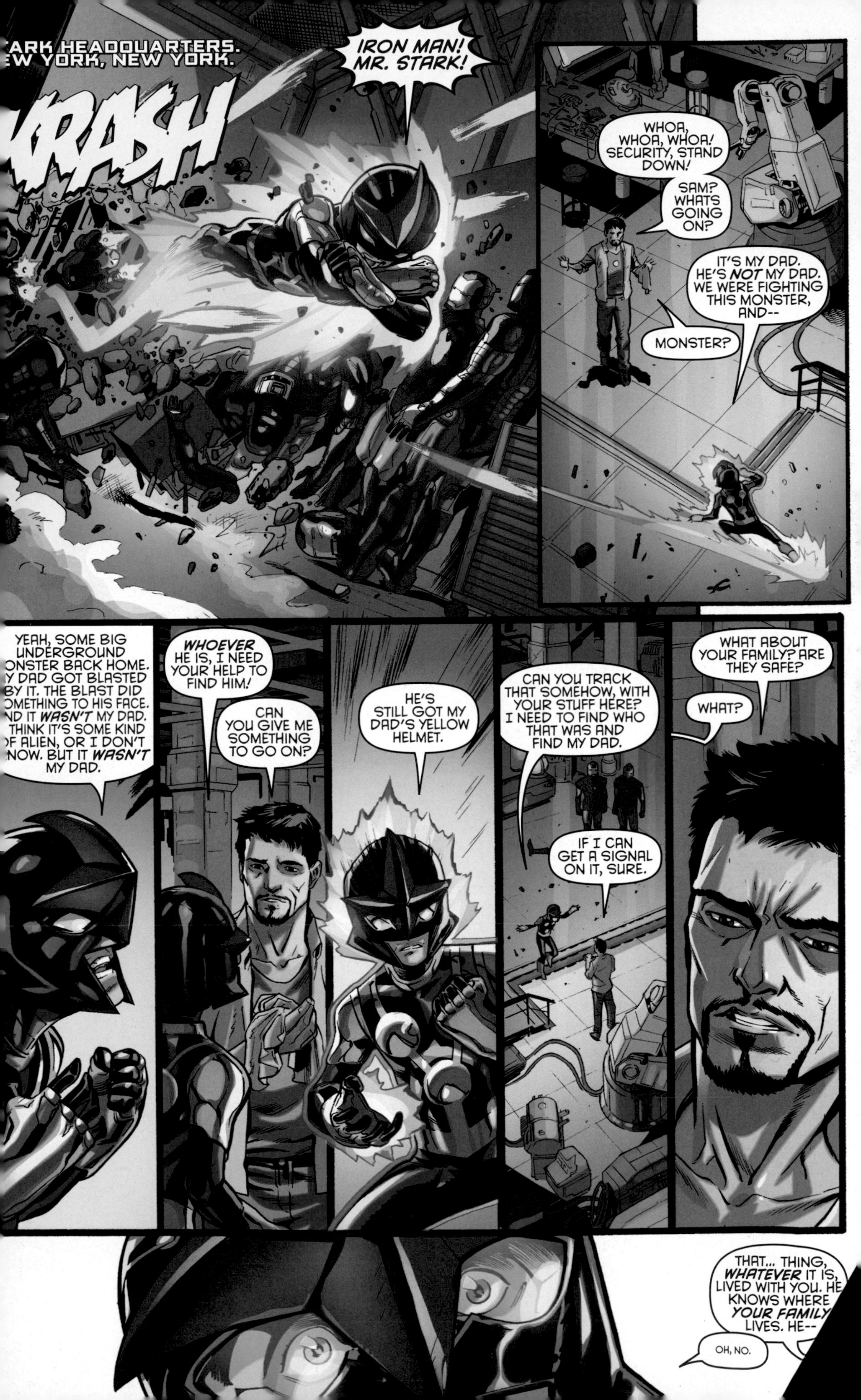

ARK HEADQUARTERS.
EW YORK, NEW YORK.
IRON MAN! MR. STARK!
KRASH
WHOA, WHOA, WHOA! SECURITY, STAND DOWN!
SAM? WHATS GOING ON?
IT'S MY DAD. HE'S NOT MY DAD. WE WERE FIGHTING THIS MONSTER, AND--
MONSTER?
YEAH, SOME BIG UNDERGROUND ONSTER BACK HOME. Y DAD GOT BLASTED BY IT. THE BLAST DID OMETHING TO HIS FACE. ND IT WASN'T MY DAD. THINK IT'S SOME KIND F ALIEN, OR I DON'T NOW. BUT IT WASN'T MY DAD.
WHOEVER HE IS, I NEED YOUR HELP TO FIND HIM!
CAN YOU GIVE ME SOMETHING TO GO ON?
HE'S STILL GOT MY DAD'S YELLOW HELMET.
CAN YOU TRACK THAT SOMEHOW, WITH YOUR STUFF HERE? I NEED TO FIND WHO THAT WAS AND FIND MY DAD.
IF I CAN GET A SIGNAL ON IT, SURE.
WHAT ABOUT YOUR FAMILY? ARE THEY SAFE?
WHAT?
THAT... THING, WHATEVER IT IS, LIVED WITH YOU. HE KNOWS WHERE YOUR FAMILY LIVES. HE--
OH, NO.

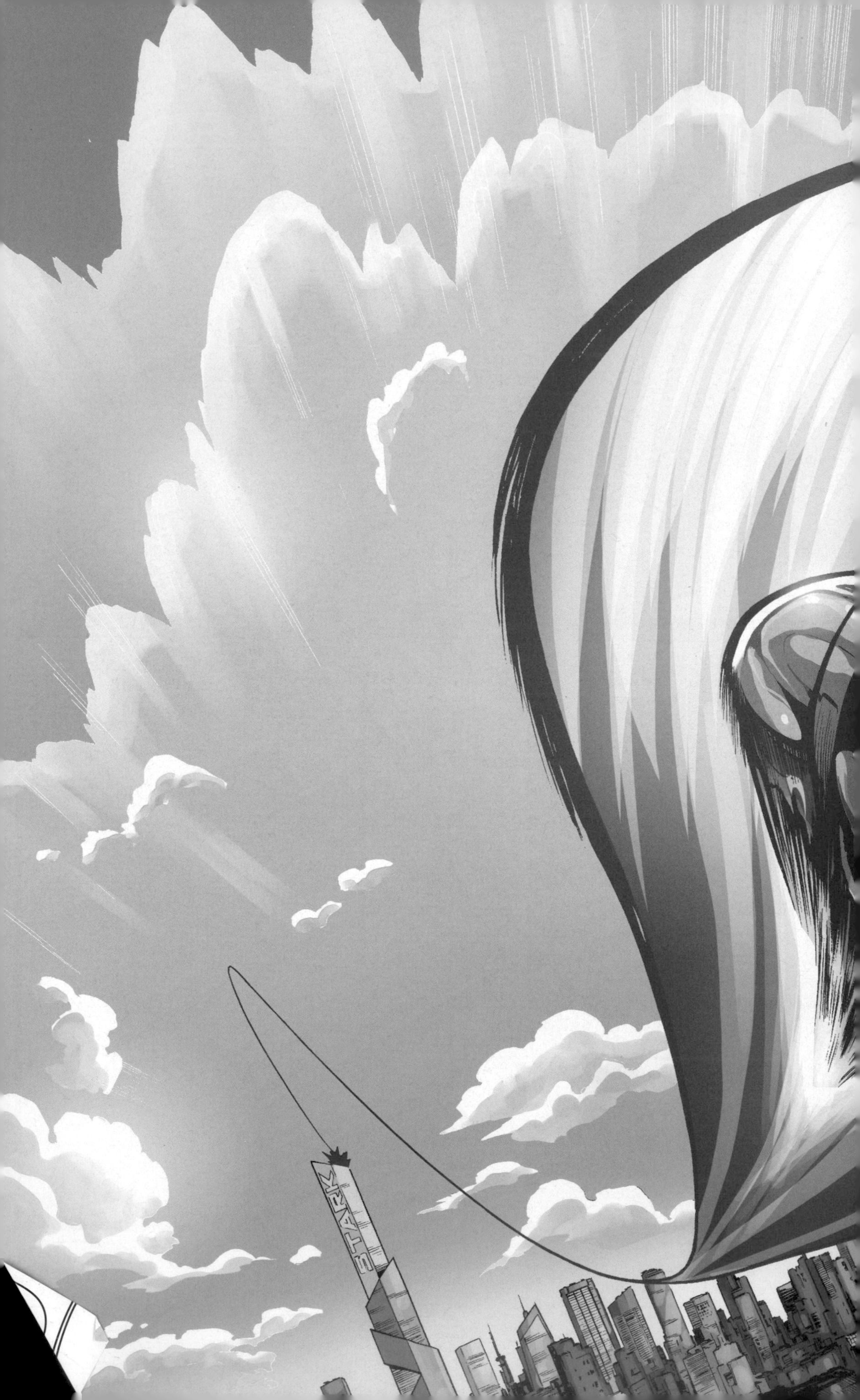
STARK

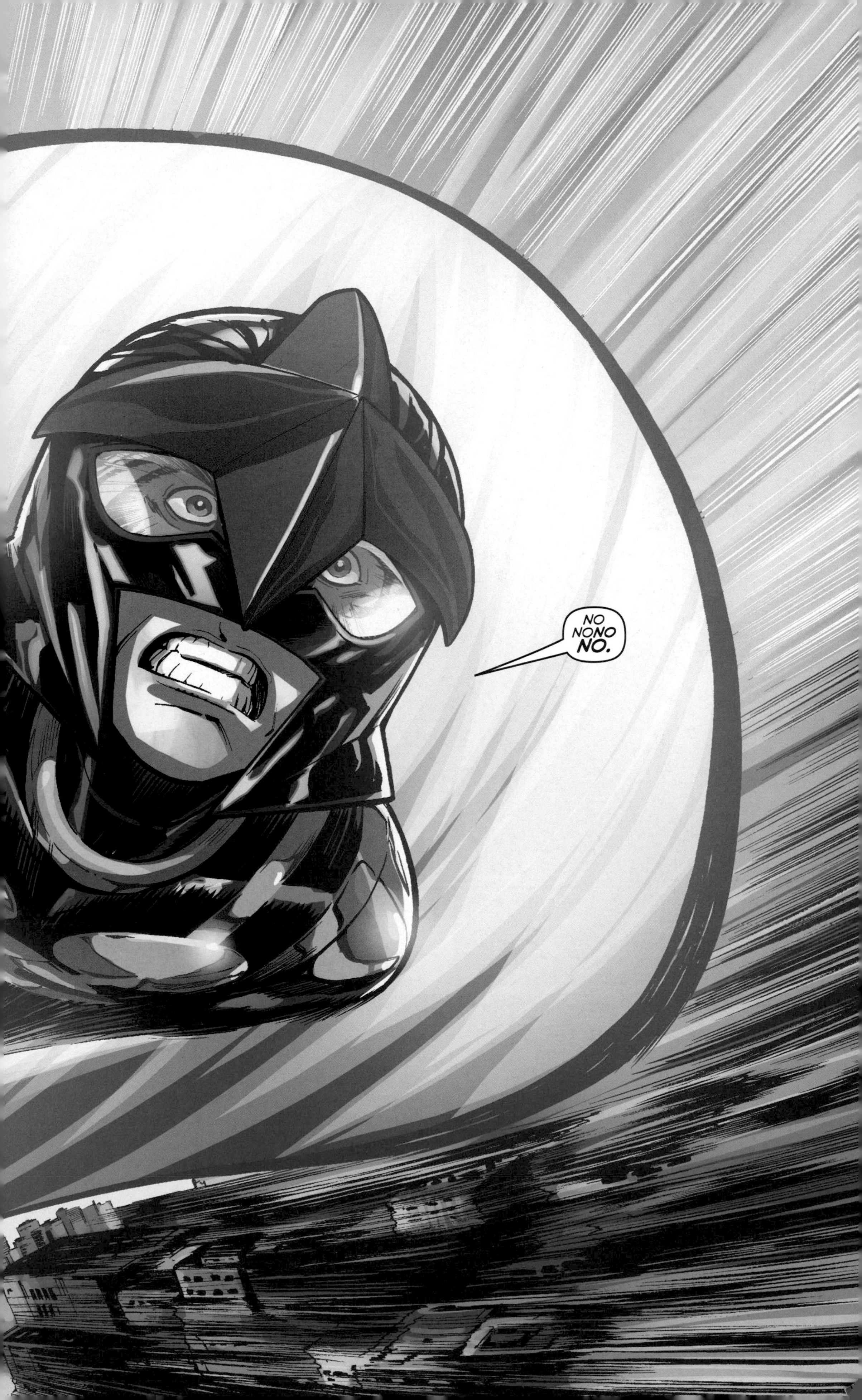
NO NONO NO.

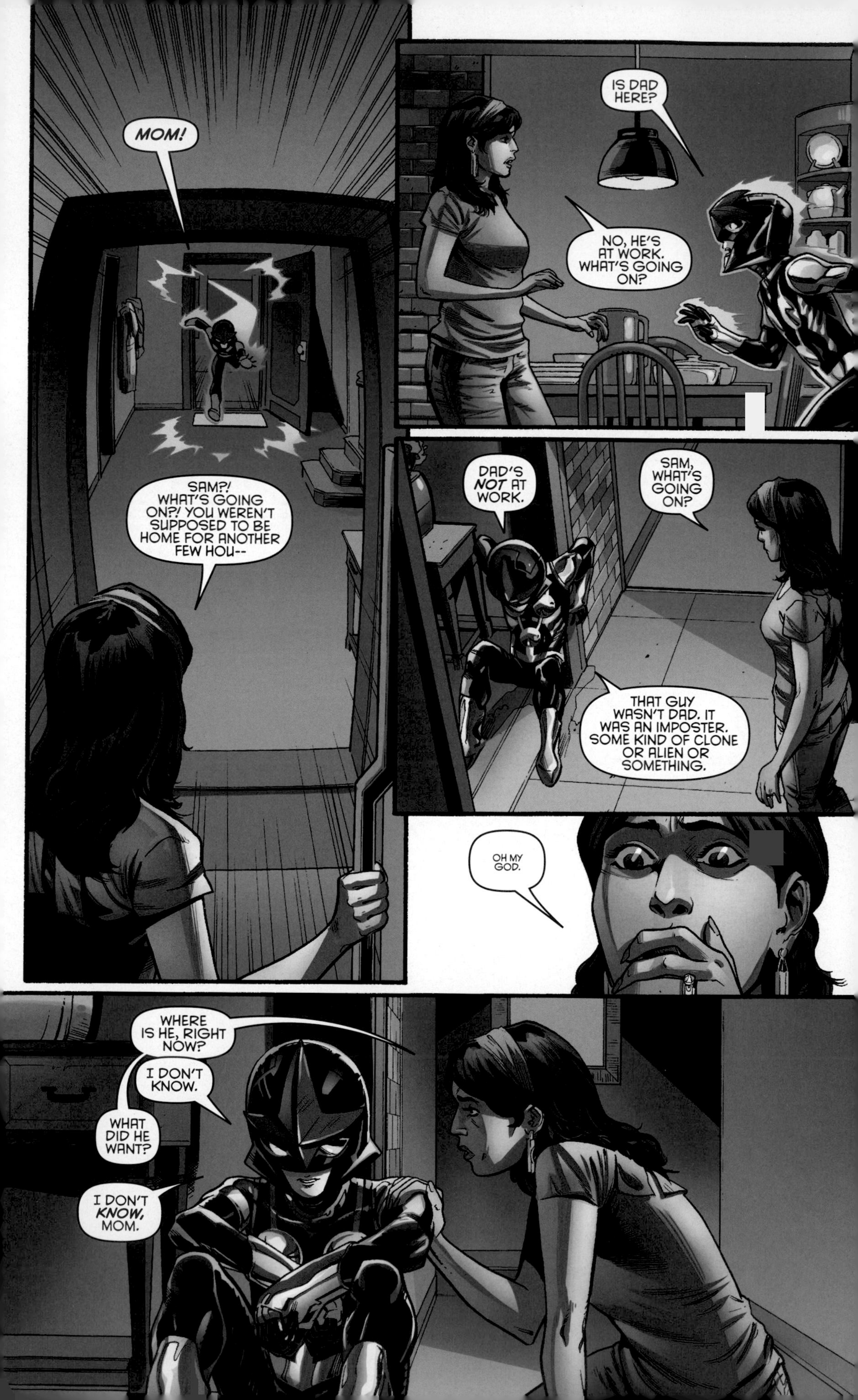
MOM!
SAM?! WHAT'S GOING ON?! YOU WEREN'T SUPPOSED TO BE HOME FOR ANOTHER FEW HOU--
IS DAD HERE?
NO, HE'S AT WORK. WHAT'S GOING ON?
DAD'S NOT AT WORK.
SAM, WHAT'S GOING ON?
THAT GUY WASN'T DAD. IT WAS AN IMPOSTER. SOME KIND OF CLONE OR ALIEN OR SOMETHING.
OH MY GOD.
WHERE IS HE, RIGHT NOW?
I DON'T KNOW.
WHAT DID HE WANT?
I DON'T KNOW, MOM.

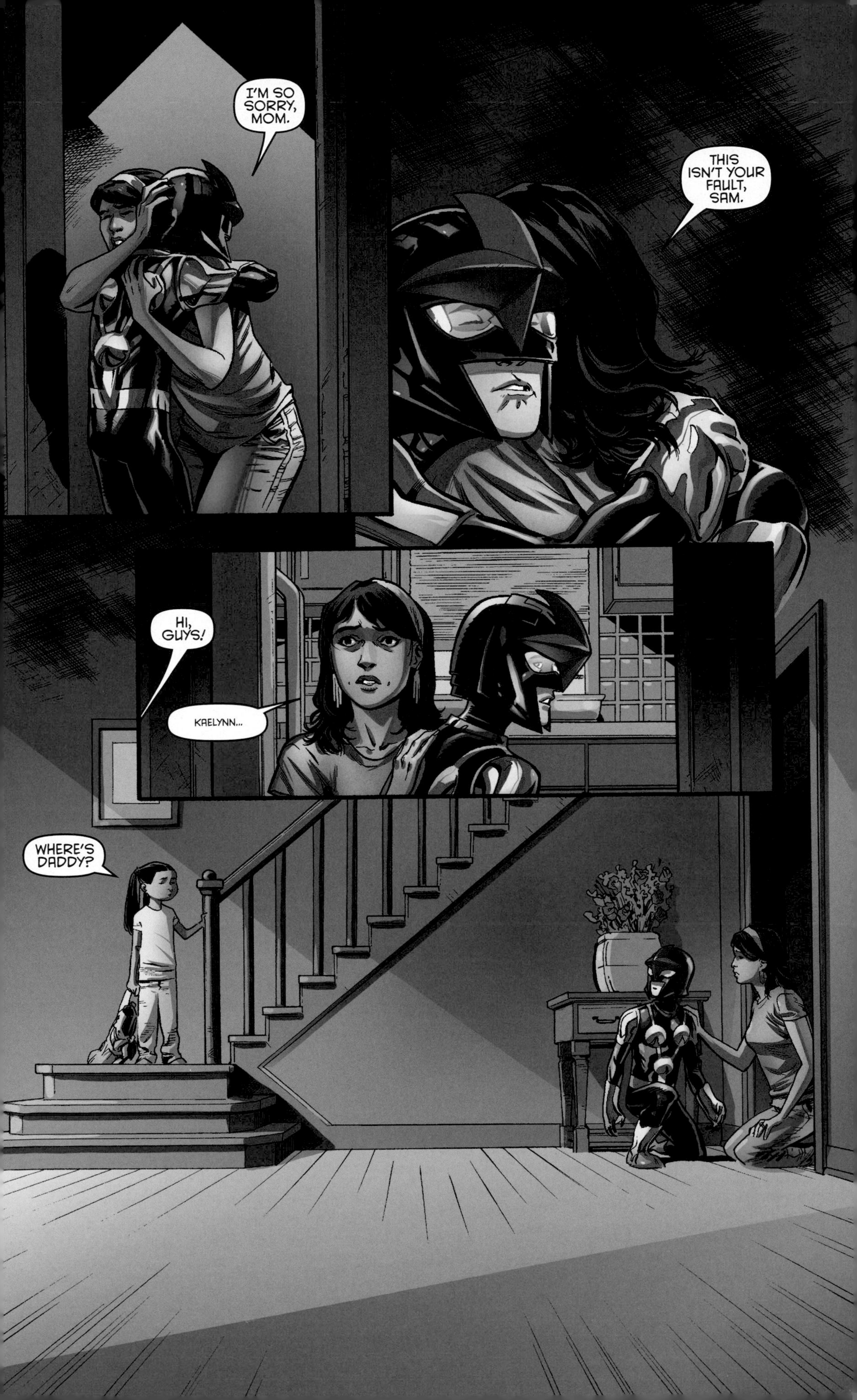
I'M SO SORRY, MOM.
THIS ISN'T YOUR FAULT, SAM.
HI, GUYS!
KAELYNN...
WHERE'S DADDY?

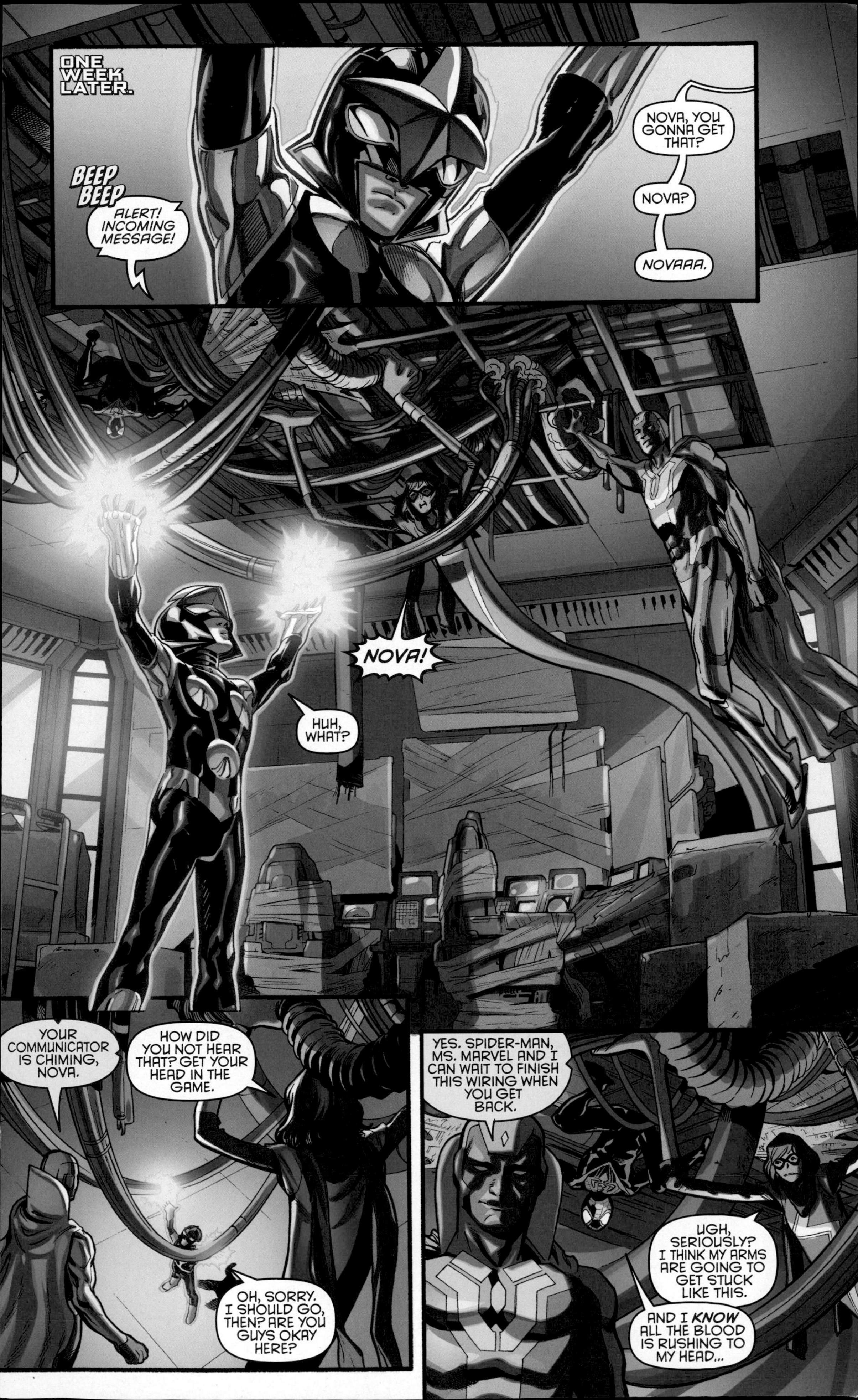
ONE WEEK LATER.
BEEP BEEP
ALERT! INCOMING MESSAGE!
NOVA, YOU GONNA GET THAT?
NOVA?
NOVAAA.
NOVA!
HUH, WHAT?
YOUR COMMUNICATOR IS CHIMING, NOVA.
HOW DID YOU NOT HEAR THAT? GET YOUR HEAD IN THE GAME.
OH, SORRY. I SHOULD GO, THEN? ARE YOU GUYS OKAY HERE?
YES. SPIDER-MAN, MS. MARVEL AND I CAN WAIT TO FINISH THIS WIRING WHEN YOU GET BACK.
UGH, SERIOUSLY? I THINK MY ARMS ARE GOING TO GET STUCK LIKE THIS.
AND I KNOW ALL THE BLOOD IS RUSHING TO MY HEAD...

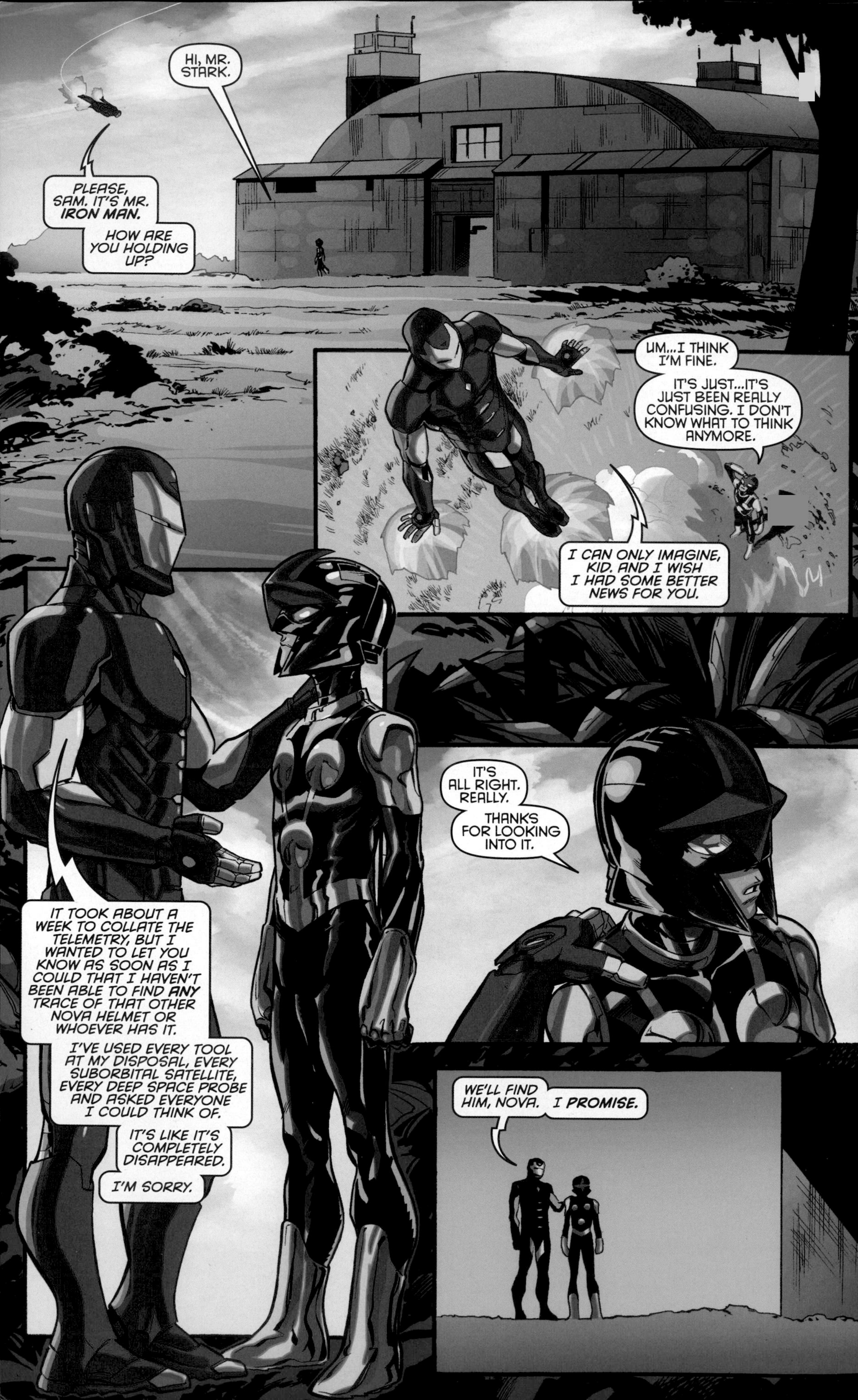
HI, MR. STARK.
PLEASE, SAM. IT'S MR. IRON MAN.
HOW ARE YOU HOLDING UP?
UM...I THINK I'M FINE.
IT'S JUST...IT'S JUST BEEN REALLY CONFUSING. I DON'T KNOW WHAT TO THINK ANYMORE.
I CAN ONLY IMAGINE, KID. AND I WISH I HAD SOME BETTER NEWS FOR YOU.
IT TOOK ABOUT A WEEK TO COLLATE THE TELEMETRY, BUT I WANTED TO LET YOU KNOW AS SOON AS I COULD THAT I HAVEN'T BEEN ABLE TO FIND ANY TRACE OF THAT OTHER NOVA HELMET OR WHOEVER HAS IT.
I'VE USED EVERY TOOL AT MY DISPOSAL, EVERY SUBORBITAL SATELLITE, EVERY DEEP SPACE PROBE AND ASKED EVERYONE I COULD THINK OF.
IT'S LIKE IT'S COMPLETELY DISAPPEARED.
I'M SORRY.
IT'S ALL RIGHT. REALLY.
THANKS FOR LOOKING INTO IT.
WE'LL FIND HIM, NOVA. I PROMISE.

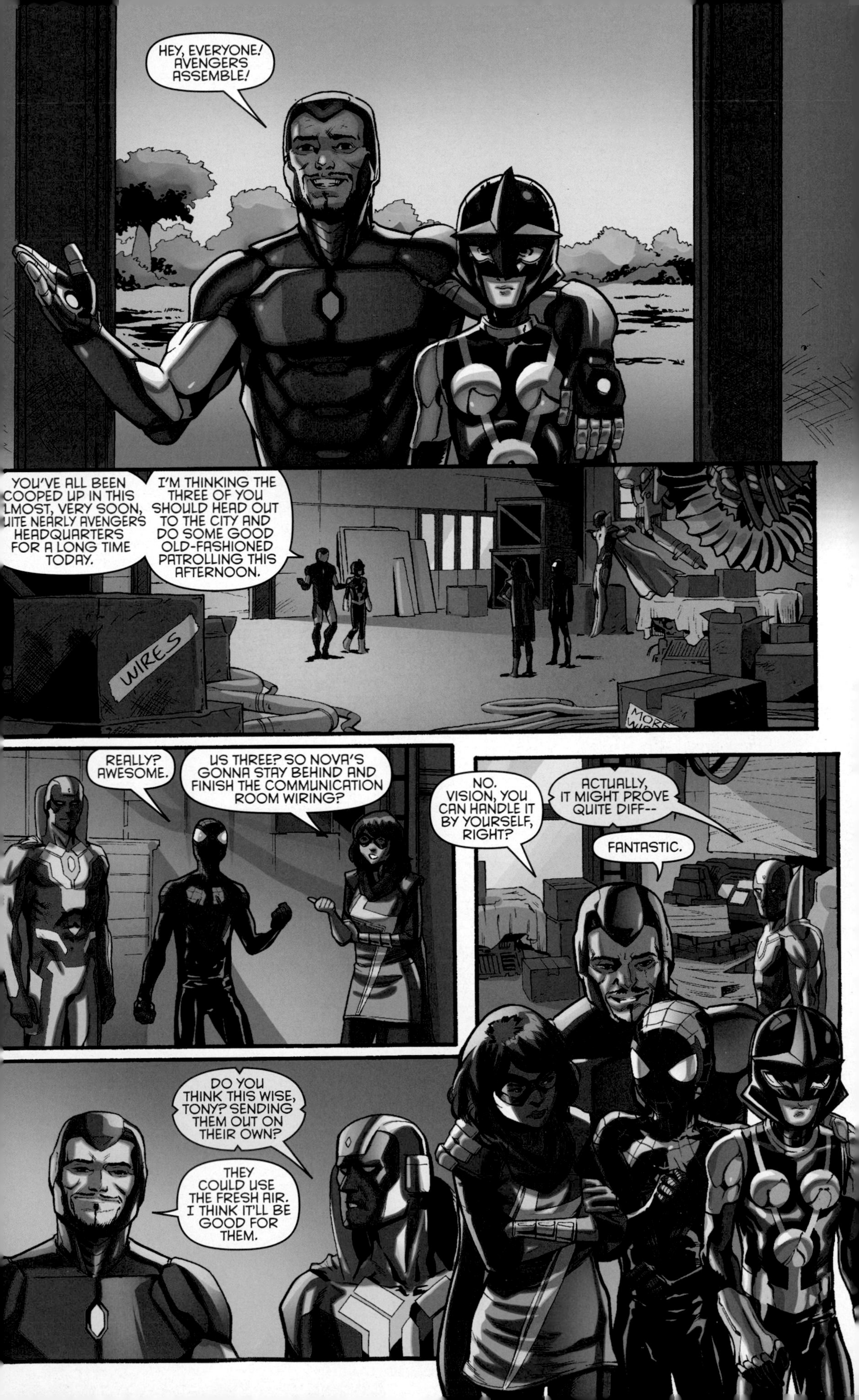
HEY, EVERYONE! AVENGERS ASSEMBLE!
YOU'VE ALL BEEN COOPED UP IN THIS LMOST, VERY SOON, UITE NEARLY AVENGERS HEADQUARTERS FOR A LONG TIME TODAY.
I'M THINKING THE THREE OF YOU SHOULD HEAD OUT TO THE CITY AND DO SOME GOOD OLD-FASHIONED PATROLLING THIS AFTERNOON.
WIRES
REALLY? AWESOME.
US THREE? SO NOVA'S GONNA STAY BEHIND AND FINISH THE COMMUNICATION ROOM WIRING?
NO. VISION, YOU CAN HANDLE IT BY YOURSELF, RIGHT?
ACTUALLY, IT MIGHT PROVE QUITE DIFF--
FANTASTIC.
DO YOU THINK THIS WISE, TONY? SENDING THEM OUT ON THEIR OWN?
THEY COULD USE THE FRESH AIR. I THINK IT'LL BE GOOD FOR THEM.

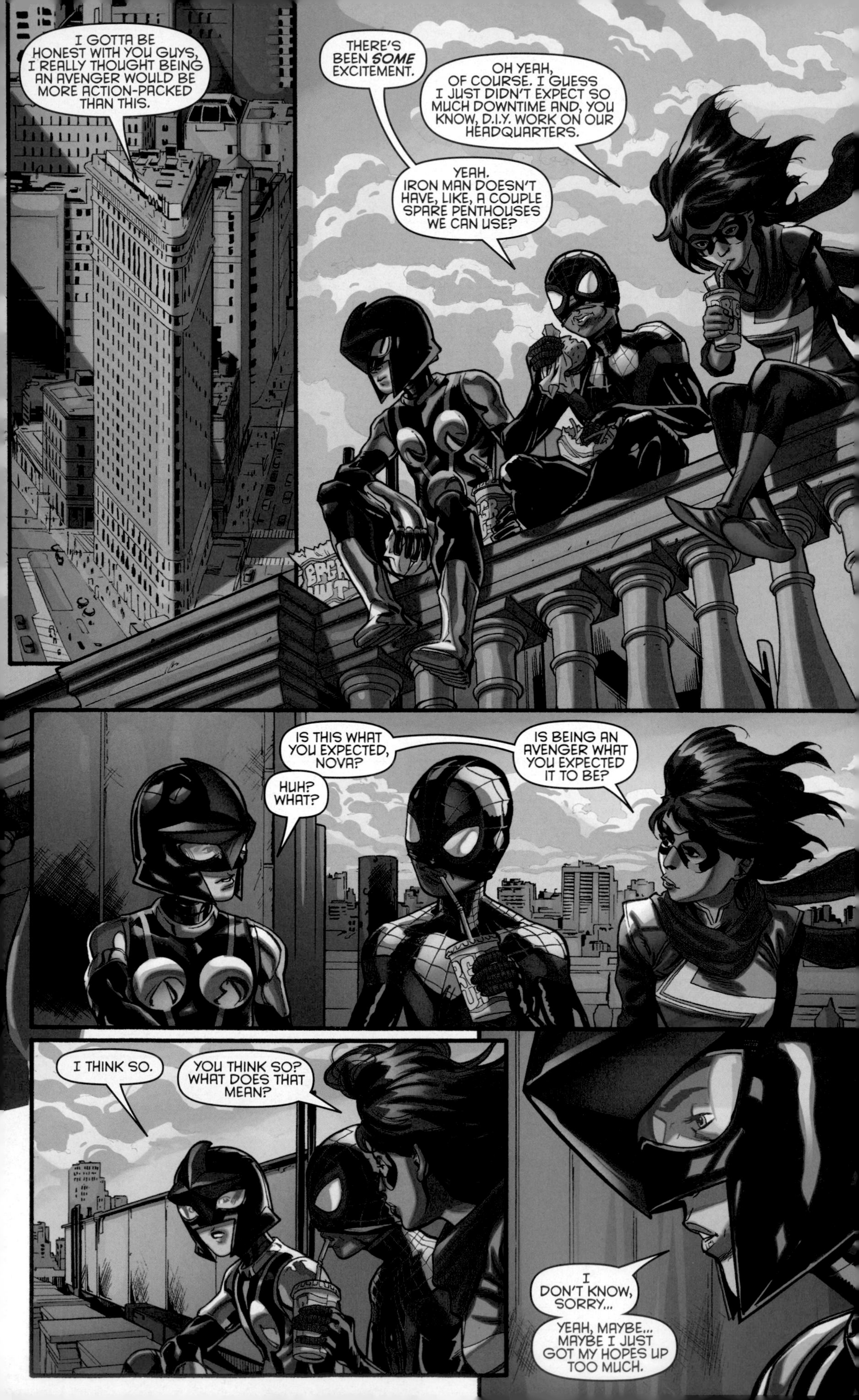
I GOTTA BE HONEST WITH YOU GUYS, I REALLY THOUGHT BEING AN AVENGER WOULD BE MORE ACTION-PACKED THAN THIS.
THERE'S BEEN *SOME* EXCITEMENT.
OH YEAH, OF COURSE. I GUESS I JUST DIDN'T EXPECT SO MUCH DOWNTIME AND, YOU KNOW, D.I.Y. WORK ON OUR HEADQUARTERS.
YEAH. IRON MAN DOESN'T HAVE, LIKE, A COUPLE SPARE PENTHOUSES WE CAN USE?
IS THIS WHAT YOU EXPECTED, NOVA?
IS BEING AN AVENGER WHAT YOU EXPECTED IT TO BE?
HUH? WHAT?
I THINK SO.
YOU THINK SO? WHAT DOES THAT MEAN?
I DON'T KNOW, SORRY...
YEAH, MAYBE... MAYBE I JUST GOT MY HOPES UP TOO MUCH.

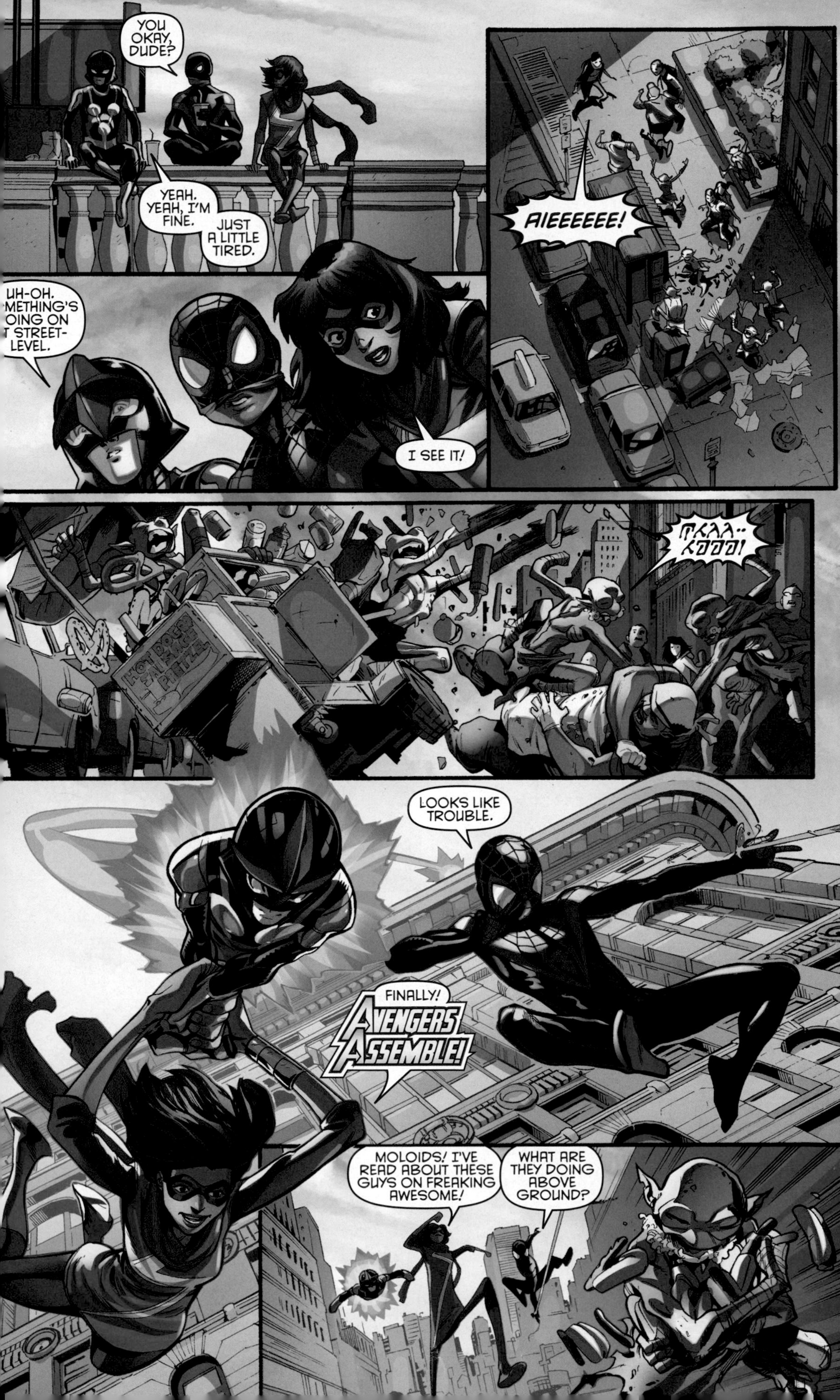

YOU OKAY, DUDE?
YEAH. YEAH, I'M FINE.
JUST A LITTLE TIRED.
AIEEEEEE!
UH-OH. METHING'S OING ON T STREET-LEVEL.
I SEE IT!
LOOKS LIKE TROUBLE.
FINALLY! AVENGERS ASSEMBLE!
MOLOIDS! I'VE READ ABOUT THESE GUYS ON FREAKING AWESOME!
WHAT ARE THEY DOING ABOVE GROUND?

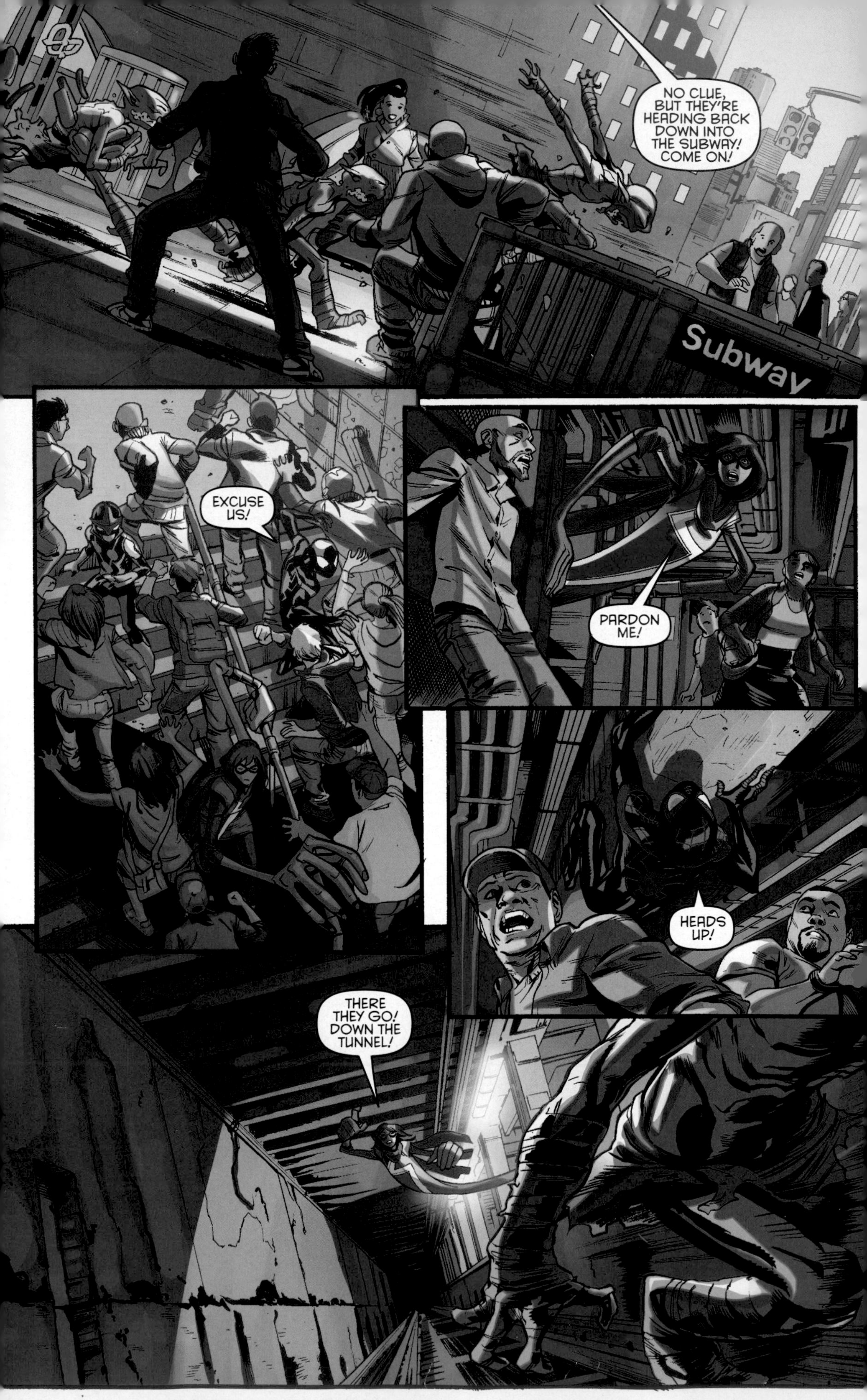
NO CLUE, BUT THEY'RE HEADING BACK DOWN INTO THE SUBWAY! COME ON!
Subway
EXCUSE US!
PARDON ME!
HEADS UP!
THERE THEY GO! DOWN THE TUNNEL!

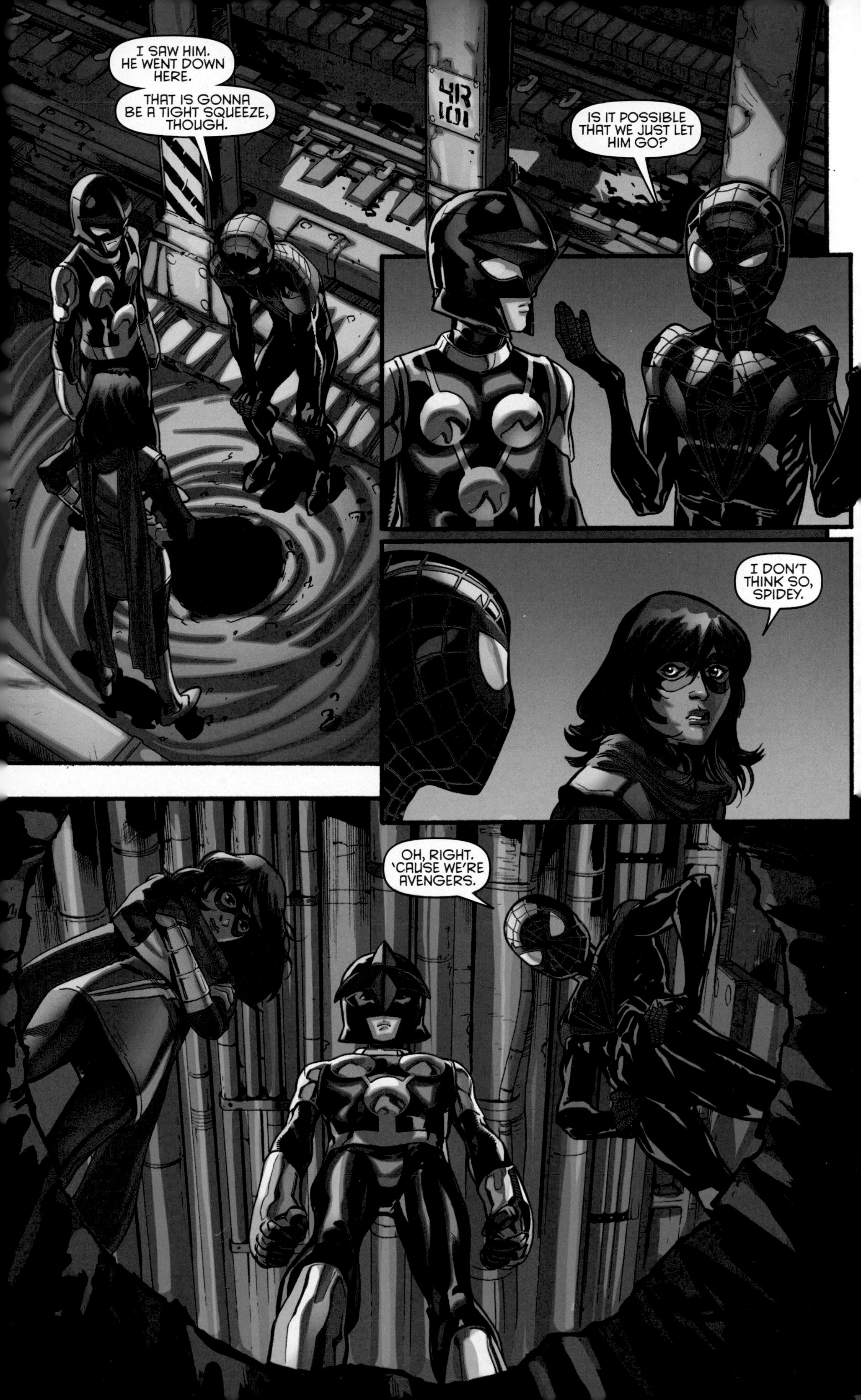
I SAW HIM. HE WENT DOWN HERE.
THAT IS GONNA BE A TIGHT SQUEEZE, THOUGH.
4R 101
IS IT POSSIBLE THAT WE JUST LET HIM GO?
I DON'T THINK SO, SPIDEY.
OH, RIGHT. 'CAUSE WE'RE AVENGERS.

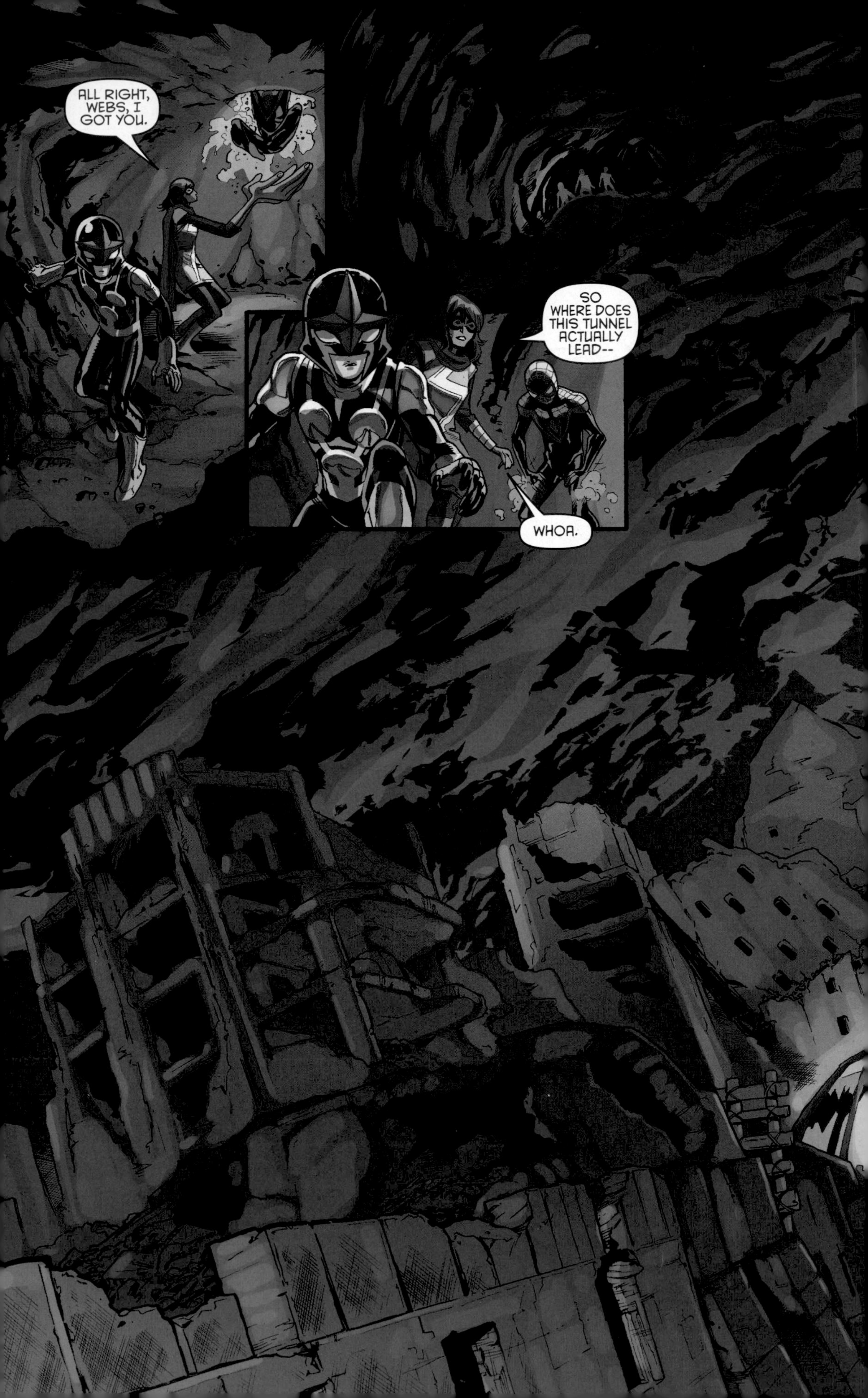
ALL RIGHT, WEBS, I GOT YOU.
SO WHERE DOES THIS TUNNEL ACTUALLY LEAD--
WHOA.

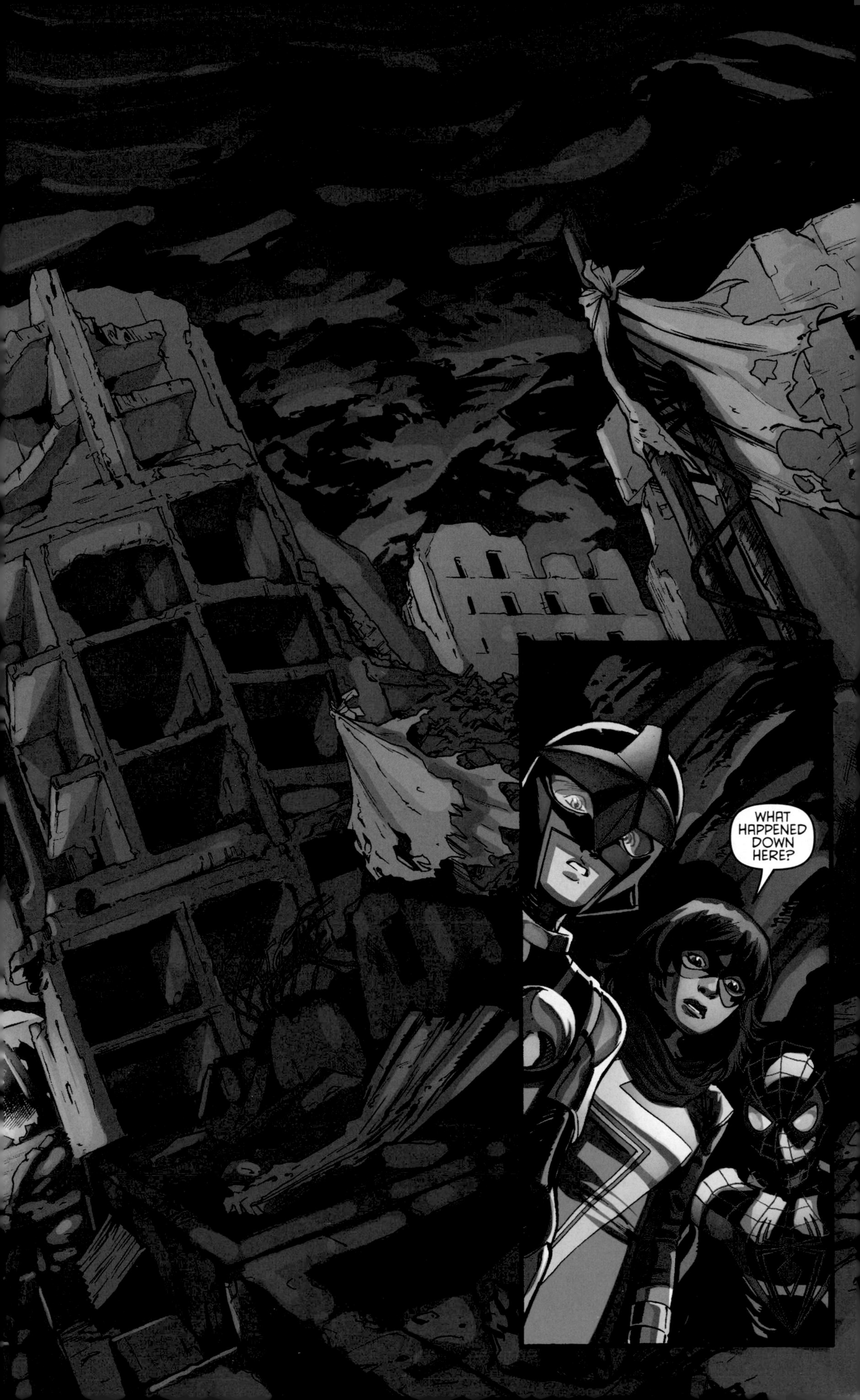
WHAT HAPPENED DOWN HERE?

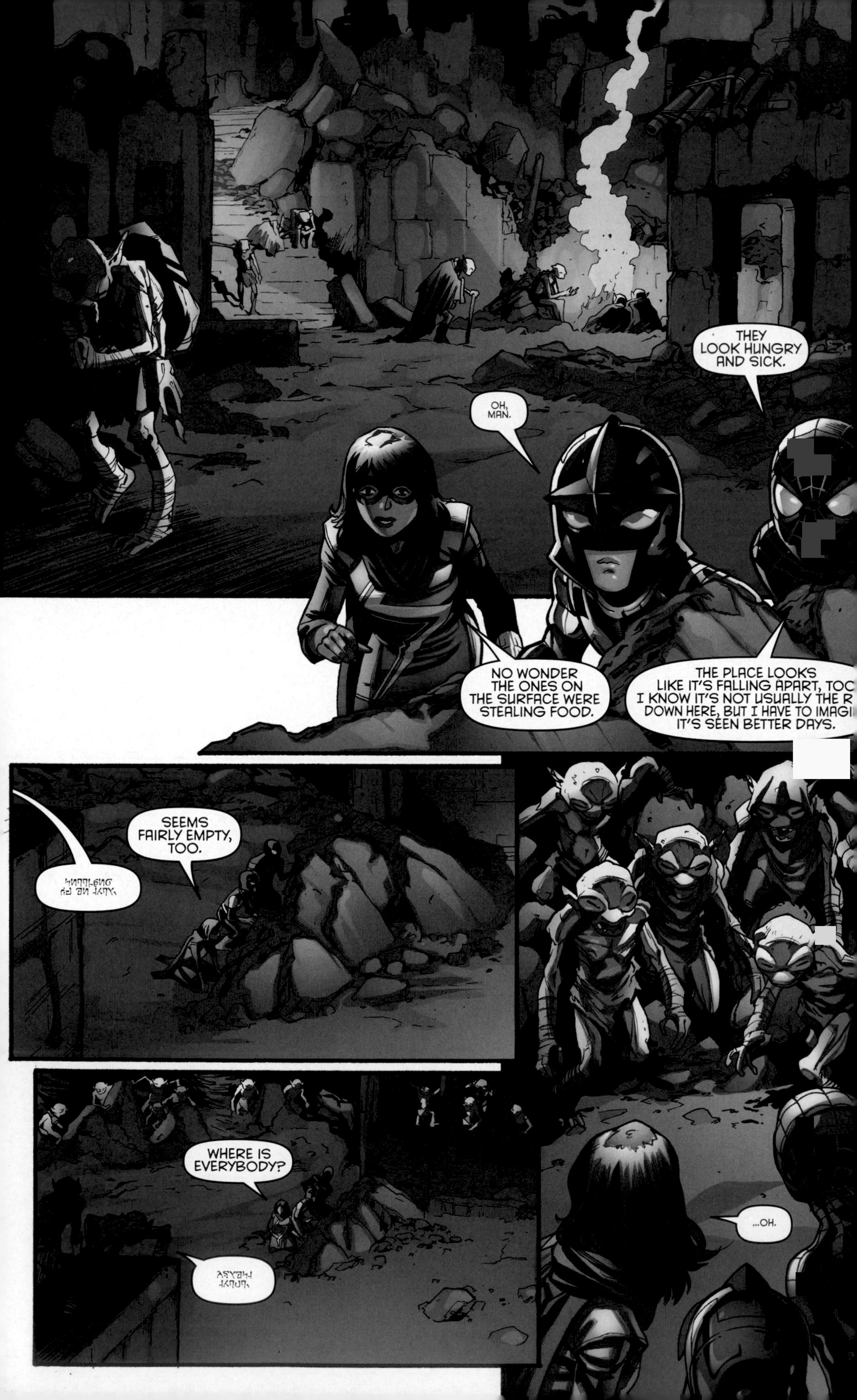

OH, MAN.
THEY LOOK HUNGRY AND SICK.
NO WONDER THE ONES ON THE SURFACE WERE STEALING FOOD.
THE PLACE LOOKS LIKE IT'S FALLING APART, TOO I KNOW IT'S NOT USUALLY THE R DOWN HERE, BUT I HAVE TO IMAGI IT'S SEEN BETTER DAYS.
SEEMS FAIRLY EMPTY, TOO.
WHERE IS EVERYBODY?
...OH.

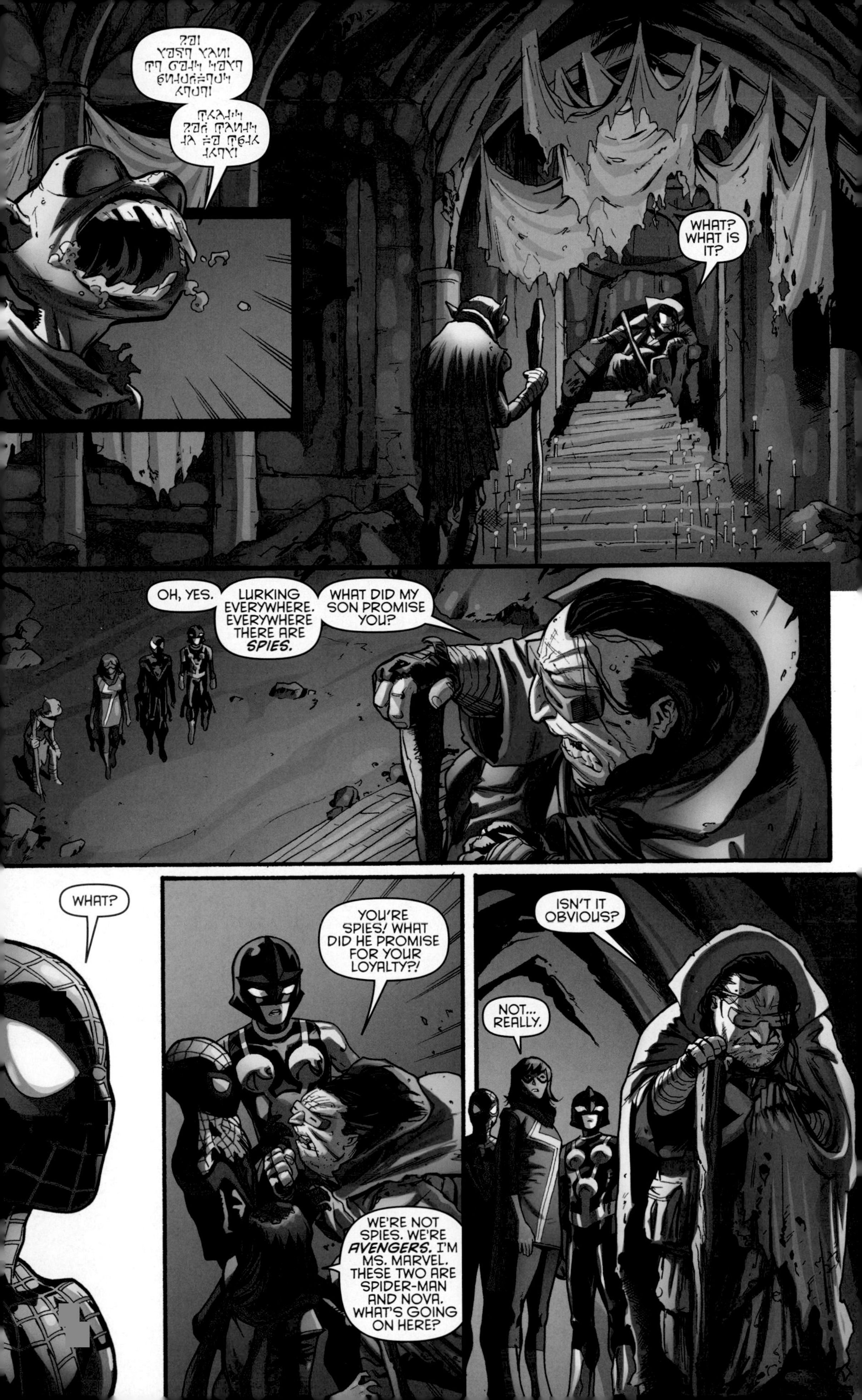
WHAT? WHAT IS IT?
OH, YES.
LURKING EVERYWHERE. EVERYWHERE THERE ARE SPIES.
WHAT DID MY SON PROMISE YOU?
WHAT?
YOU'RE SPIES! WHAT DID HE PROMISE FOR YOUR LOYALTY?!
WE'RE NOT SPIES. WE'RE AVENGERS. I'M MS. MARVEL. THESE TWO ARE SPIDER-MAN AND NOVA. WHAT'S GOING ON HERE?
ISN'T IT OBVIOUS?
NOT... REALLY.

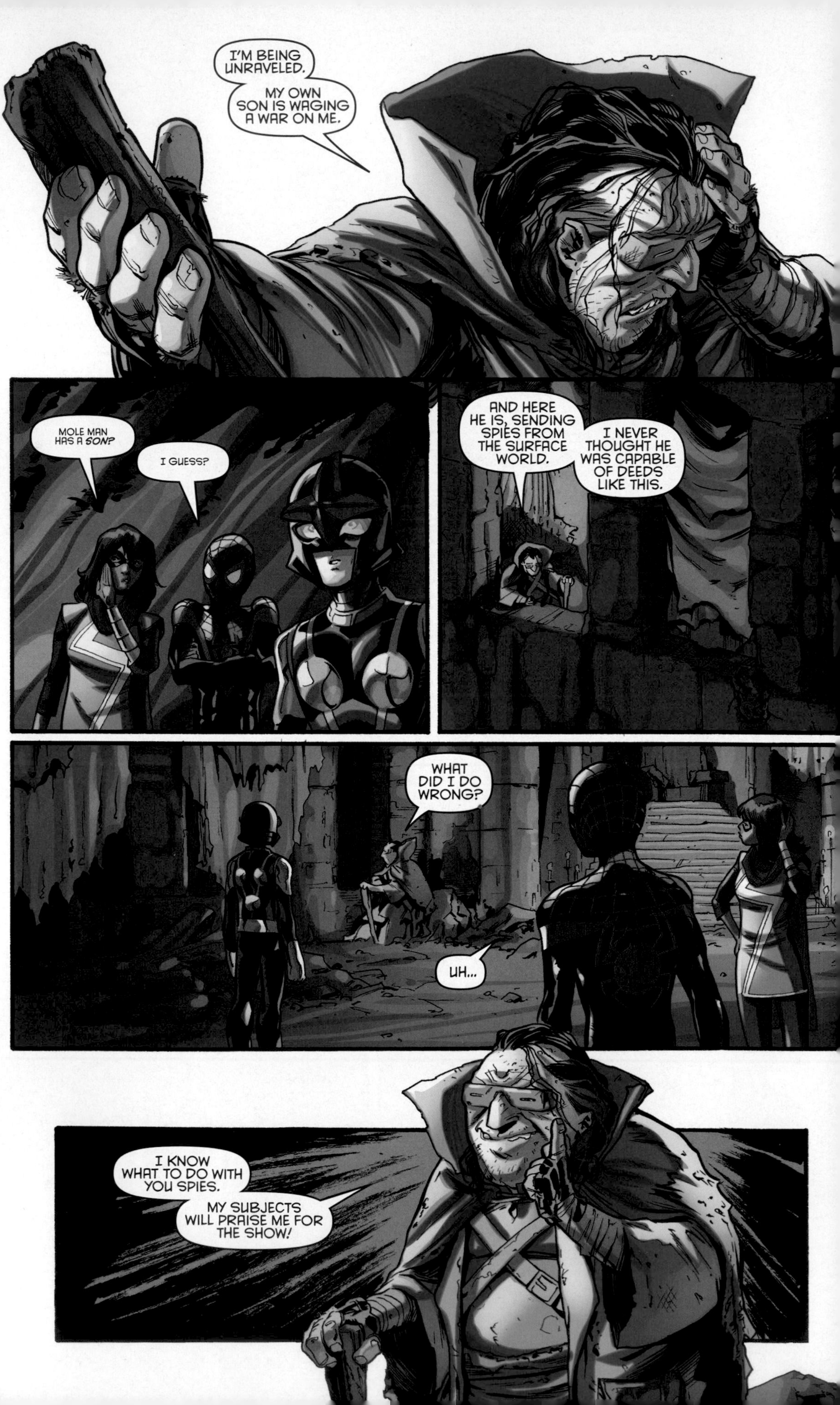
I'M BEING UNRAVELED.
MY OWN SON IS WAGING A WAR ON ME.
MOLE MAN HAS A SON?
I GUESS?
AND HERE HE IS, SENDING SPIES FROM THE SURFACE WORLD.
I NEVER THOUGHT HE WAS CAPABLE OF DEEDS LIKE THIS.
WHAT DID I DO WRONG?
UH...
I KNOW WHAT TO DO WITH YOU SPIES.
MY SUBJECTS WILL PRAISE ME FOR THE SHOW!

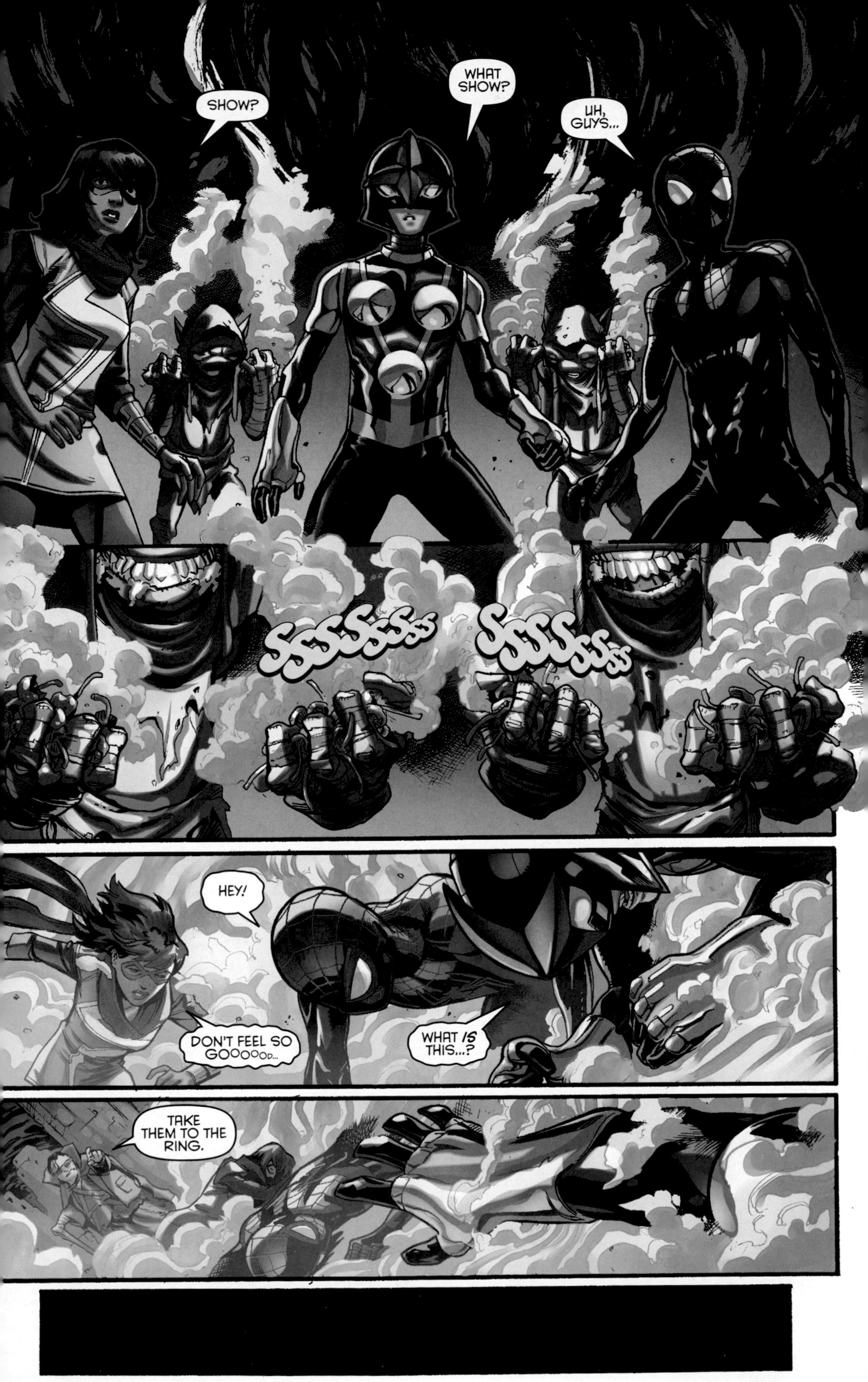
SHOW?
WHAT SHOW?
UH, GUYS...
SSSSSSSSS
SSSSSSSS
HEY!
DON'T FEEL SO GOOooOD...
WHAT IS THIS...?
TAKE THEM TO THE RING.

[redacted]

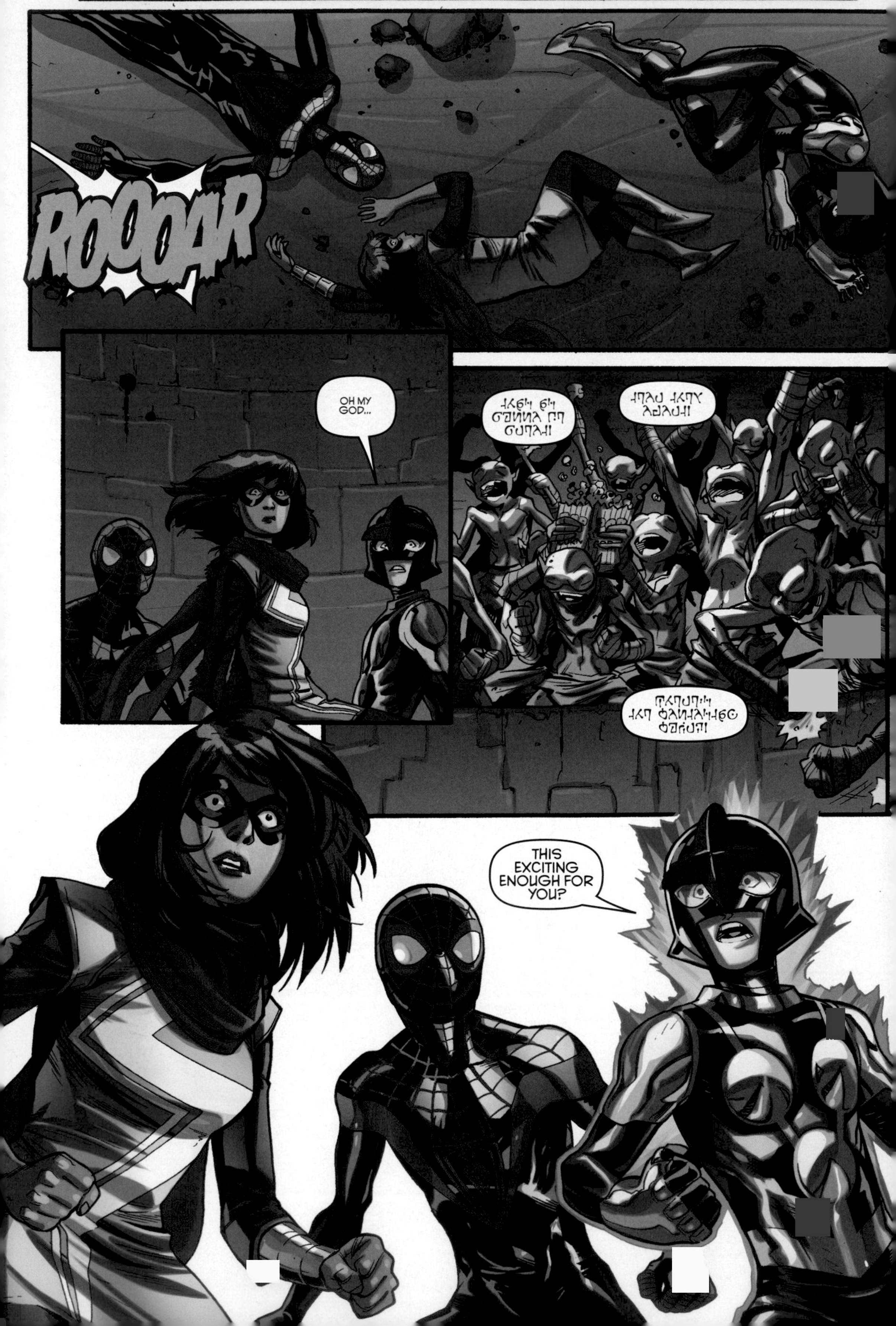
ROOOAR
OH MY GOD...
THIS EXCITING ENOUGH FOR YOU?

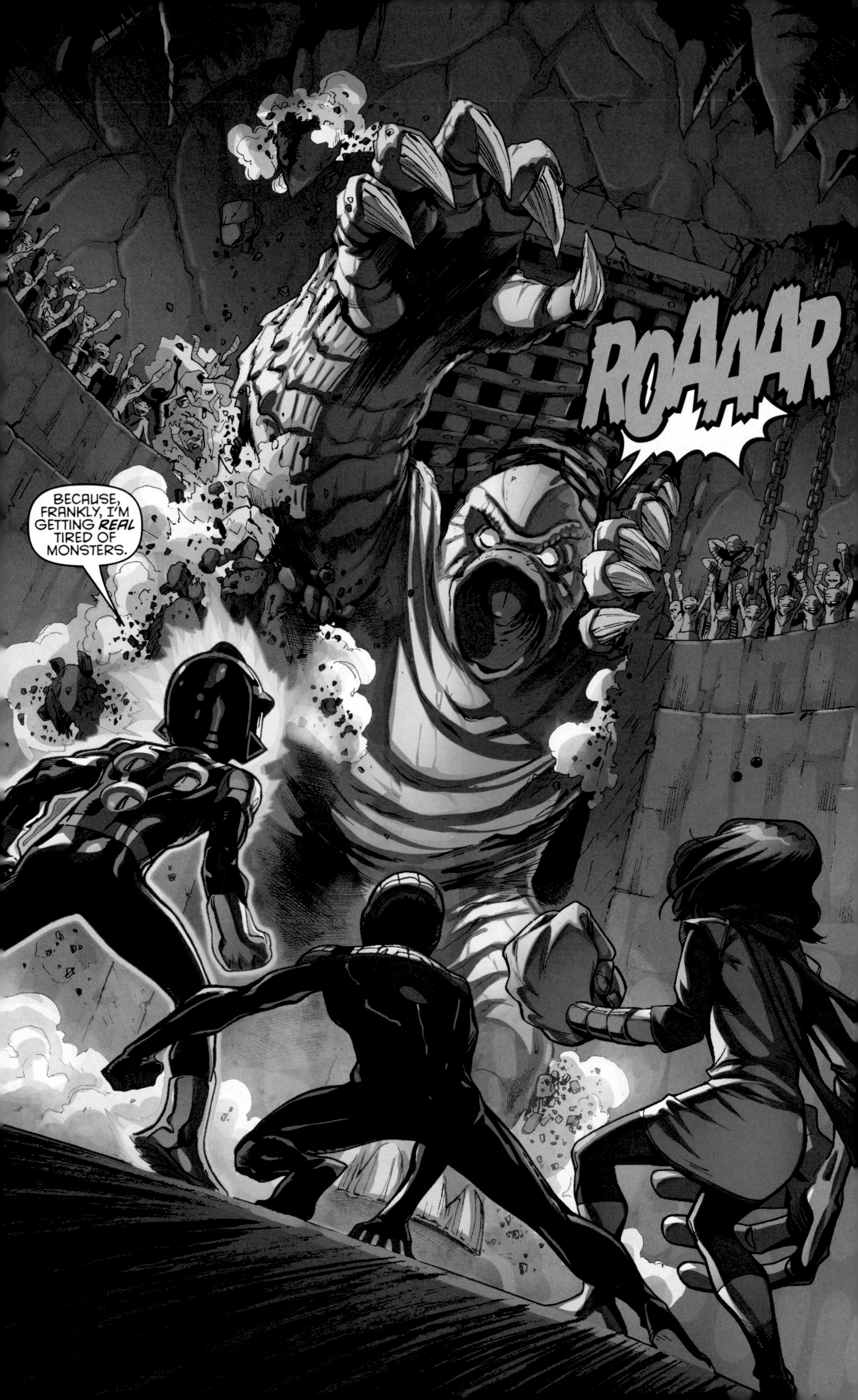
ROAAAR
BECAUSE, FRANKLY, I'M GETTING REAL TIRED OF MONSTERS.

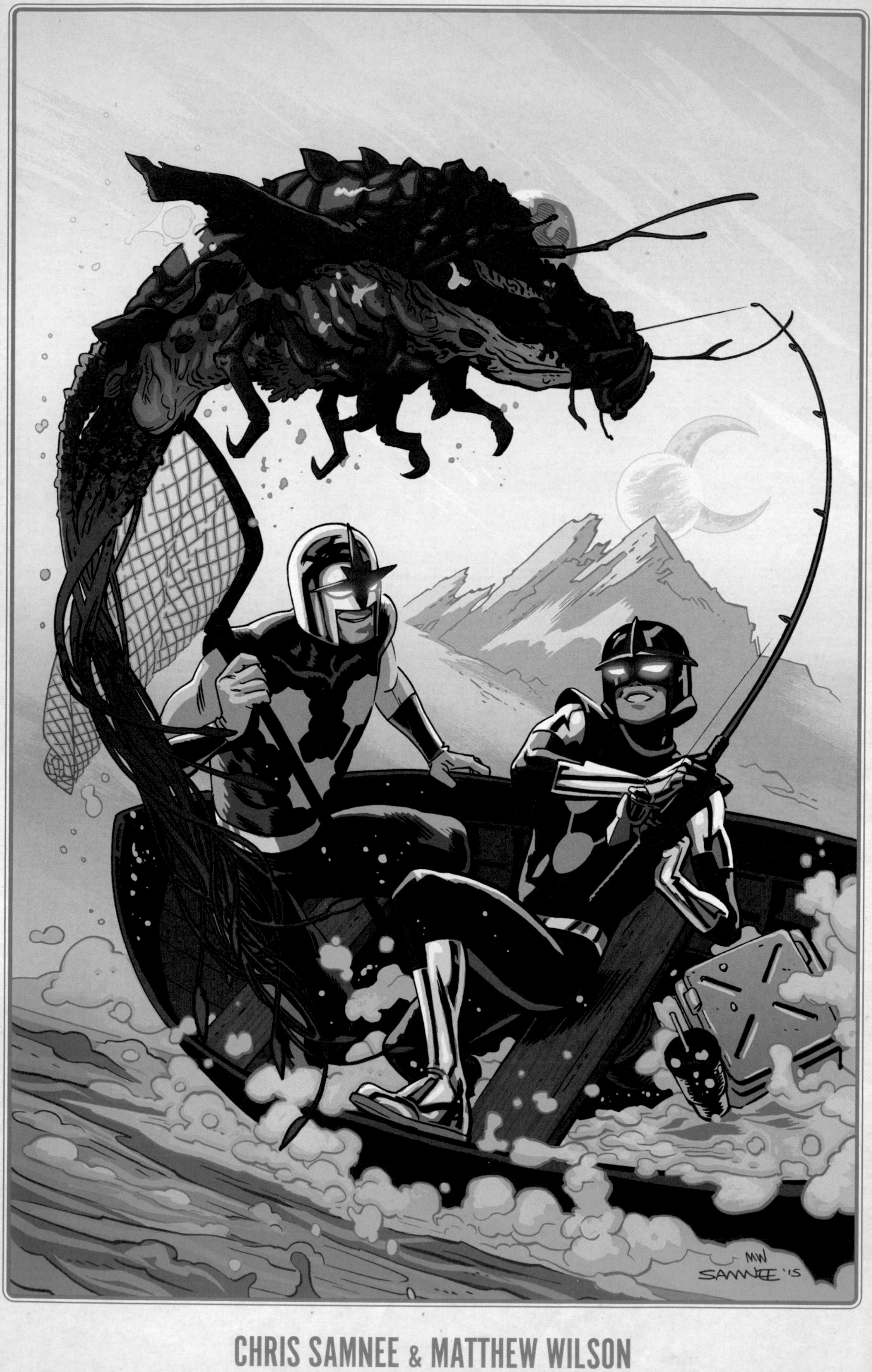
MW
SAMNEE '15

CHRIS SAMNEE & MATTHEW WILSON
No. 1 VARIANT

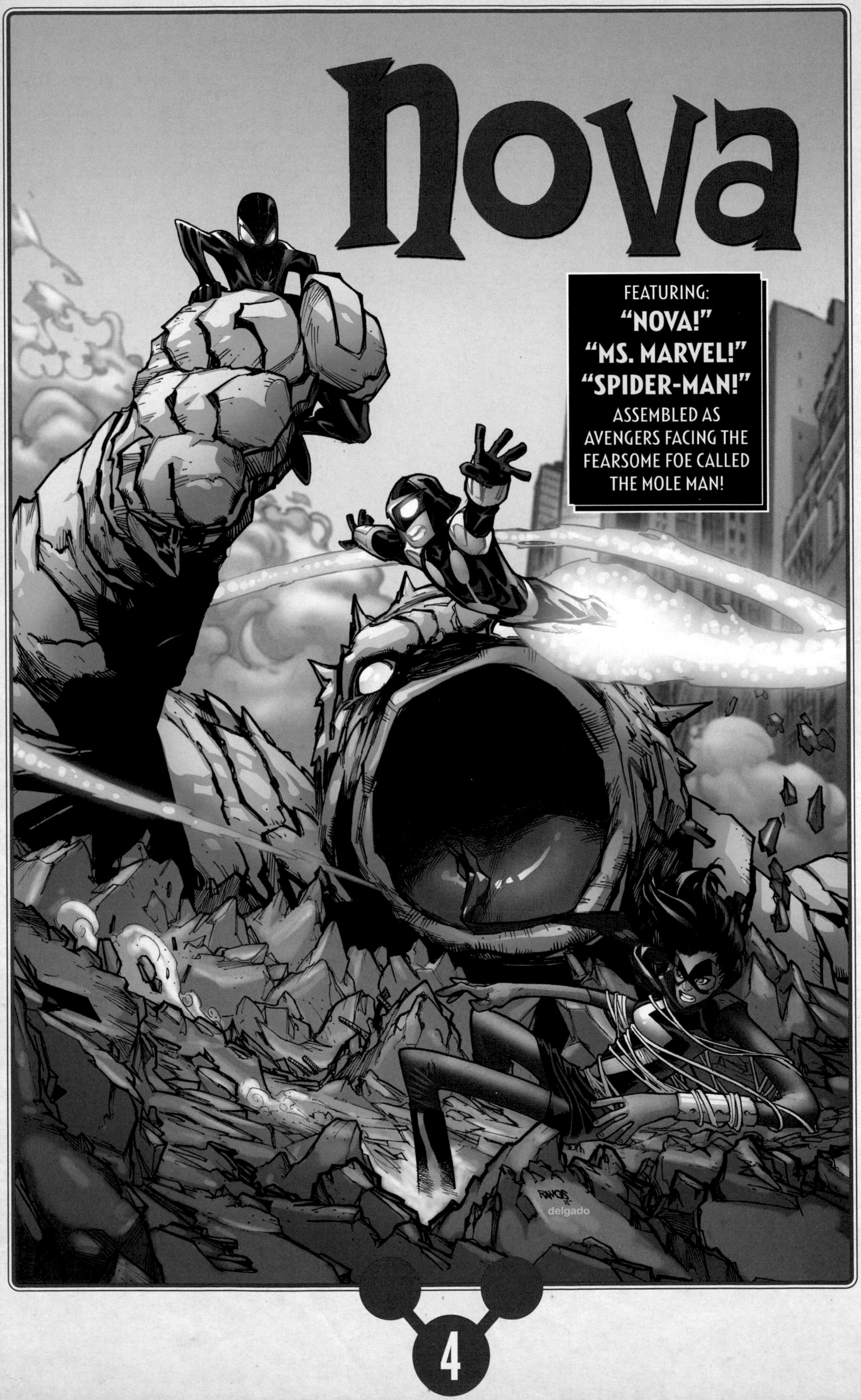

Nova
FEATURING:
"NOVA!"
"MS. MARVEL!"
"SPIDER-MAN!"
ASSEMBLED AS
AVENGERS FACING THE
FEARSOME FOE CALLED
THE MOLE MAN!
delgado
4

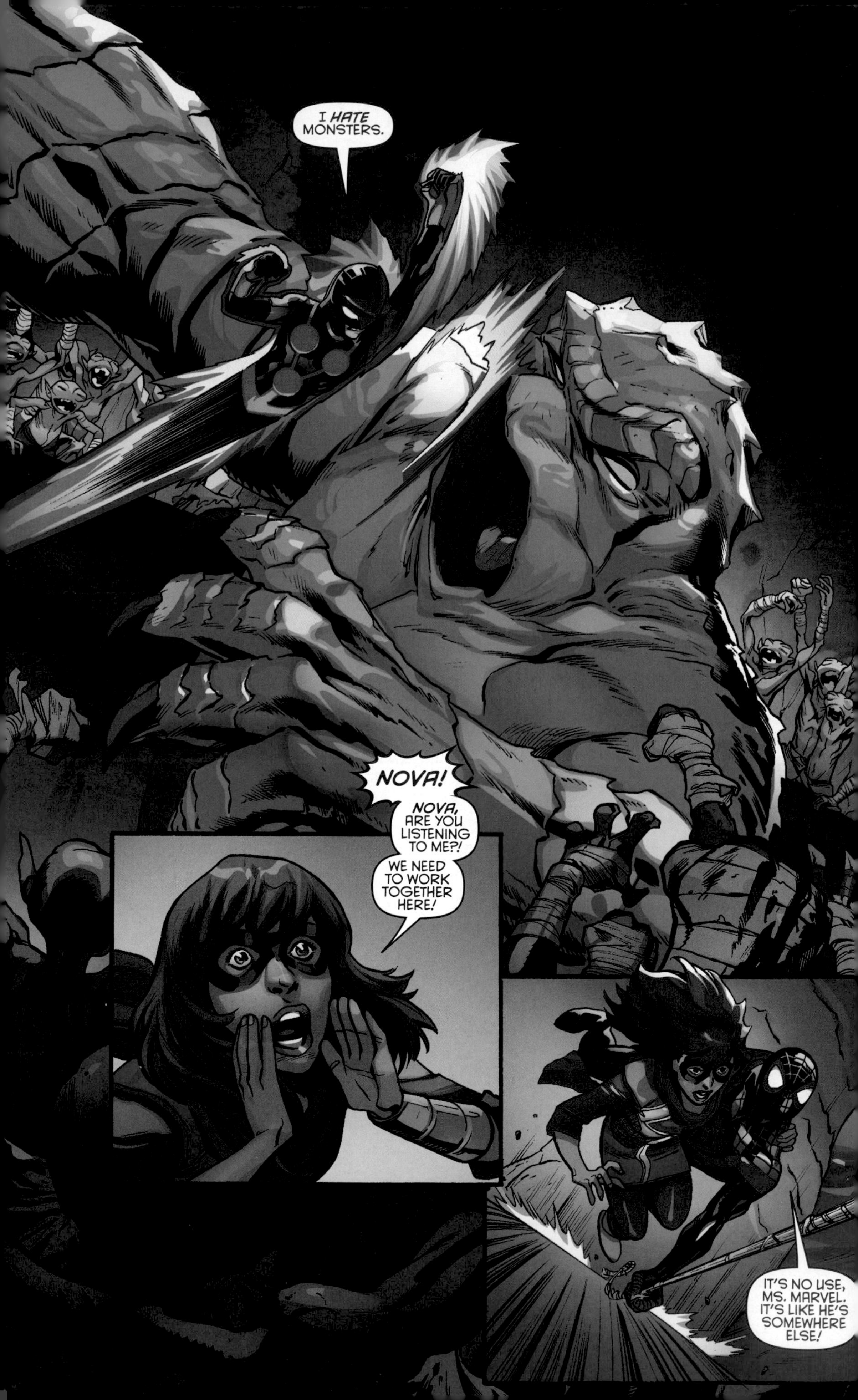
I *HATE* MONSTERS.
NOVA!
NOVA, ARE YOU LISTENING TO ME?!
WE NEED TO WORK TOGETHER HERE!
IT'S NO USE, MS. MARVEL. IT'S LIKE HE'S SOMEWHERE ELSE!

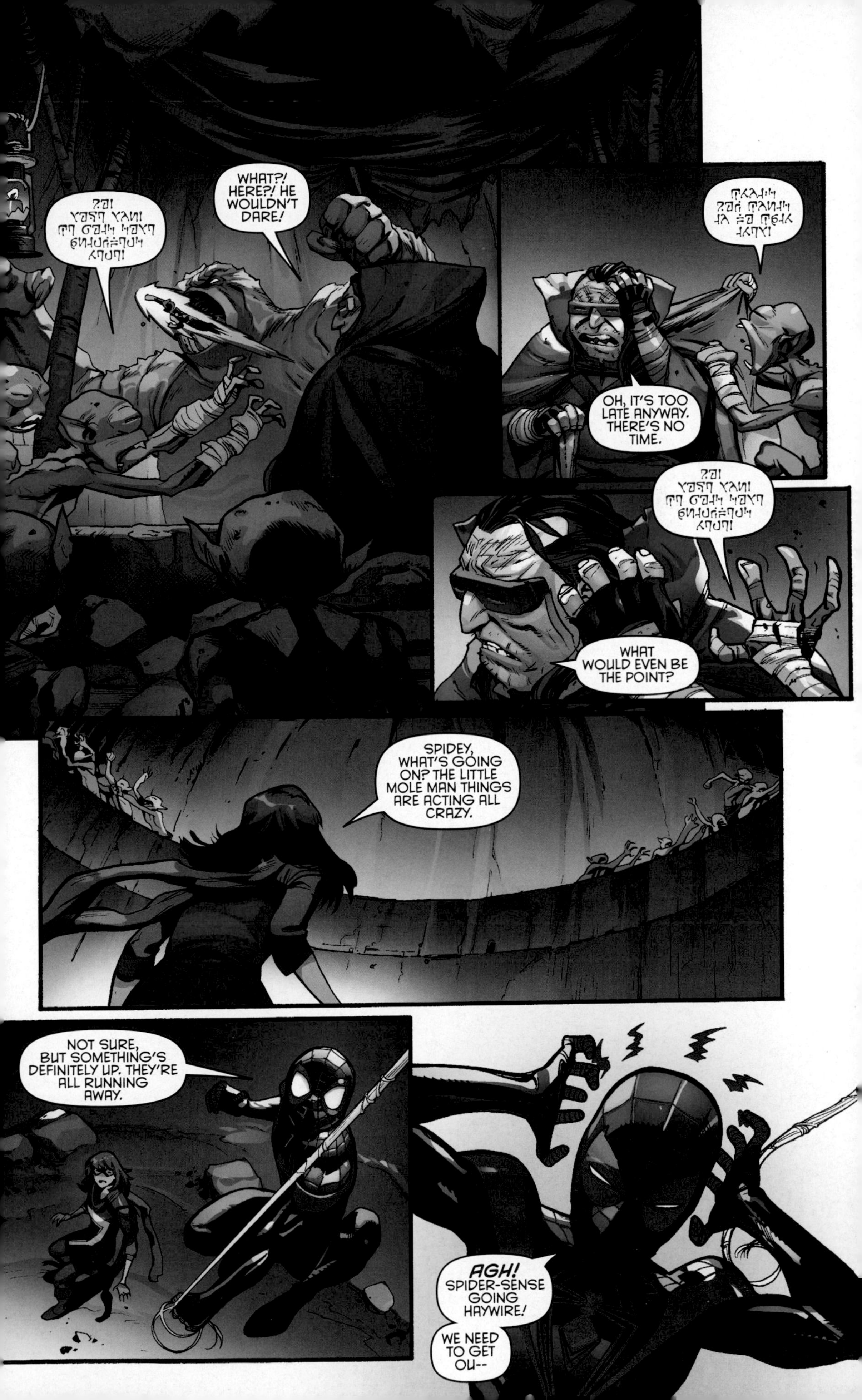
WHAT?! HERE?! HE WOULDN'T DARE!
OH, IT'S TOO LATE ANYWAY. THERE'S NO TIME.
WHAT WOULD EVEN BE THE POINT?
SPIDEY, WHAT'S GOING ON? THE LITTLE MOLE MAN THINGS ARE ACTING ALL CRAZY.
NOT SURE, BUT SOMETHING'S DEFINITELY UP. THEY'RE ALL RUNNING AWAY.
AGH! SPIDER-SENSE GOING HAYWIRE!
WE NEED TO GET OU--

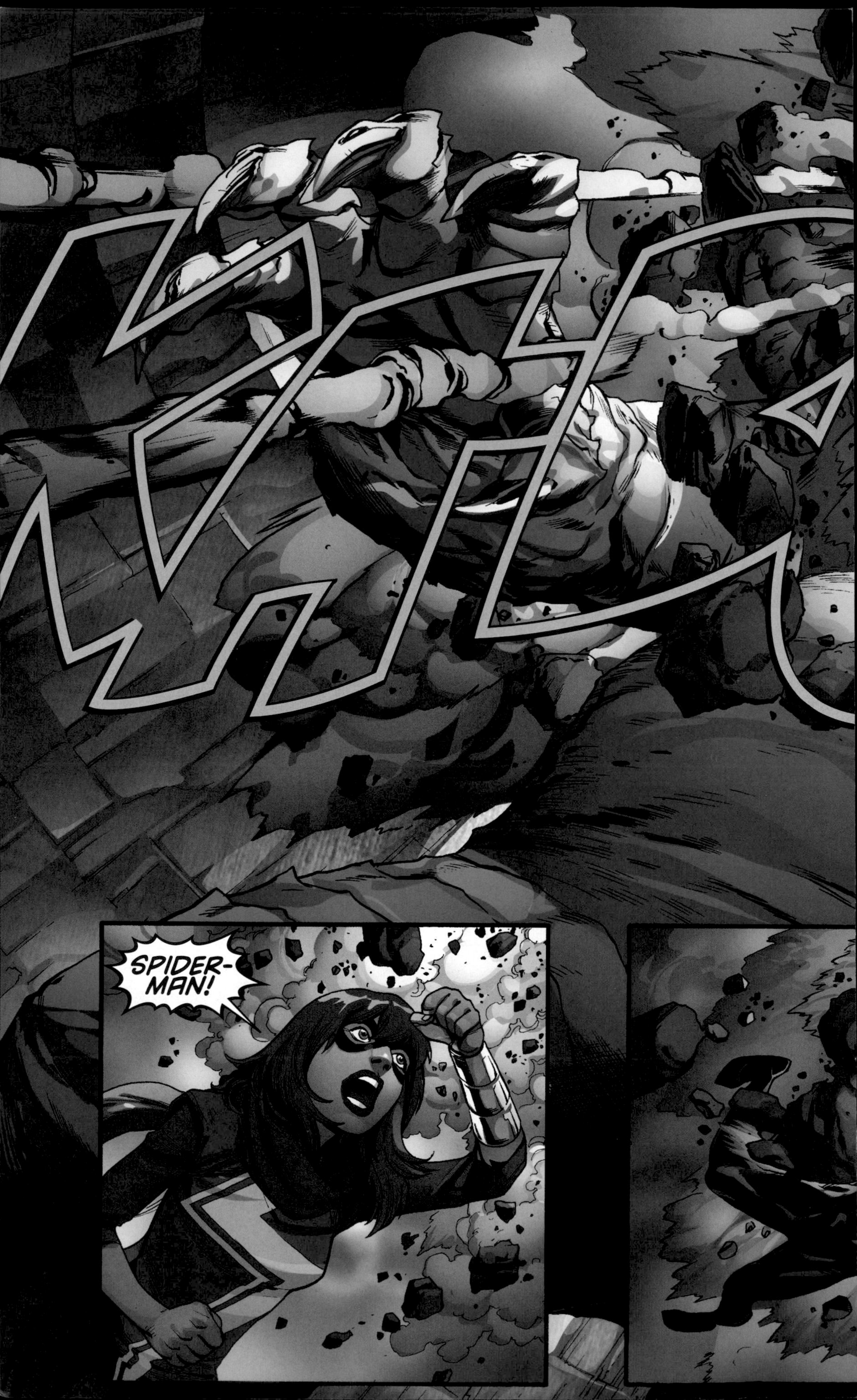
SPIDER-
MAN!

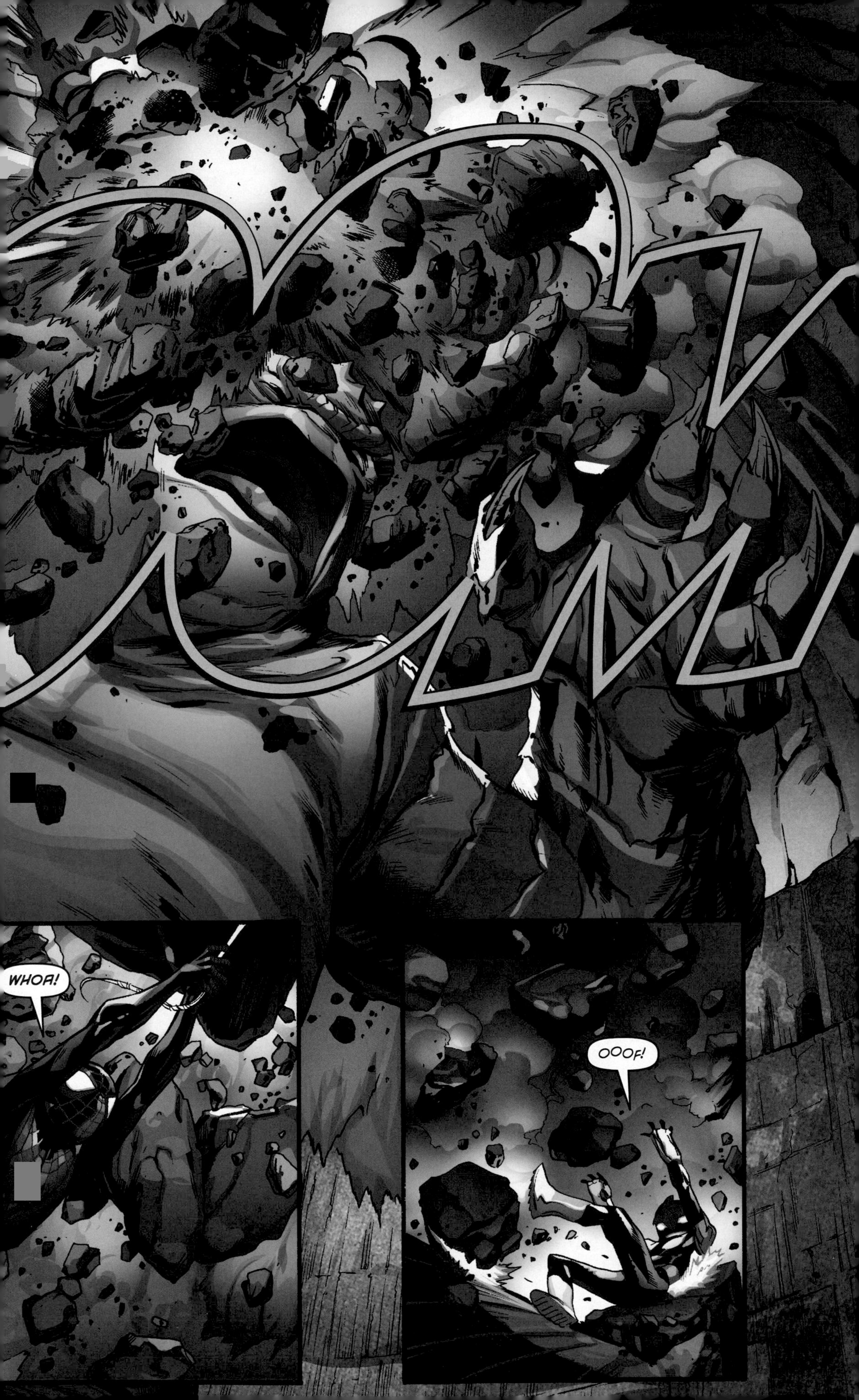
WHOA!
OOOF!

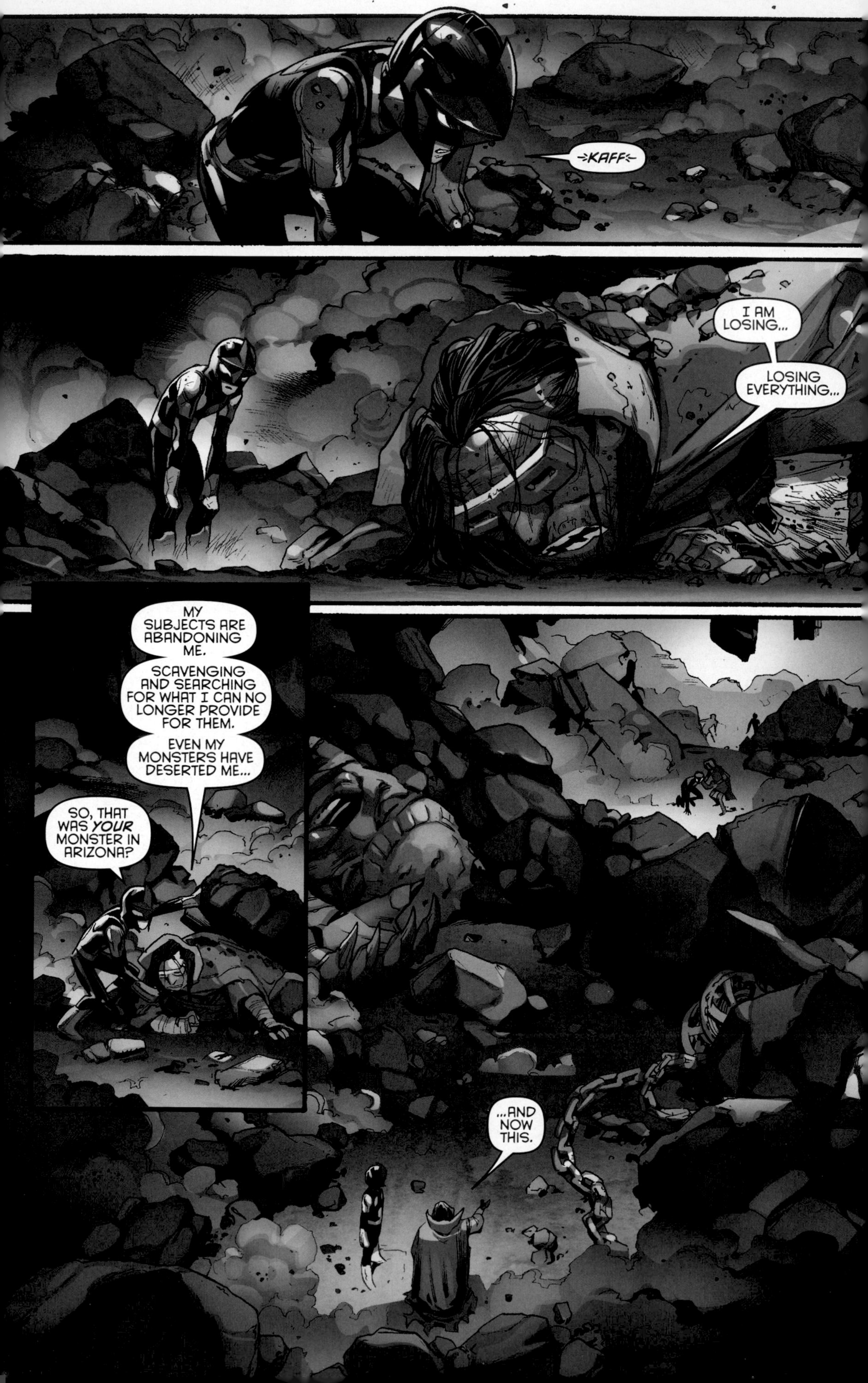
~KAFF~
I AM LOSING...
LOSING EVERYTHING...
MY SUBJECTS ARE ABANDONING ME.
SCAVENGING AND SEARCHING FOR WHAT I CAN NO LONGER PROVIDE FOR THEM.
EVEN MY MONSTERS HAVE DESERTED ME...
SO, THAT WAS *YOUR* MONSTER IN ARIZONA?
...AND NOW THIS.

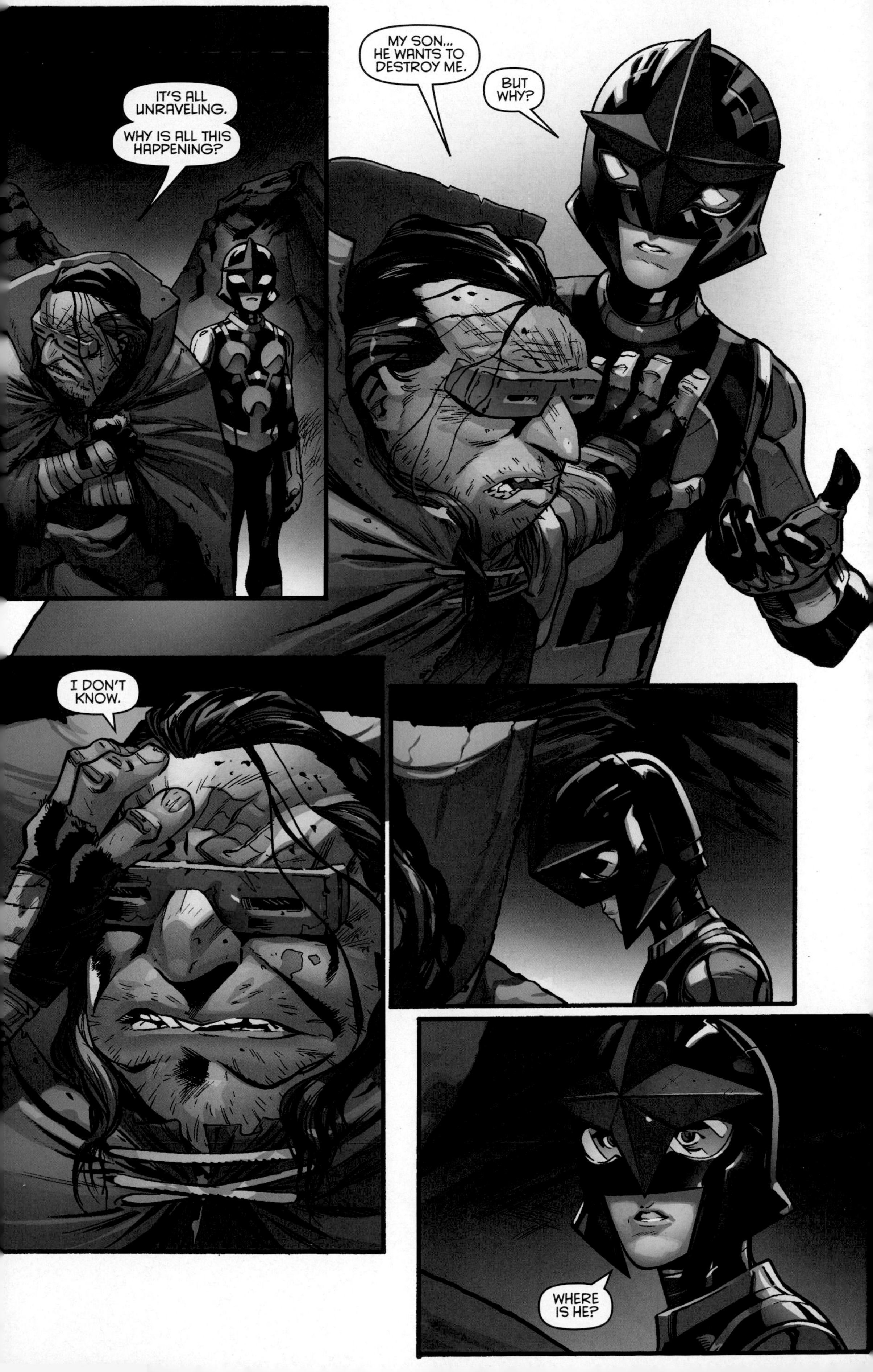
IT'S ALL UNRAVELING.
WHY IS ALL THIS HAPPENING?
MY SON... HE WANTS TO DESTROY ME.
BUT WHY?
I DON'T KNOW.
WHERE IS HE?

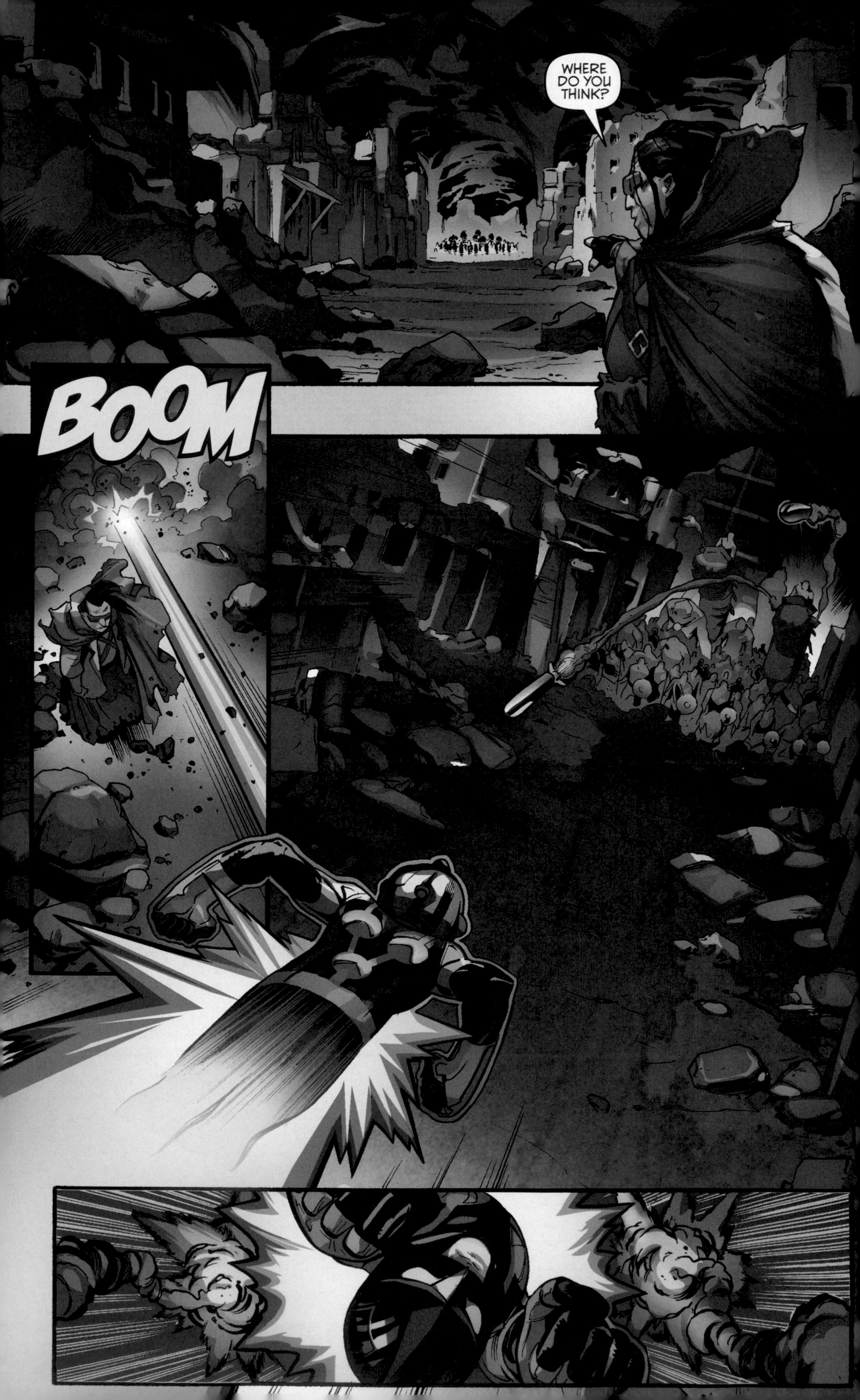
WHERE DO YOU THINK?
BOOM

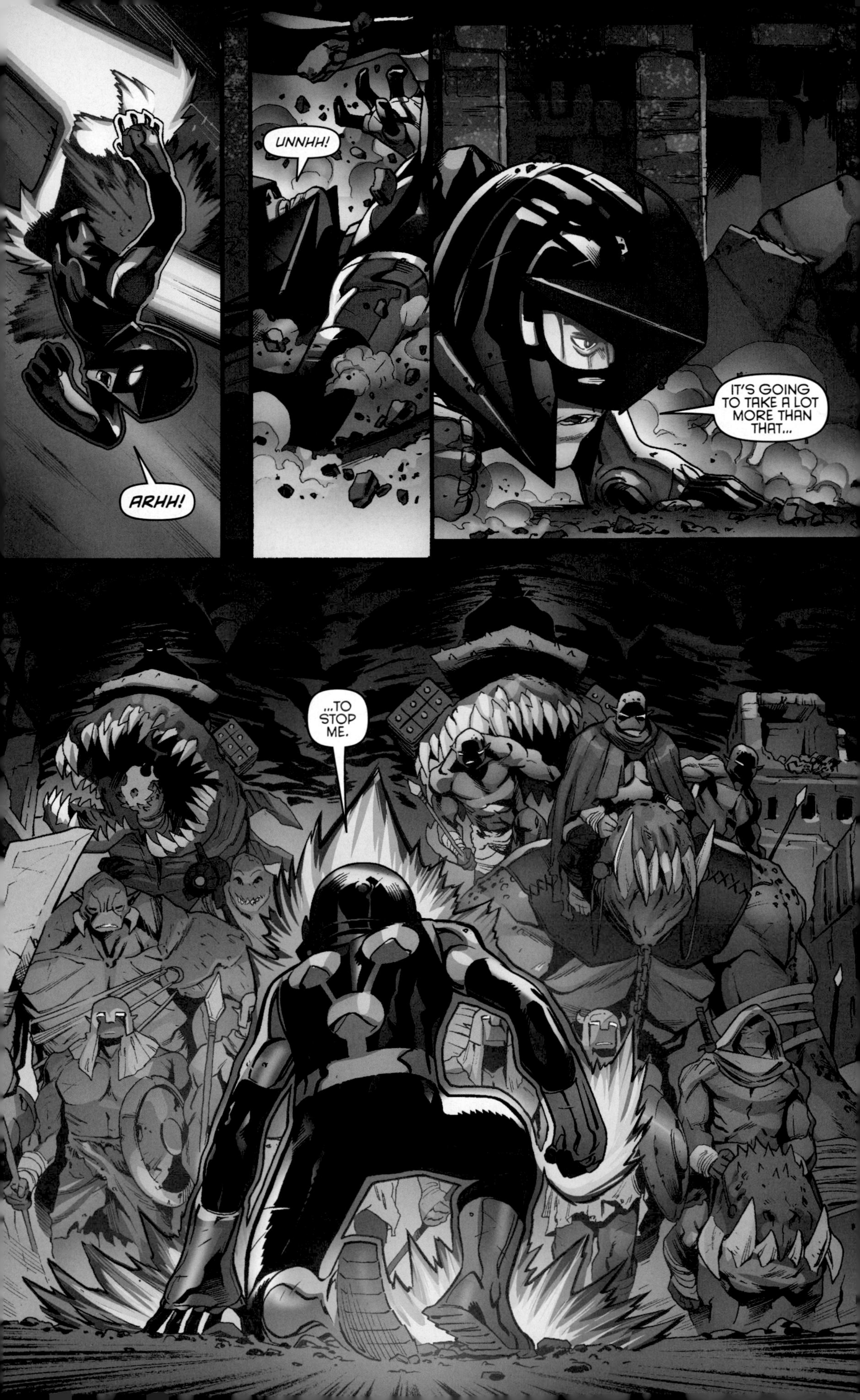
ARHH!
UNNHH!
IT'S GOING TO TAKE A LOT MORE THAN THAT...
...TO STOP ME.

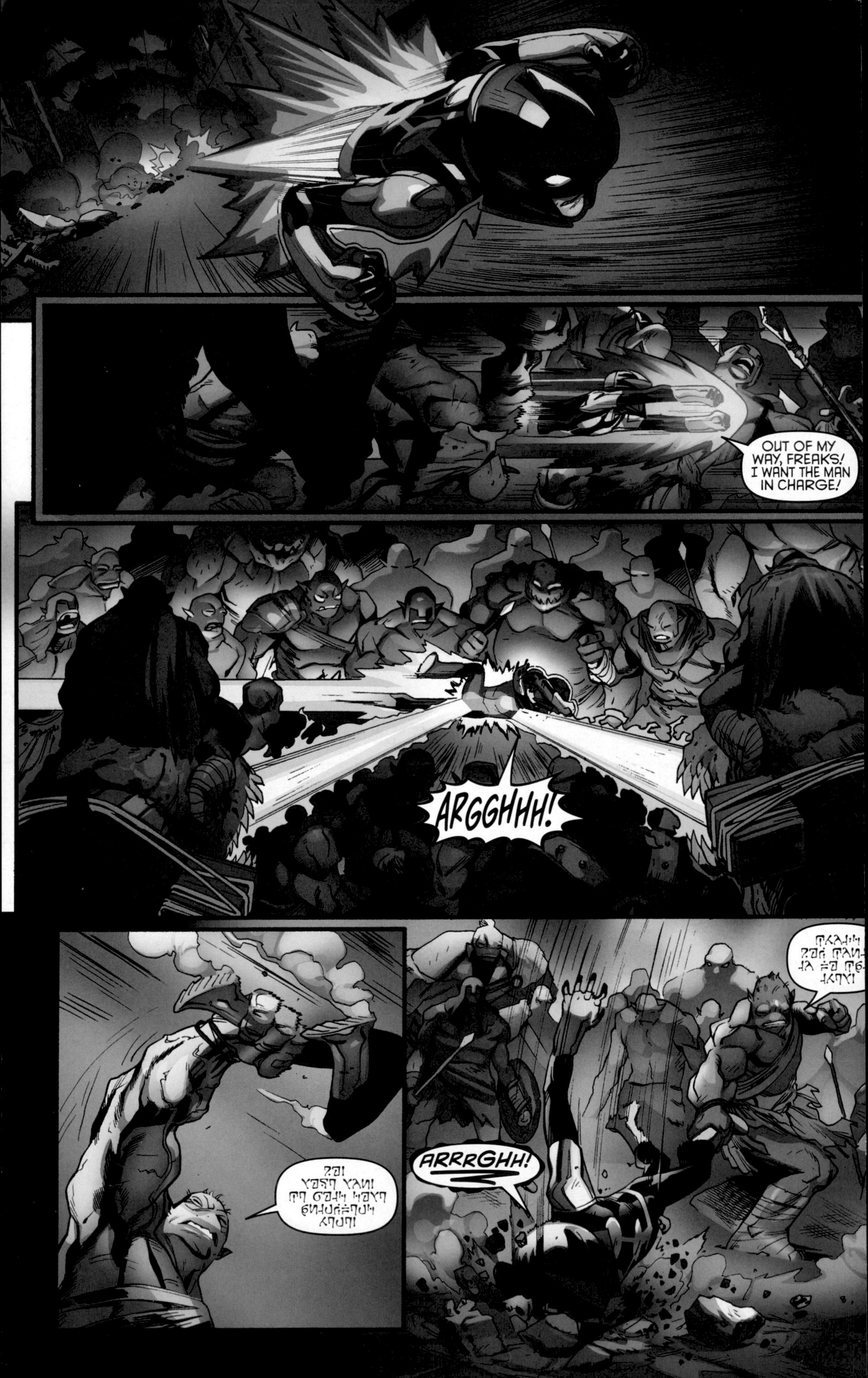
OUT OF MY WAY, FREAKS! I WANT THE MAN IN CHARGE!
ARGGHHH!
ARRRGHH!

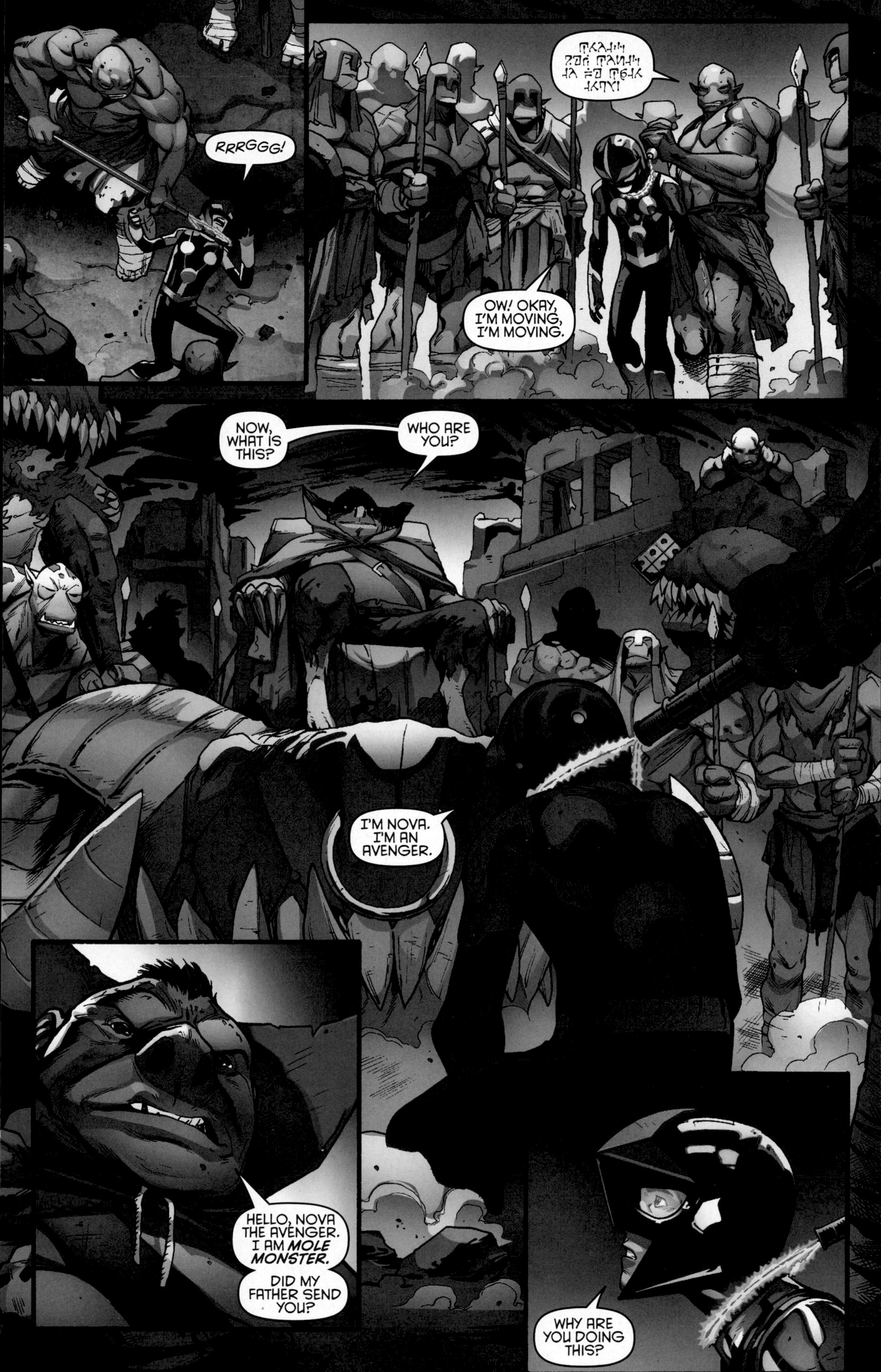
RRRGGG!
OW! OKAY, I'M MOVING, I'M MOVING.
NOW, WHAT IS THIS?
WHO ARE YOU?
I'M NOVA. I'M AN AVENGER.
HELLO, NOVA THE AVENGER. I AM *MOLE MONSTER.*
DID MY FATHER SEND YOU?
WHY ARE YOU DOING THIS?

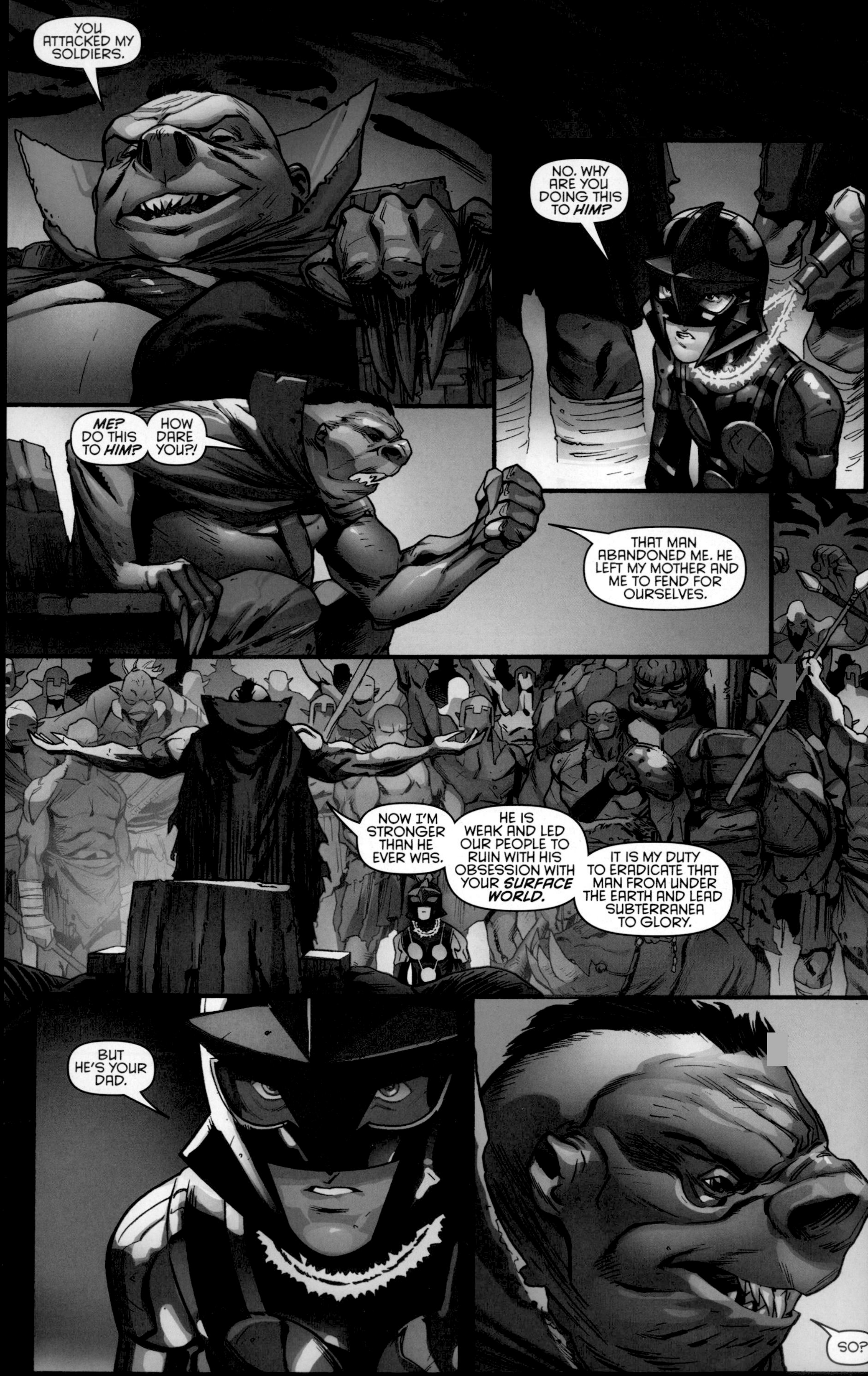
YOU ATTACKED MY SOLDIERS.
NO. WHY ARE YOU DOING THIS TO *HIM?*
ME? DO THIS TO *HIM?*
HOW DARE YOU?!
THAT MAN ABANDONED ME. HE LEFT MY MOTHER AND ME TO FEND FOR OURSELVES.
NOW I'M STRONGER THAN HE EVER WAS.
HE IS WEAK AND LED OUR PEOPLE TO RUIN WITH HIS OBSESSION WITH YOUR *SURFACE WORLD.*
IT IS MY DUTY TO ERADICATE THAT MAN FROM UNDER THE EARTH AND LEAD SUBTERRANEA TO GLORY.
BUT HE'S YOUR DAD.
SO?

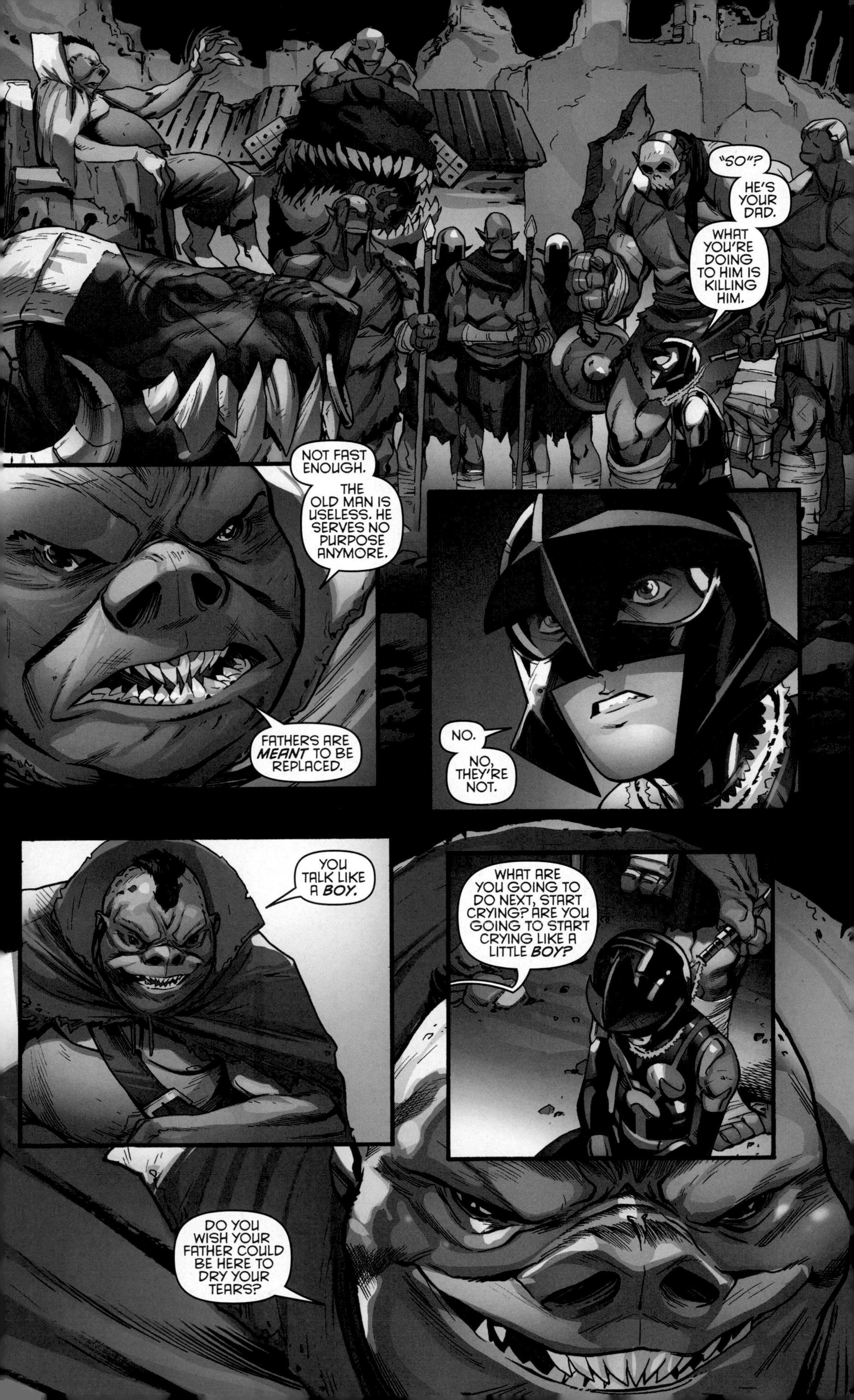
"SO"?
HE'S YOUR DAD.
WHAT YOU'RE DOING TO HIM IS KILLING HIM.
NOT FAST ENOUGH.
THE OLD MAN IS USELESS. HE SERVES NO PURPOSE ANYMORE.
FATHERS ARE MEANT TO BE REPLACED.
NO.
NO, THEY'RE NOT.
YOU TALK LIKE A BOY.
WHAT ARE YOU GOING TO DO NEXT, START CRYING? ARE YOU GOING TO START CRYING LIKE A LITTLE BOY?
DO YOU WISH YOUR FATHER COULD BE HERE TO DRY YOUR TEARS?

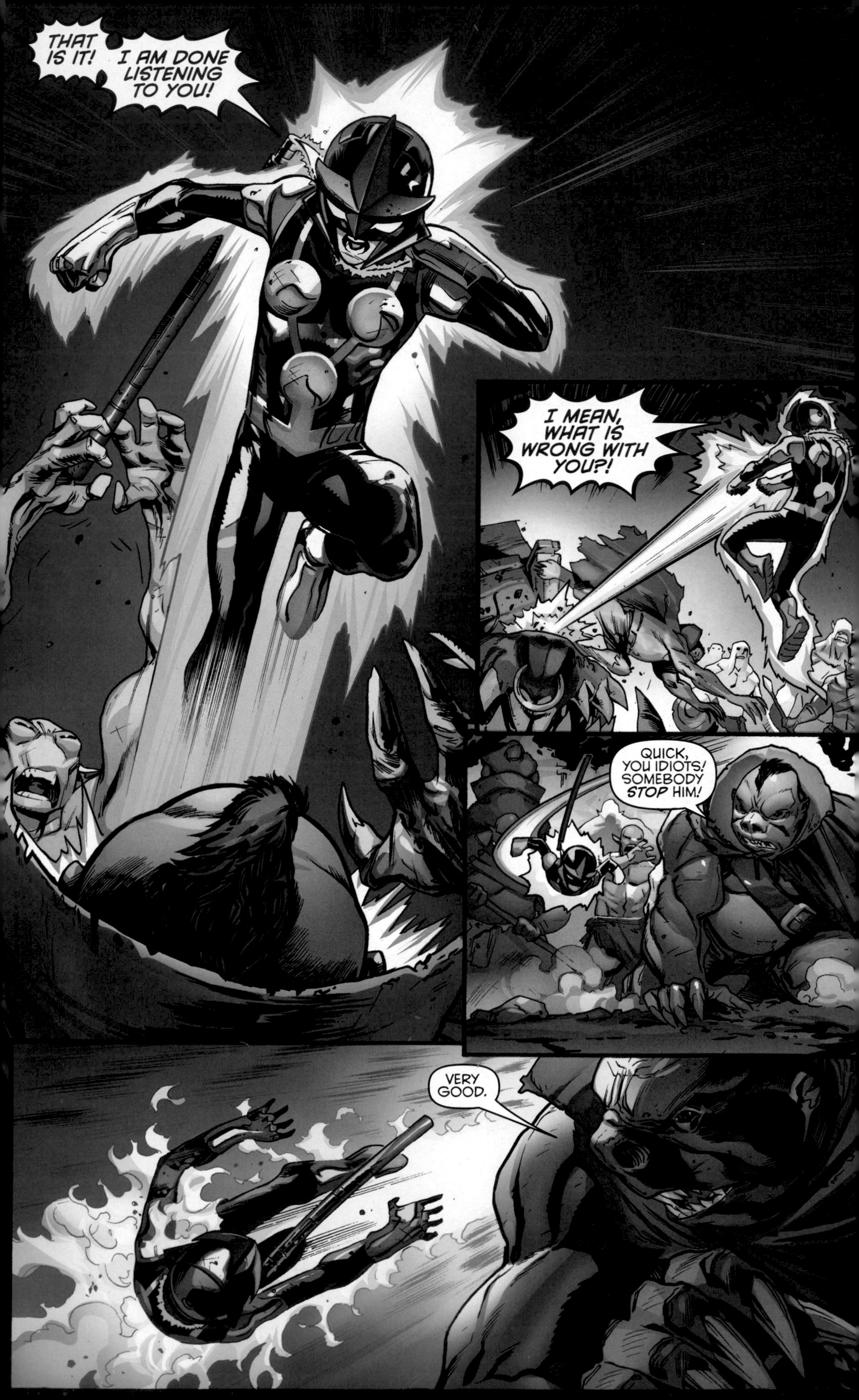
THAT IS IT!
I AM DONE LISTENING TO YOU!
I MEAN, WHAT IS WRONG WITH YOU?!
QUICK, YOU IDIOTS! SOMEBODY STOP HIM!
VERY GOOD.

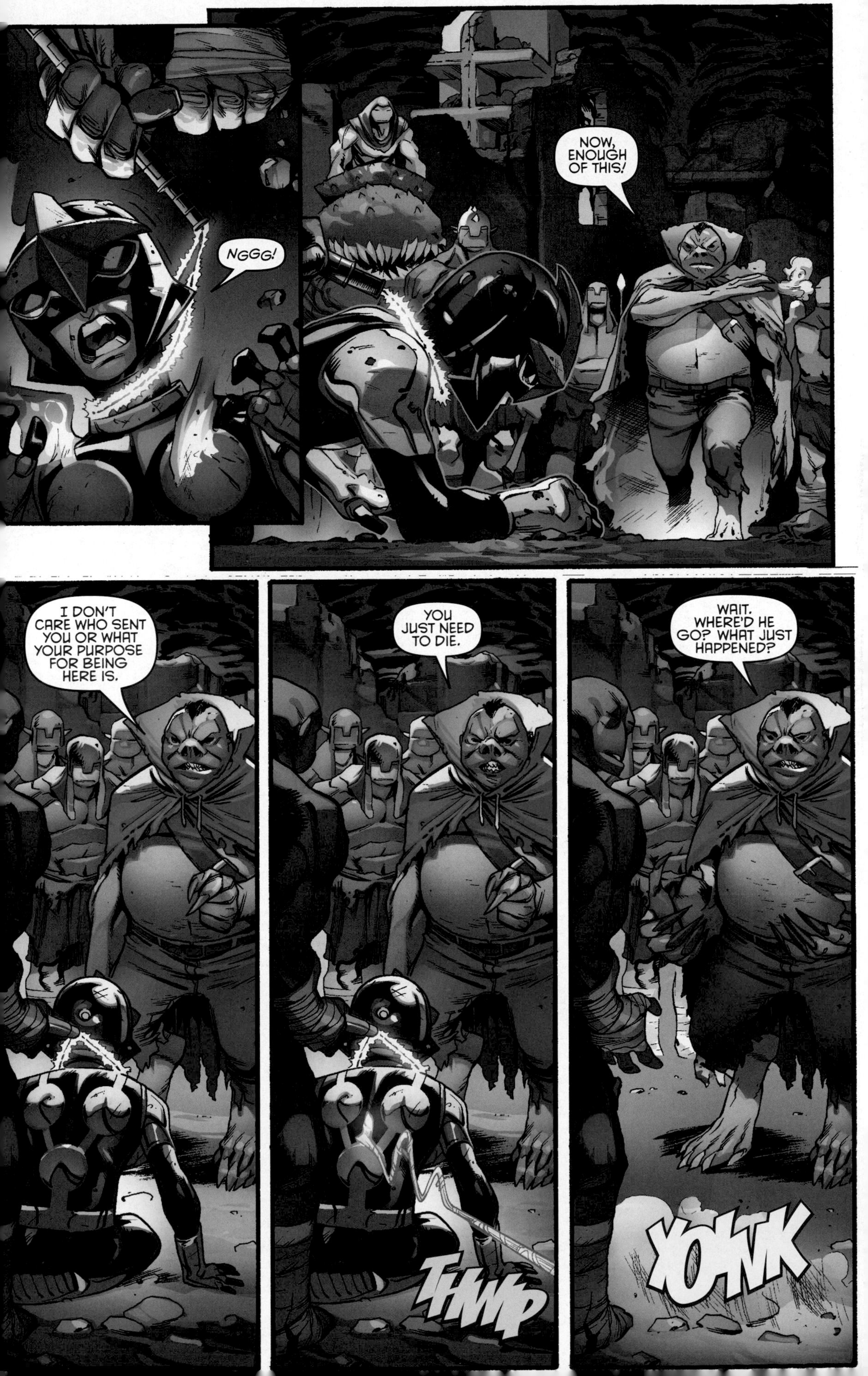
NGGG!
NOW, ENOUGH OF THIS!
I DON'T CARE WHO SENT YOU OR WHAT YOUR PURPOSE FOR BEING HERE IS.
YOU JUST NEED TO DIE.
THWP
WAIT. WHERE'D HE GO? WHAT JUST HAPPENED?
YOINK

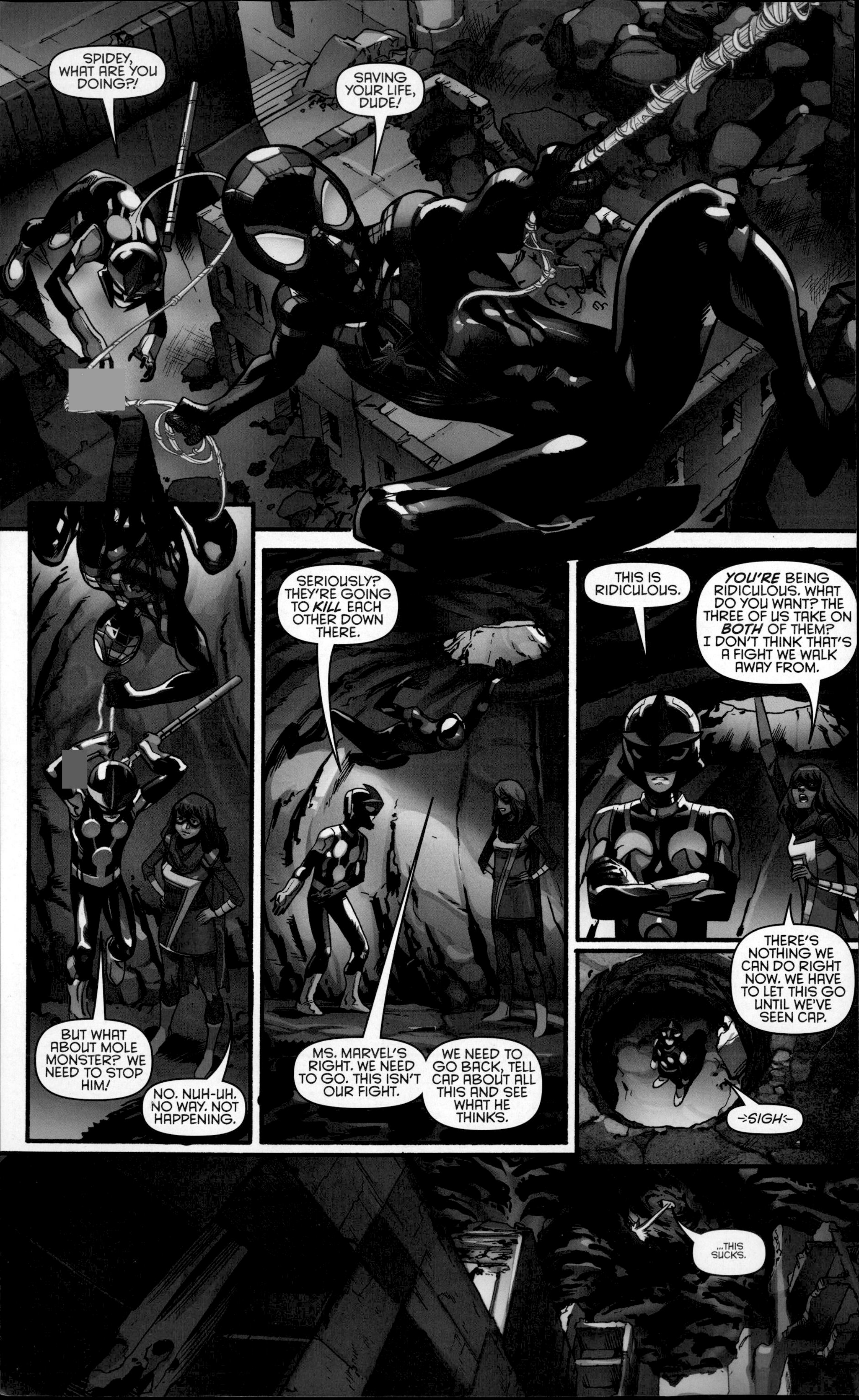
SPIDEY, WHAT ARE YOU DOING?!
SAVING YOUR LIFE, DUDE!
BUT WHAT ABOUT MOLE MONSTER? WE NEED TO STOP HIM!
NO. NUH-UH. NO WAY. NOT HAPPENING.
SERIOUSLY? THEY'RE GOING TO *KILL* EACH OTHER DOWN THERE.
MS. MARVEL'S RIGHT. WE NEED TO GO. THIS ISN'T OUR FIGHT.
WE NEED TO GO BACK, TELL CAP ABOUT ALL THIS AND SEE WHAT HE THINKS.
THIS IS RIDICULOUS.
YOU'RE BEING RIDICULOUS. WHAT DO YOU WANT? THE THREE OF US TAKE ON *BOTH* OF THEM? I DON'T THINK THAT'S A FIGHT WE WALK AWAY FROM.
THERE'S NOTHING WE CAN DO RIGHT NOW. WE HAVE TO LET THIS GO UNTIL WE'VE SEEN CAP.
SIGH
...THIS SUCKS.

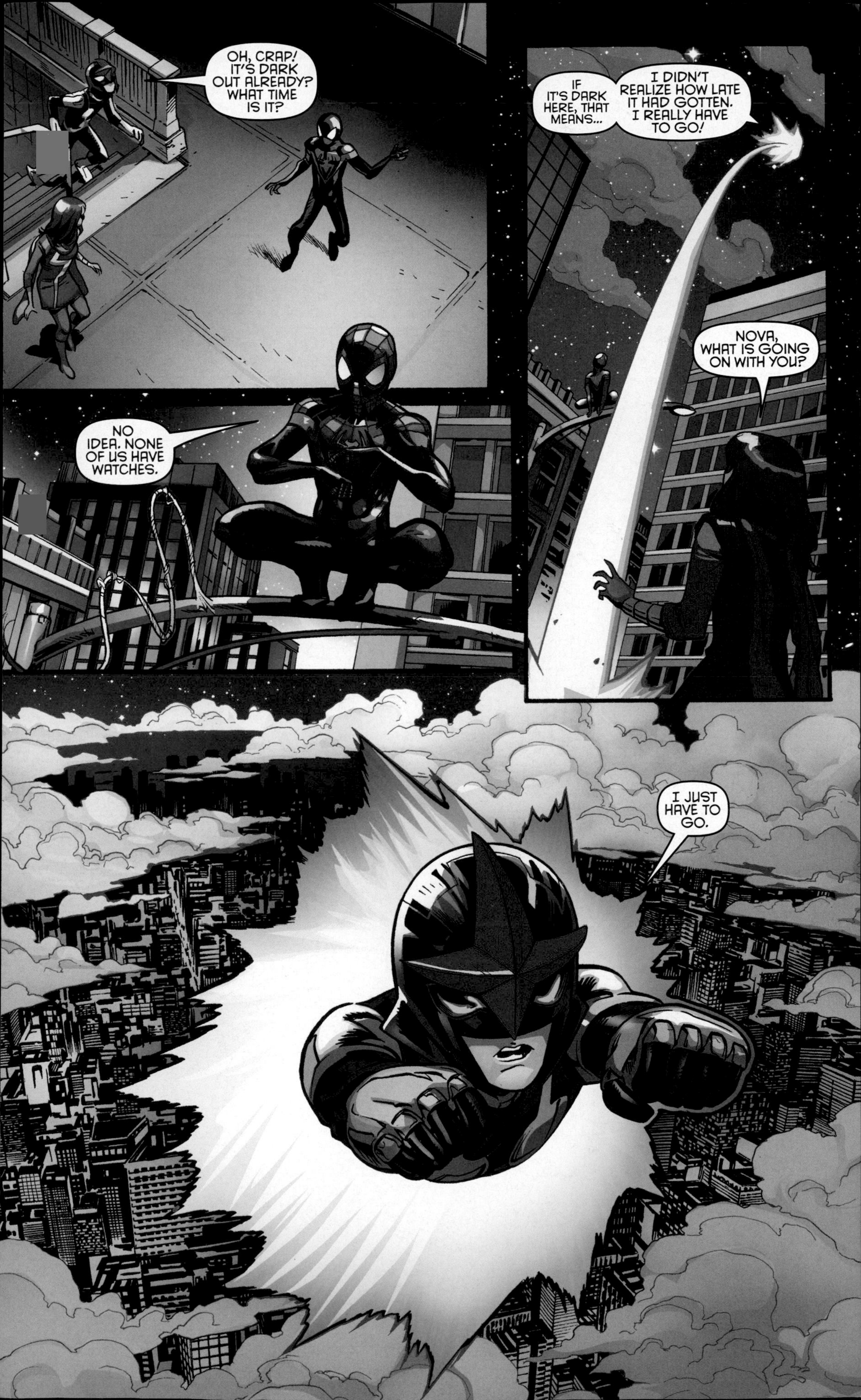
OH, CRAP! IT'S DARK OUT ALREADY? WHAT TIME IS IT?
NO IDEA. NONE OF US HAVE WATCHES.
IF IT'S DARK HERE, THAT MEANS...
I DIDN'T REALIZE HOW LATE IT HAD GOTTEN. I REALLY HAVE TO GO!
NOVA, WHAT IS GOING ON WITH YOU?
I JUST HAVE TO GO.

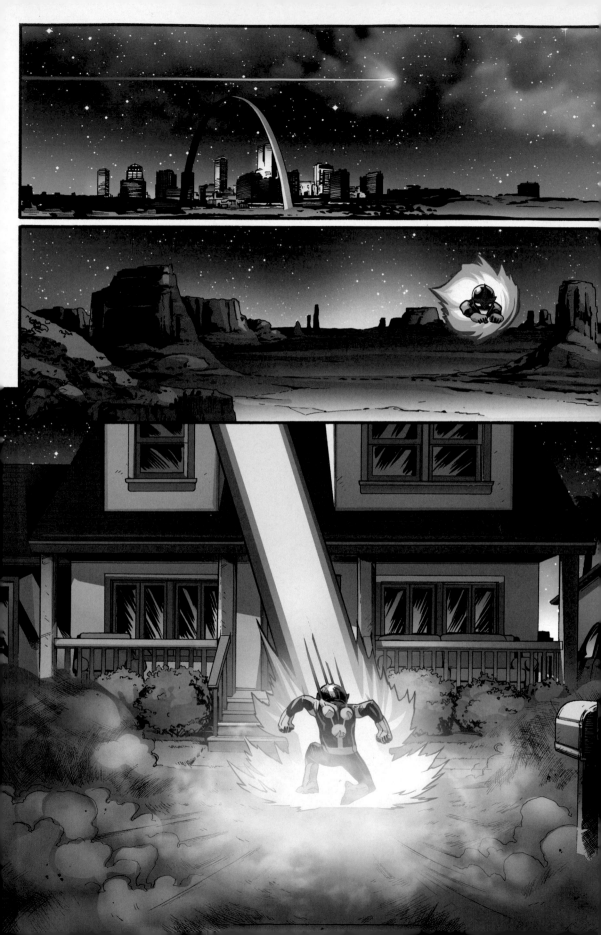

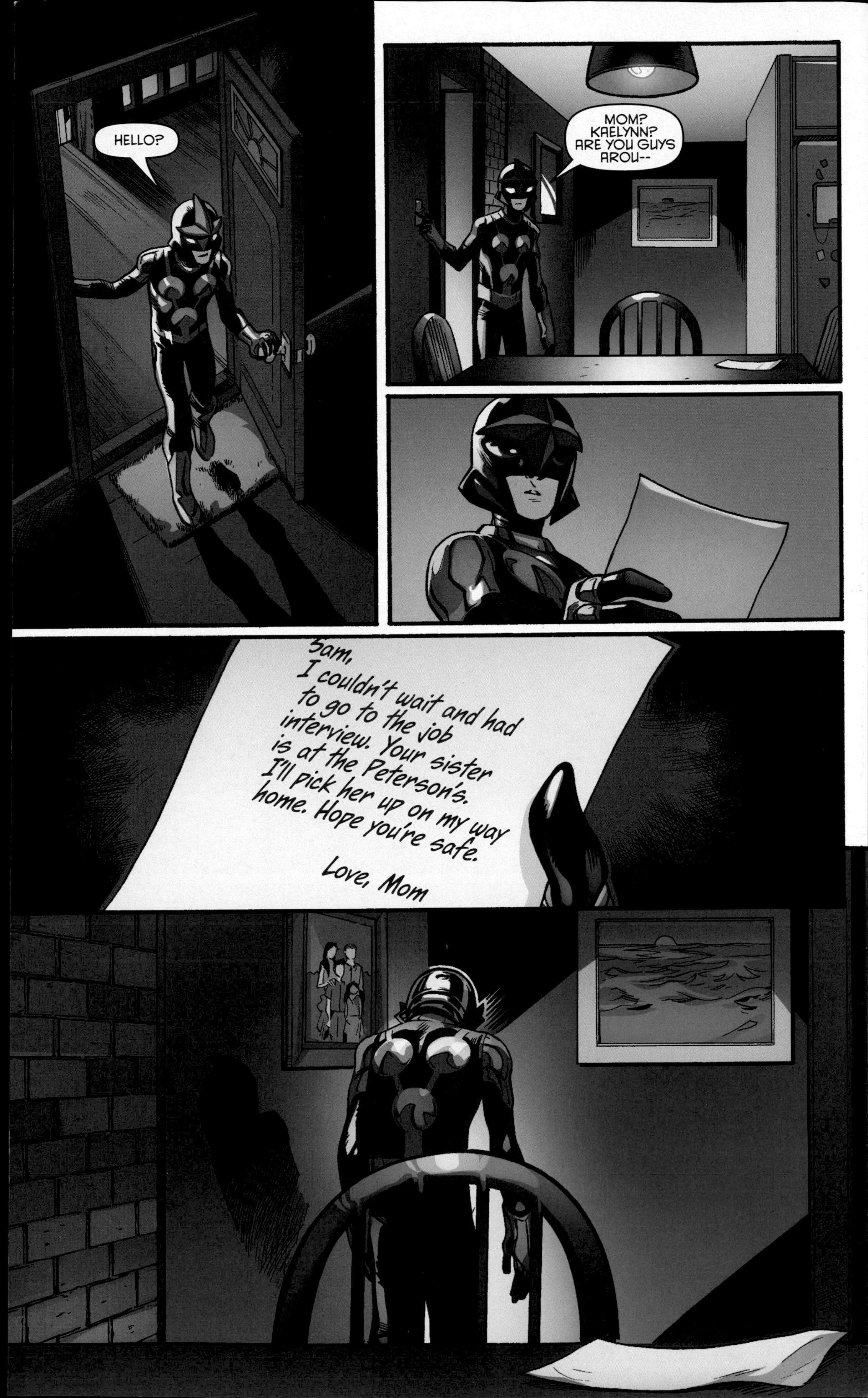
HELLO?
MOM? KAELYNN? ARE YOU GUYS AROU--
Sam,
I couldn't wait and had to go to the job interview. Your sister is at the Peterson's. I'll pick her up on my way home. Hope you're safe.
Love, Mom

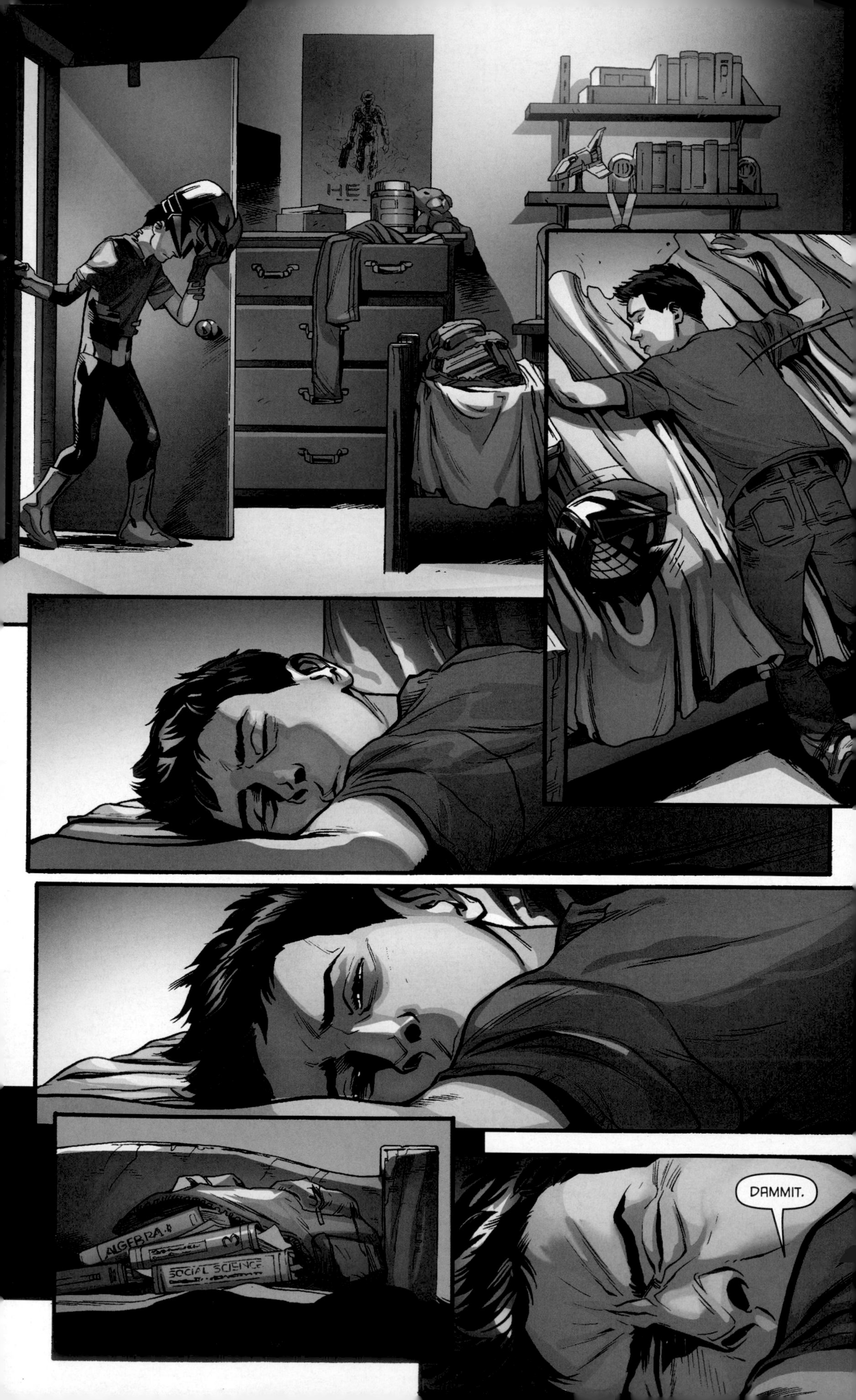
ALGEBRA
SOCIAL SCIENCE
DAMMIT.

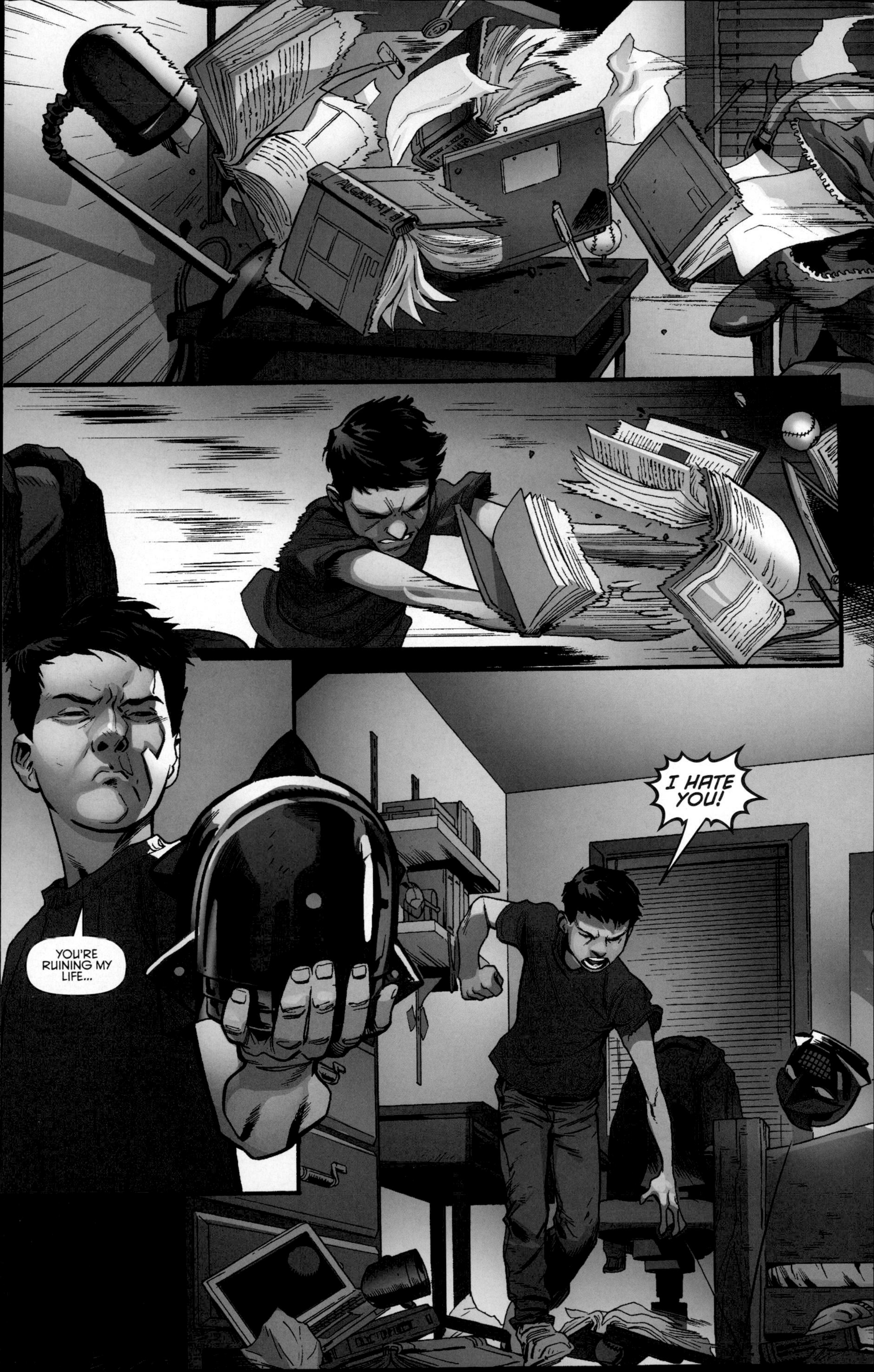
I HATE YOU!
YOU'RE RUINING MY LIFE...

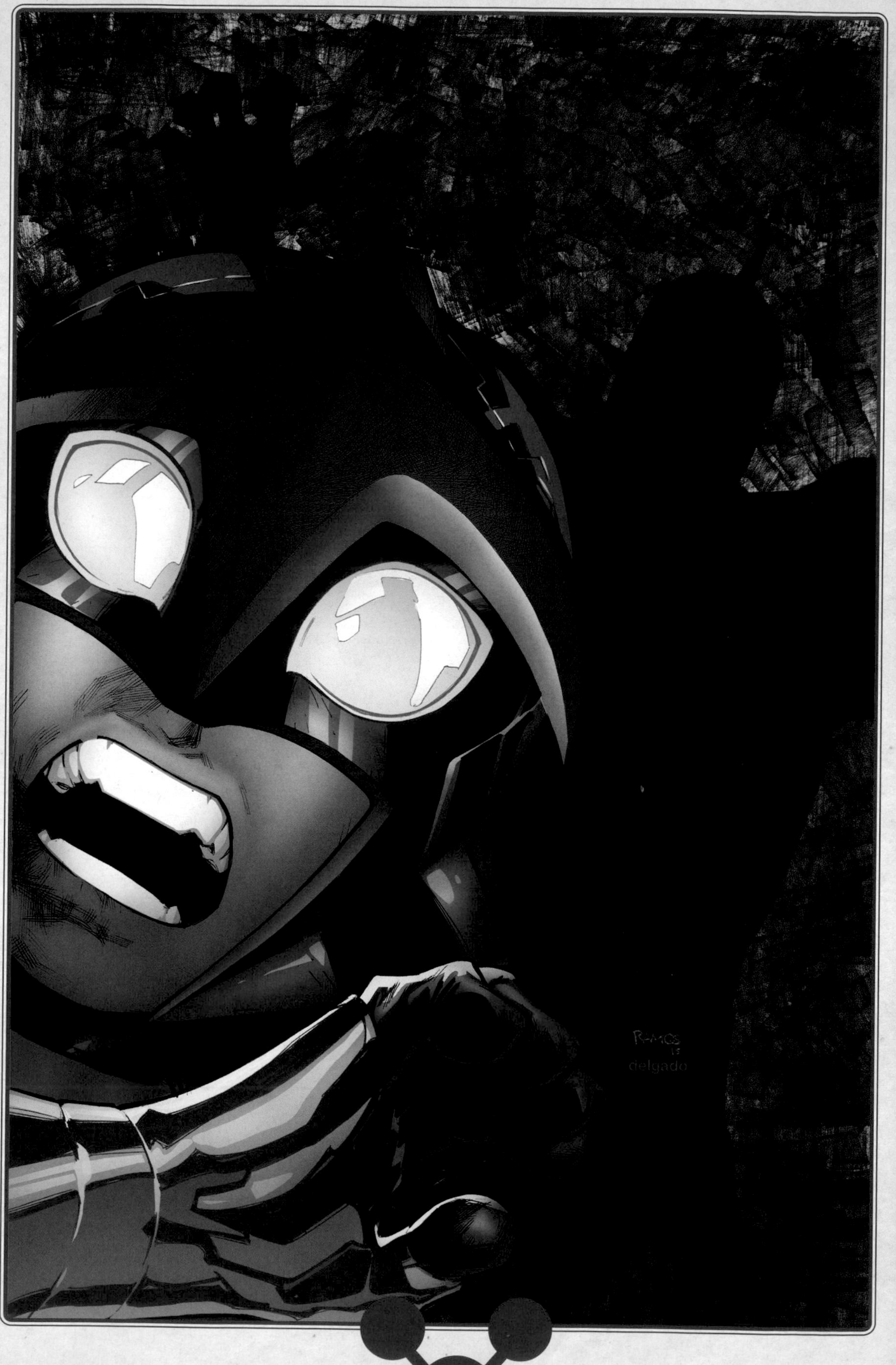

5

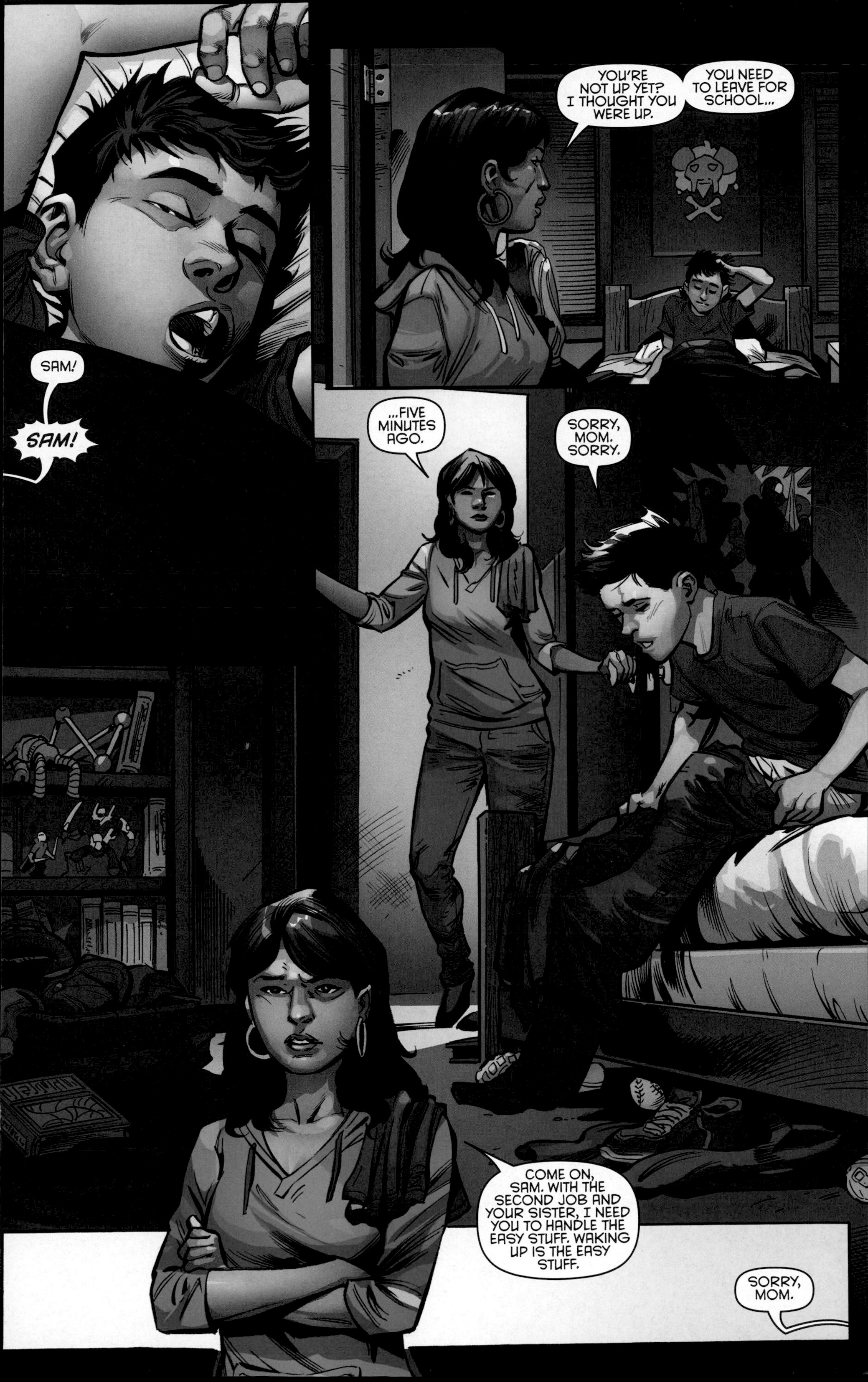

SAM!
SAM!
YOU'RE NOT UP YET? I THOUGHT YOU WERE UP.
YOU NEED TO LEAVE FOR SCHOOL...
...FIVE MINUTES AGO.
SORRY, MOM. SORRY.
COME ON, SAM. WITH THE SECOND JOB AND YOUR SISTER, I NEED YOU TO HANDLE THE EASY STUFF. WAKING UP IS THE EASY STUFF.
SORRY, MOM.

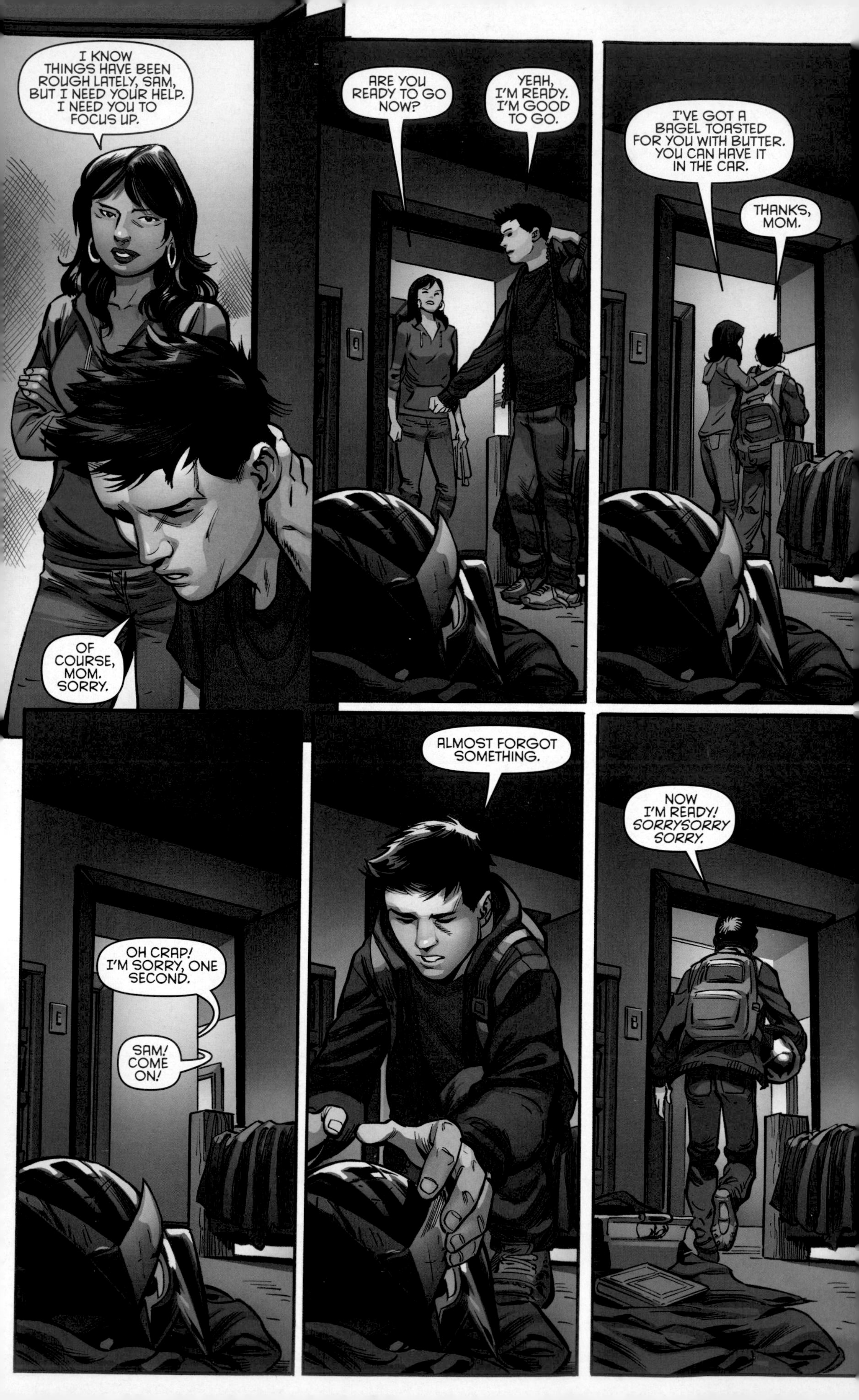
I KNOW THINGS HAVE BEEN ROUGH LATELY, SAM, BUT I NEED YOUR HELP. I NEED YOU TO FOCUS UP.
OF COURSE, MOM. SORRY.
ARE YOU READY TO GO NOW?
YEAH, I'M READY. I'M GOOD TO GO.
I'VE GOT A BAGEL TOASTED FOR YOU WITH BUTTER. YOU CAN HAVE IT IN THE CAR.
THANKS, MOM.
OH CRAP! I'M SORRY, ONE SECOND.
SAM! COME ON!
ALMOST FORGOT SOMETHING.
NOW I'M READY! SORRYSORRY SORRY.

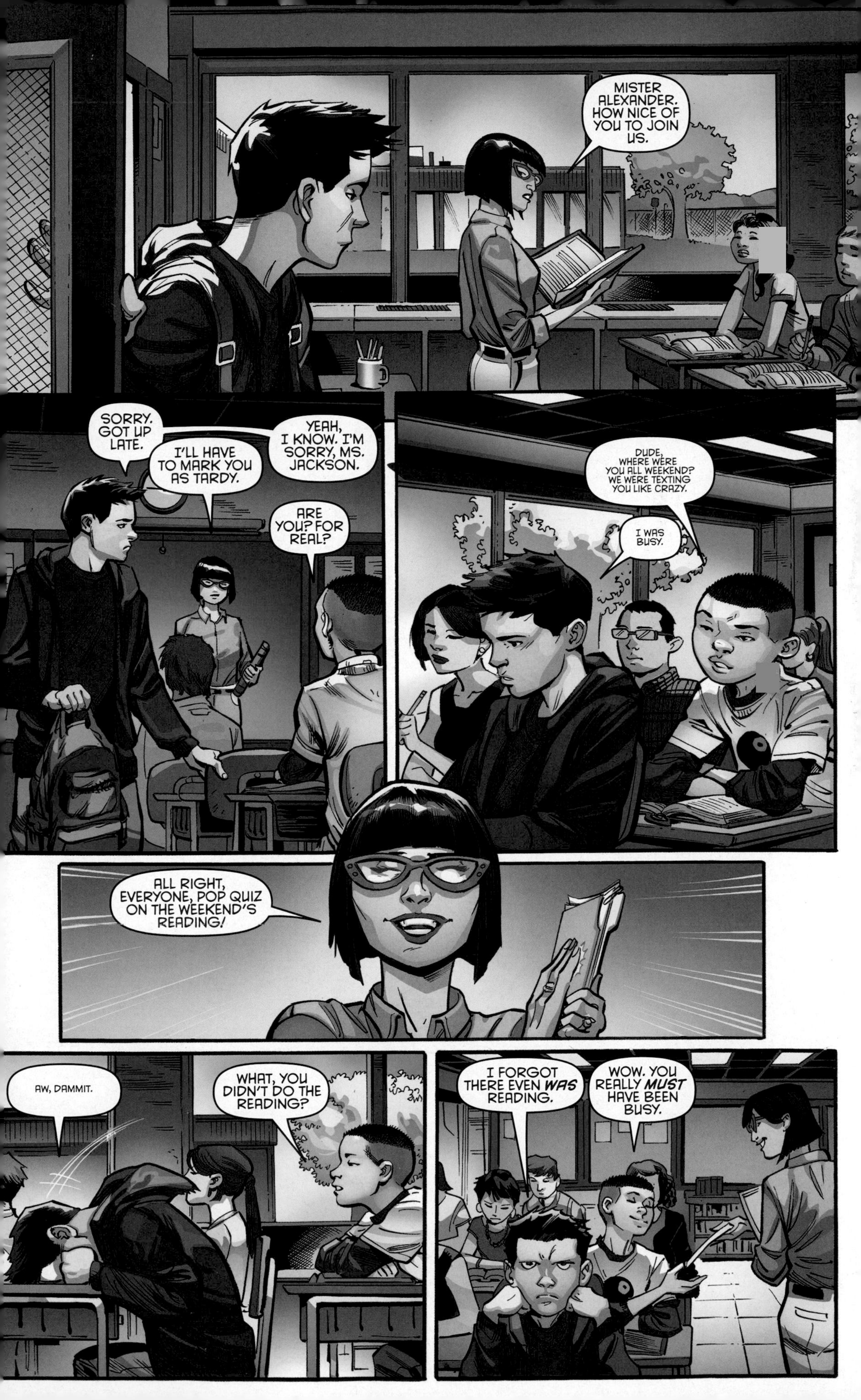

MISTER ALEXANDER. HOW NICE OF YOU TO JOIN US.
SORRY. GOT UP LATE.
I'LL HAVE TO MARK YOU AS TARDY.
YEAH, I KNOW. I'M SORRY, MS. JACKSON.
ARE YOU? FOR REAL?
DUDE, WHERE WERE YOU ALL WEEKEND? WE WERE TEXTING YOU LIKE CRAZY.
I WAS BUSY.
ALL RIGHT, EVERYONE, POP QUIZ ON THE WEEKEND'S READING!
AW, DAMMIT.
WHAT, YOU DIDN'T DO THE READING?
I FORGOT THERE EVEN ***WAS*** READING.
WOW. YOU REALLY ***MUST*** HAVE BEEN BUSY.

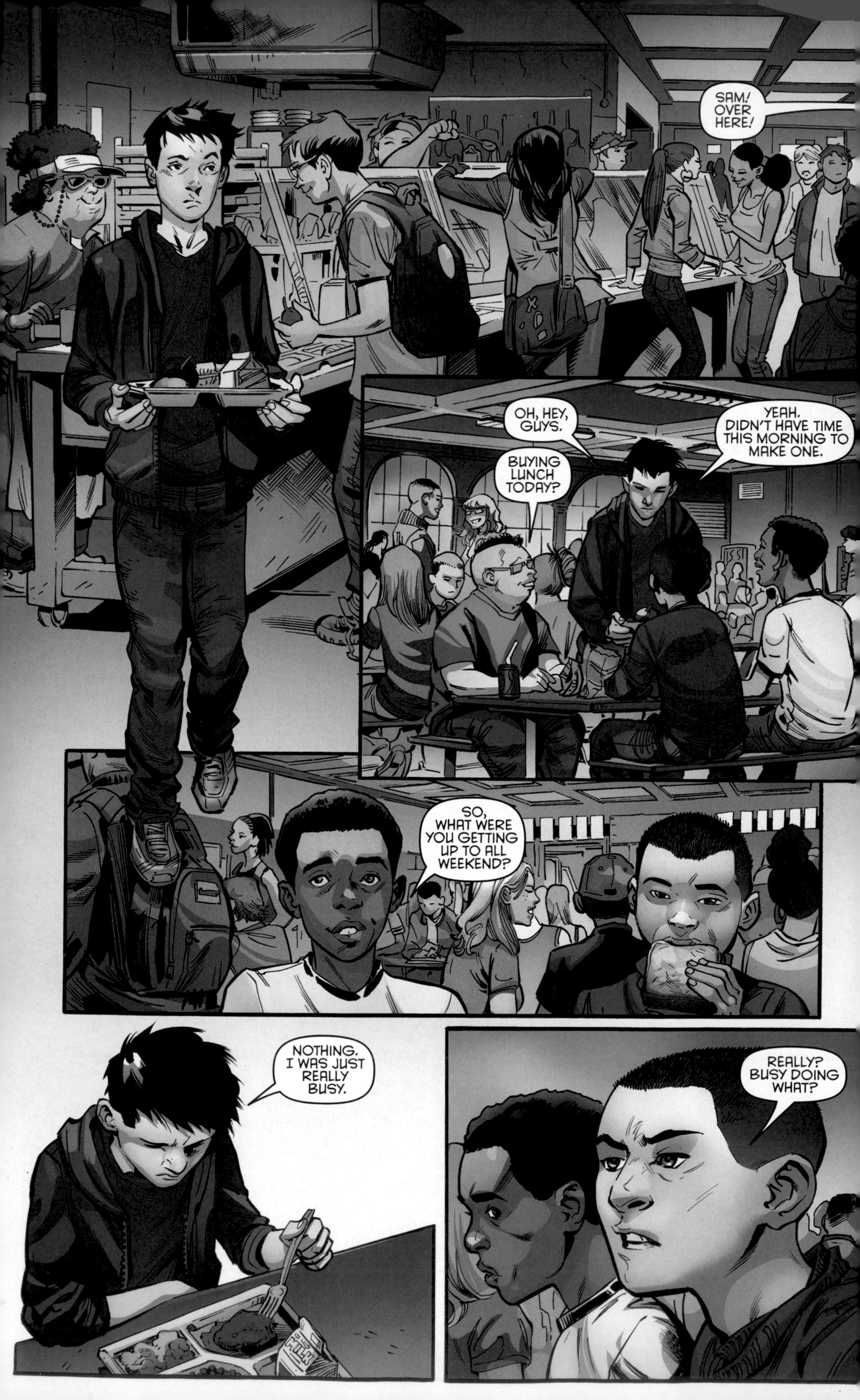
SAM! OVER HERE!
OH, HEY, GUYS.
BUYING LUNCH TODAY?
YEAH. DIDN'T HAVE TIME THIS MORNING TO MAKE ONE.
SO, WHAT WERE YOU GETTING UP TO ALL WEEKEND?
NOTHING. I WAS JUST REALLY BUSY.
REALLY? BUSY DOING WHAT?

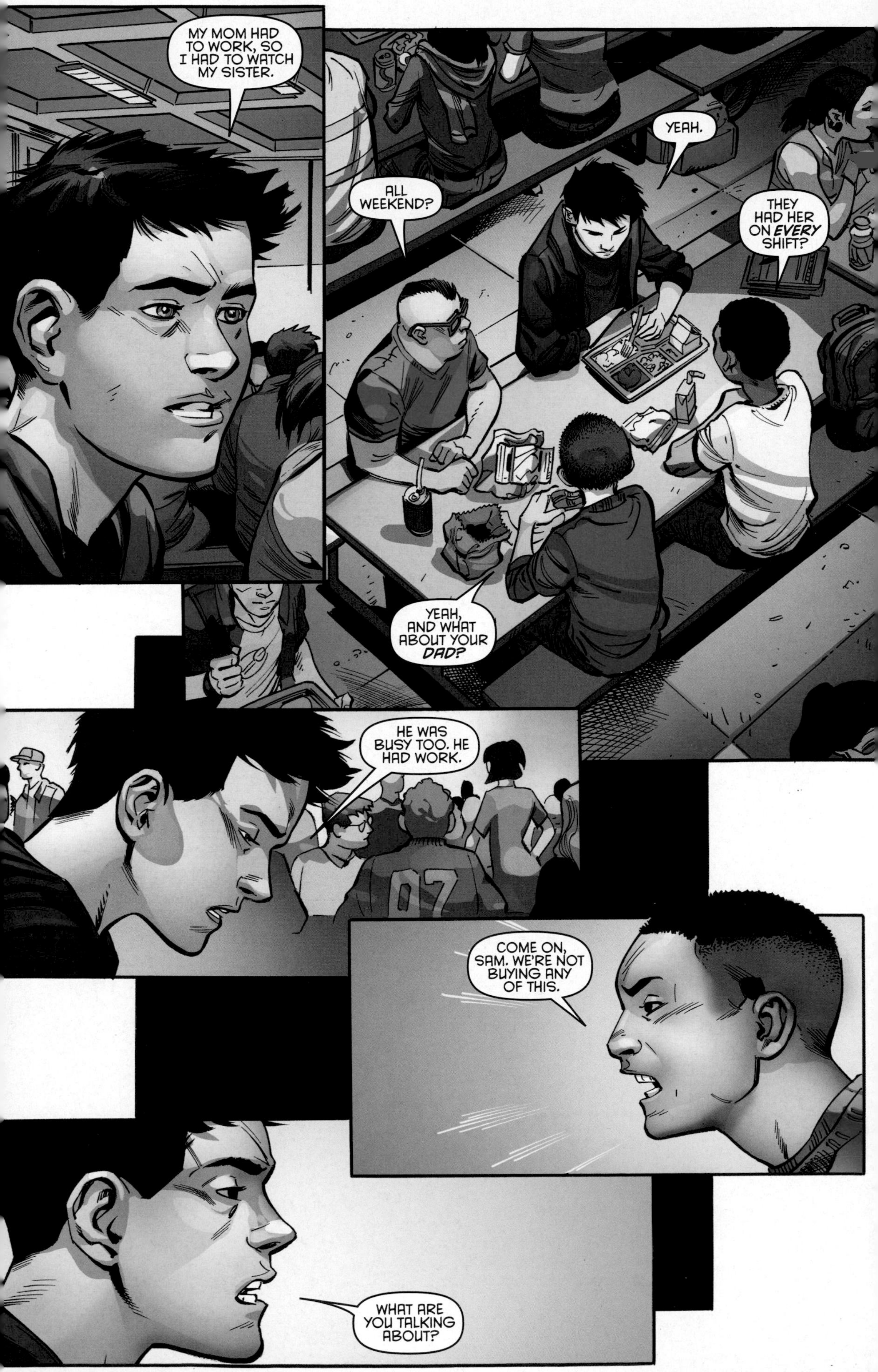
MY MOM HAD TO WORK, SO I HAD TO WATCH MY SISTER.
ALL WEEKEND?
YEAH.
THEY HAD HER ON *EVERY* SHIFT?
YEAH, AND WHAT ABOUT YOUR *DAD?*
HE WAS BUSY TOO. HE HAD WORK.
07
COME ON, SAM. WE'RE NOT BUYING ANY OF THIS.
WHAT ARE YOU TALKING ABOUT?

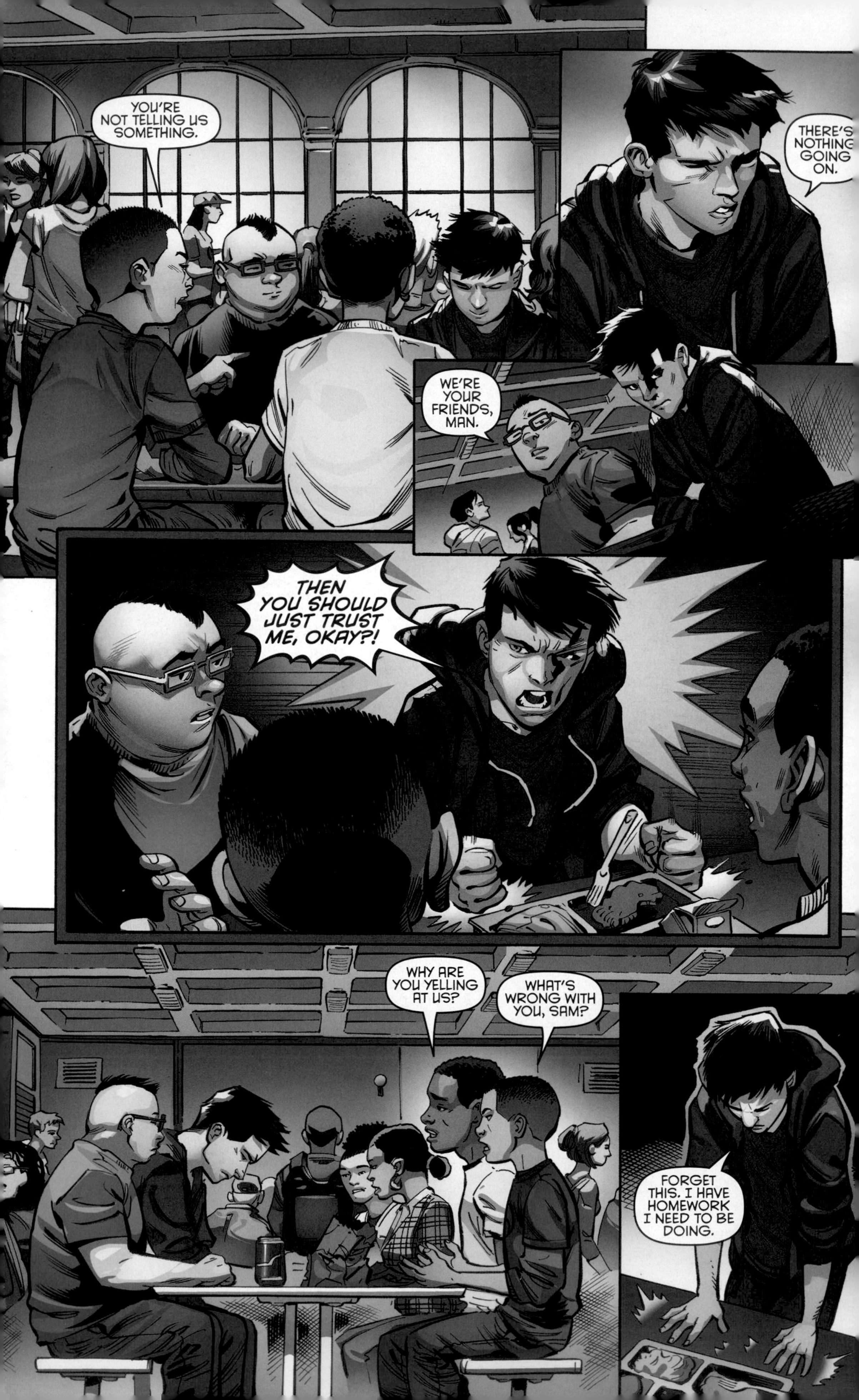

YOU'RE NOT TELLING US SOMETHING.
THERE'S NOTHING GOING ON.
WE'RE YOUR FRIENDS, MAN.
THEN YOU SHOULD JUST TRUST ME, OKAY?!
WHY ARE YOU YELLING AT US?
WHAT'S WRONG WITH YOU, SAM?
FORGET THIS. I HAVE HOMEWORK I NEED TO BE DOING.

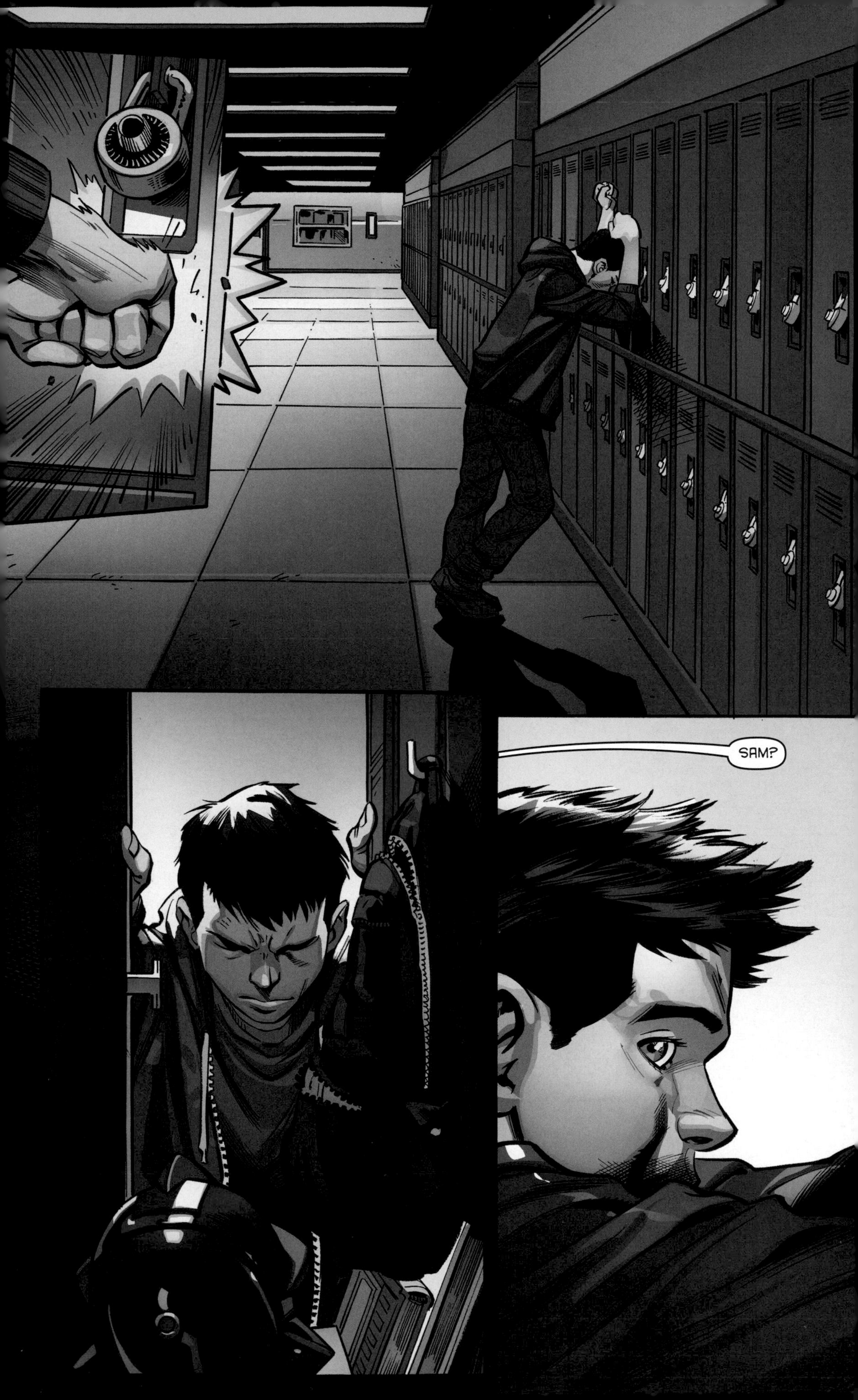
SAM?

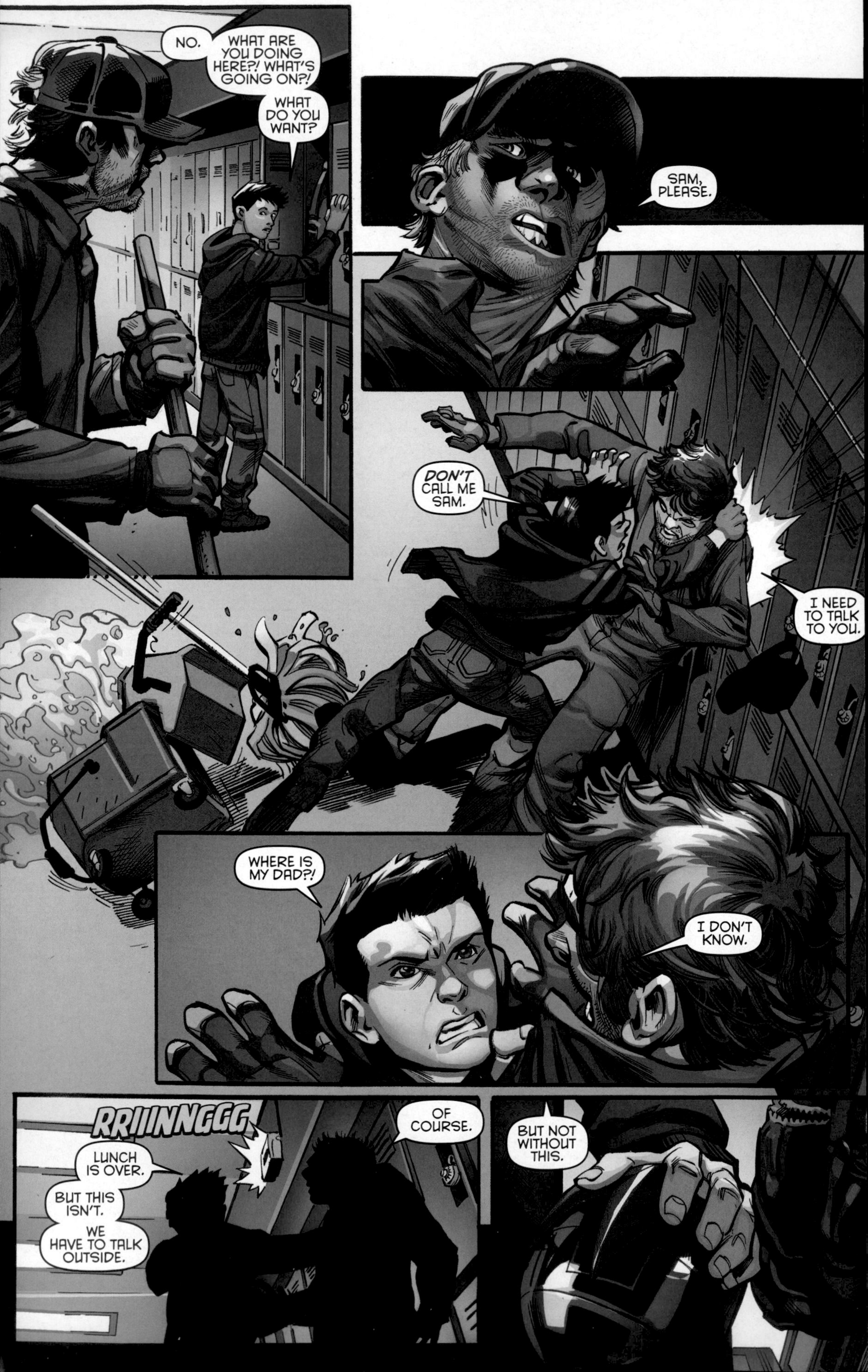
NO.
WHAT ARE YOU DOING HERE?! WHAT'S GOING ON?!
WHAT DO YOU WANT?
SAM, PLEASE.
DON'T CALL ME SAM.
I NEED TO TALK TO YOU.
WHERE IS MY DAD?!
I DON'T KNOW.
RRIIINNGGG
LUNCH IS OVER.
BUT THIS ISN'T.
WE HAVE TO TALK OUTSIDE.
OF COURSE.
BUT NOT WITHOUT THIS.

IS THIS REALLY THE MOST SECURE PLACE TO TALK?
OLDER KIDS DO ALL SORTS OF THINGS BACK HERE! WE'LL BE FINE. I KNOW WHAT I'M DOING.
YEAH, BUT WE'RE IN COSTUME BEHIND YOUR SCHOOL. THERE'S GOTTA BE A --
ANSWER THE QUESTION. WHO ARE YOU?
I'M A CLONE OF YOUR FATHER.
A *WHAT?* WHO SENT YOU?
CHITAURI SCIENTISTS CREATED ME FROM YOUR FATHER'S DNA. I GUESS I'M NOT A HUNDRED PERCENT, THOUGH.
THAT'S WHY THE HELMET KEPT SHORTING OUT ON ME. I THINK NOW, THOUGH, I'VE FIGURED OUT MOST OF THE KINKS.
BUT *WHY?*
THESE HELMETS HAVE ACCESS TO AN AMAZING POWER.
BUT *YOUR* HELMET SPECIAL. IT'S THE ONLY IE OF ITS KIND AND IT'S RE POWERFUL THAN ANY OF THE NOVA HELMETS IN THE GALAXY.
WAS SENT TO BRING BACK TO THE CHITAURI. EY WANT TO REPLICATE IT, YOU AND YOUR FATHER E THE ONLY TWO PEOPLE ALIVE WHO CAN MAKE IT WO--
MY FATHER'S ALIVE?
OH, SORRY. I DON'T ACTUALLY KNOW THAT.

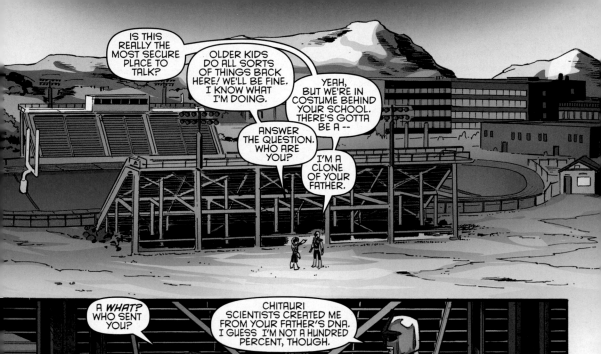

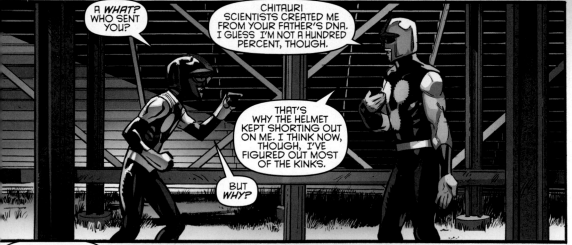

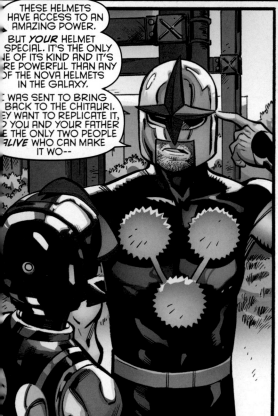

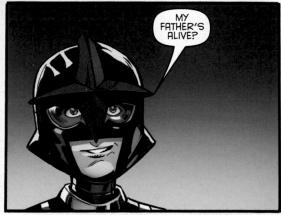

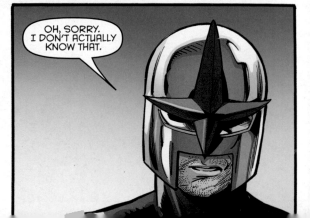

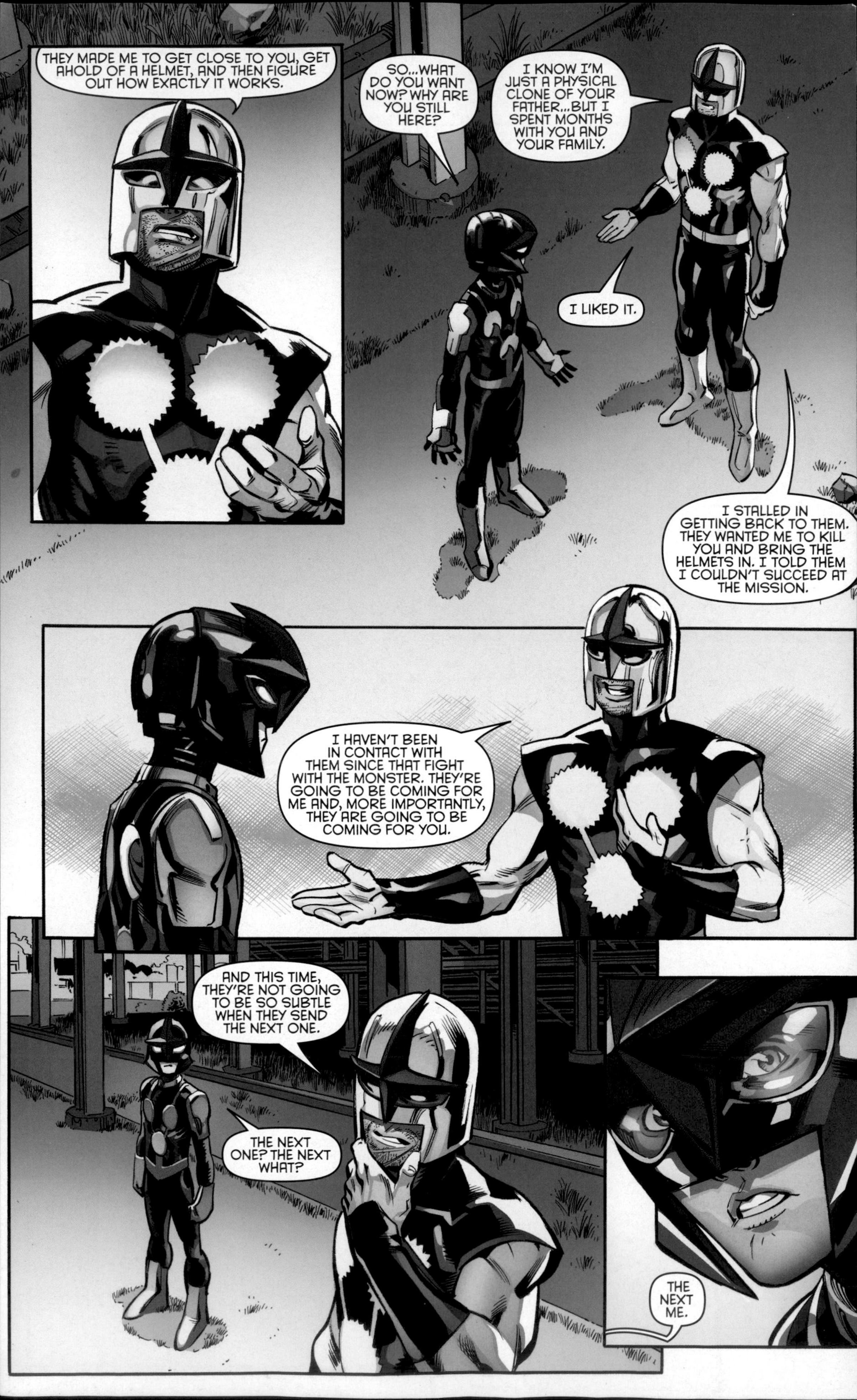
THEY MADE ME TO GET CLOSE TO YOU, GET AHOLD OF A HELMET, AND THEN FIGURE OUT HOW EXACTLY IT WORKS.
SO...WHAT DO YOU WANT NOW? WHY ARE YOU STILL HERE?
I KNOW I'M JUST A PHYSICAL CLONE OF YOUR FATHER...BUT I SPENT MONTHS WITH YOU AND YOUR FAMILY.
I LIKED IT.
I STALLED IN GETTING BACK TO THEM. THEY WANTED ME TO KILL YOU AND BRING THE HELMETS IN. I TOLD THEM I COULDN'T SUCCEED AT THE MISSION.
I HAVEN'T BEEN IN CONTACT WITH THEM SINCE THAT FIGHT WITH THE MONSTER. THEY'RE GOING TO BE COMING FOR ME AND, MORE IMPORTANTLY, THEY ARE GOING TO BE COMING FOR YOU.
AND THIS TIME, THEY'RE NOT GOING TO BE SO SUBTLE WHEN THEY SEND THE NEXT ONE.
THE NEXT ONE? THE NEXT WHAT?
THE NEXT ME.

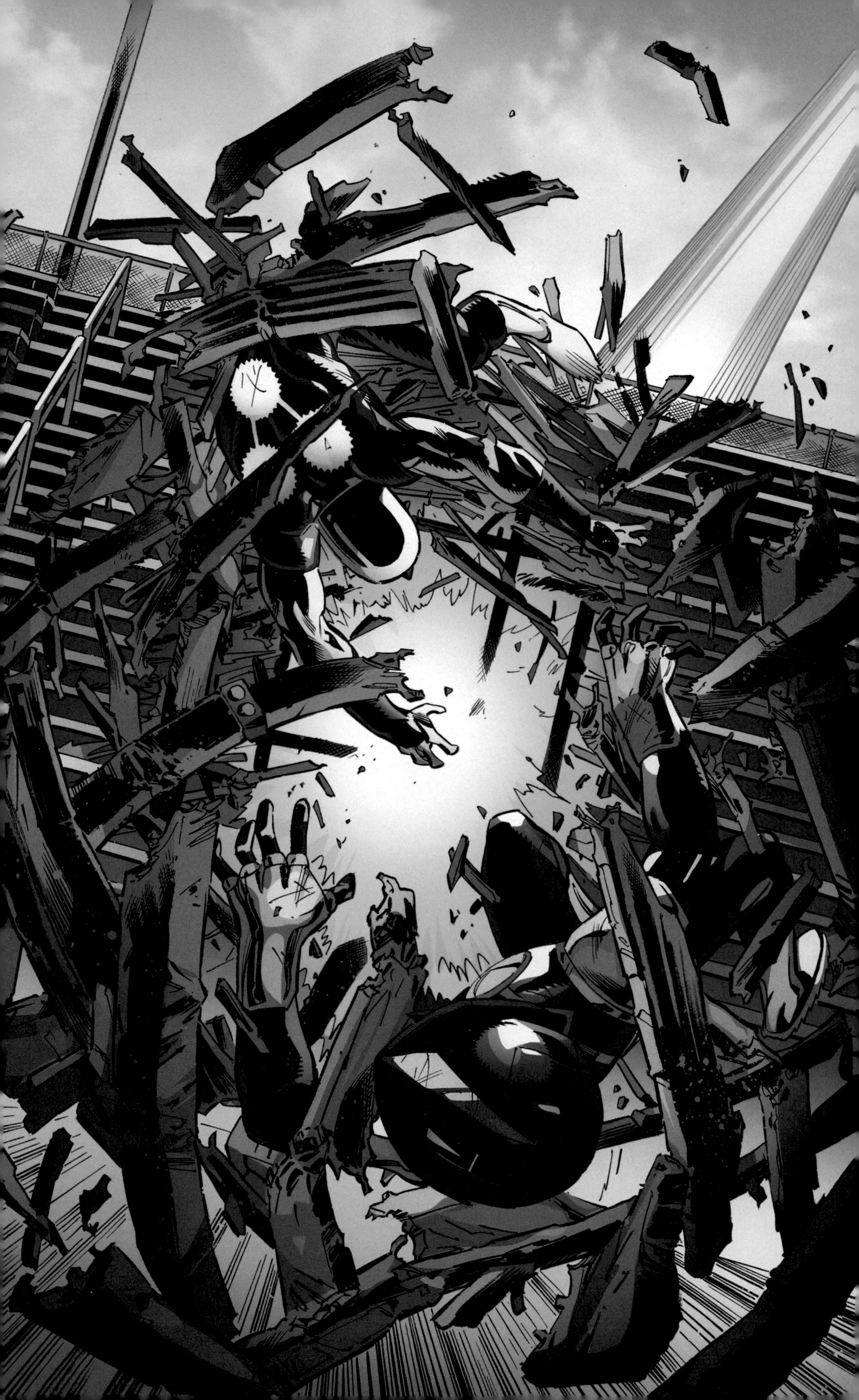

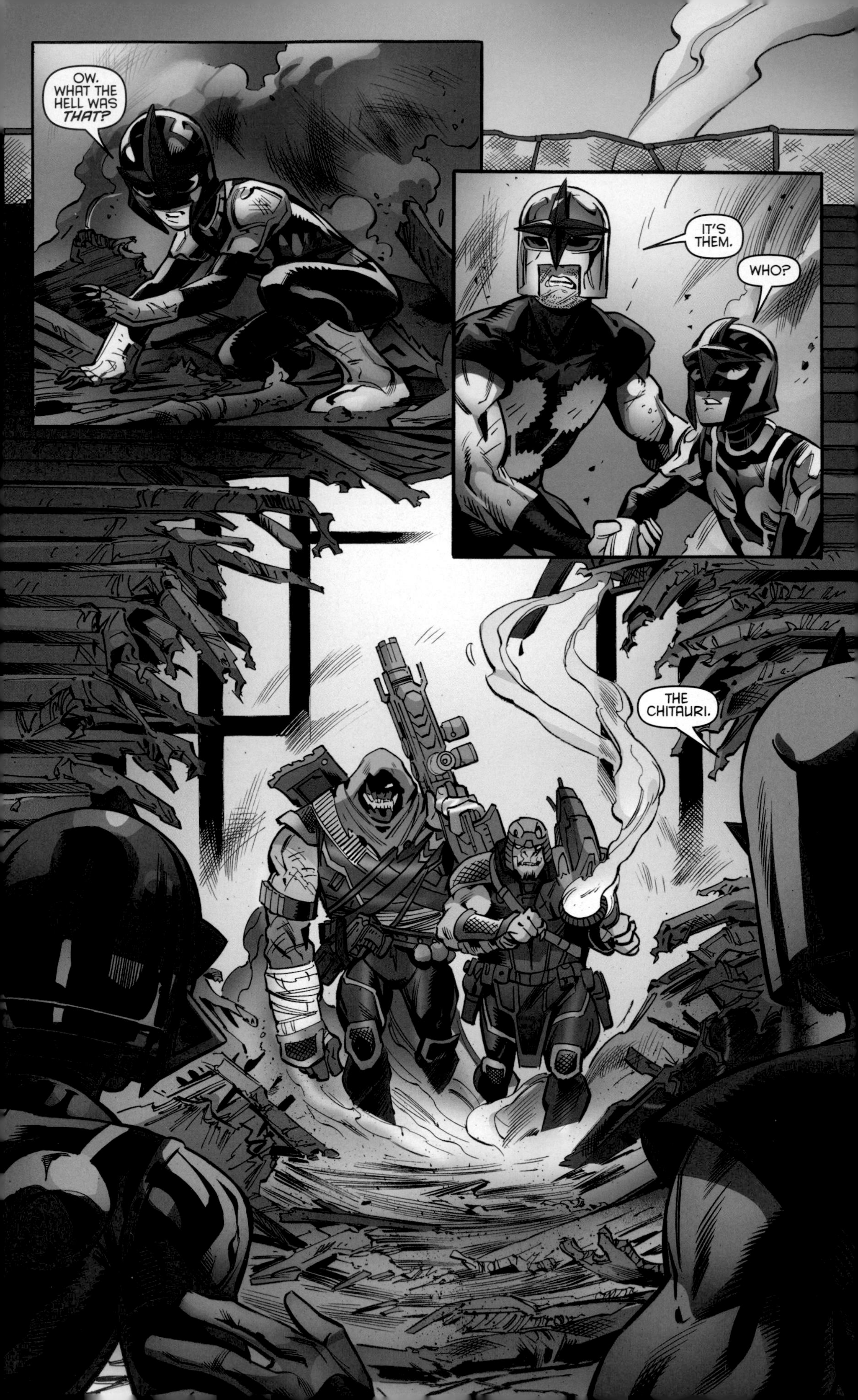
OW. WHAT THE HELL WAS *THAT?*
IT'S THEM.
WHO?
THE CHITAURI.

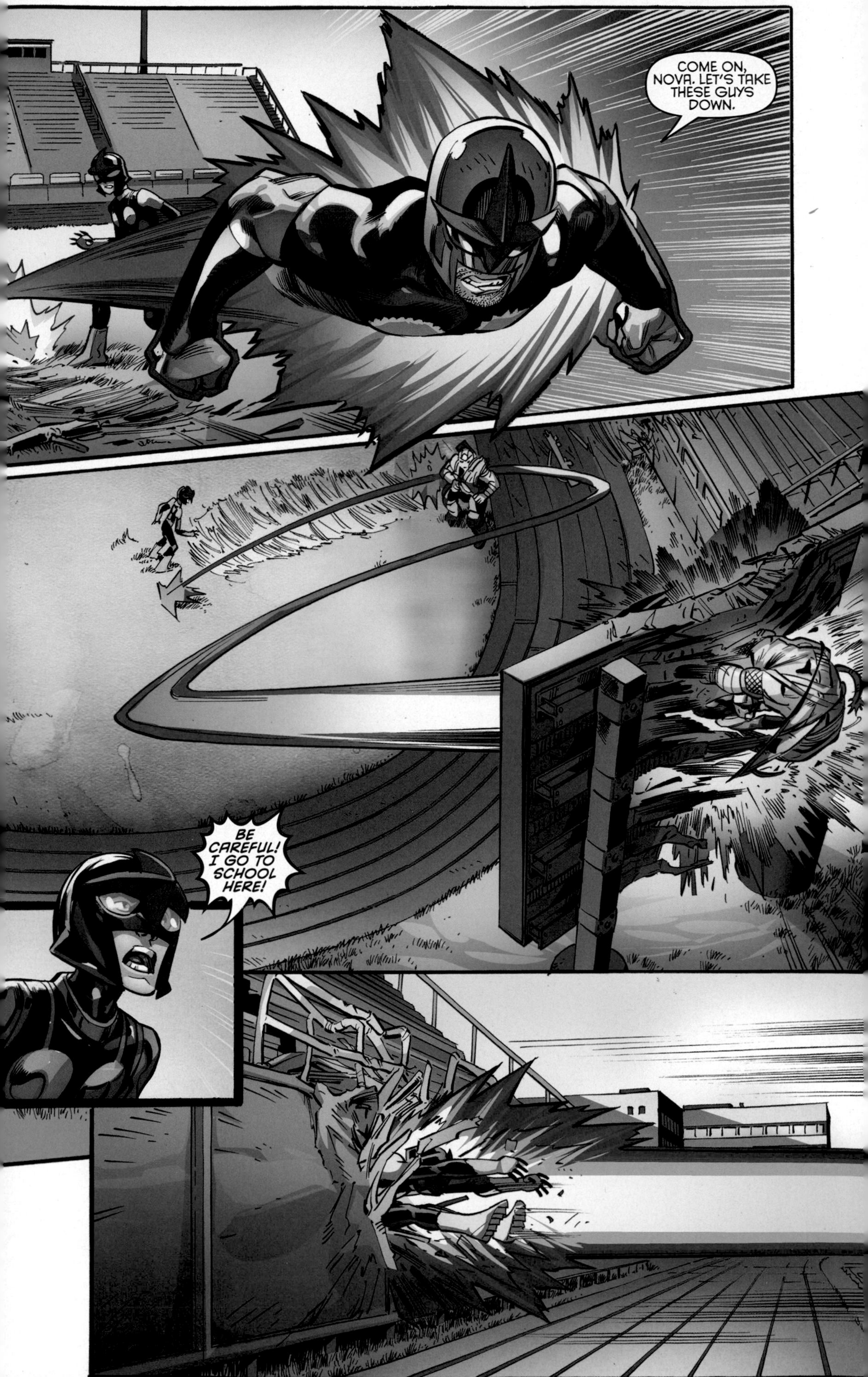
COME ON, NOVA. LET'S TAKE THESE GUYS DOWN.
BE CAREFUL! I GO TO SCHOOL HERE!

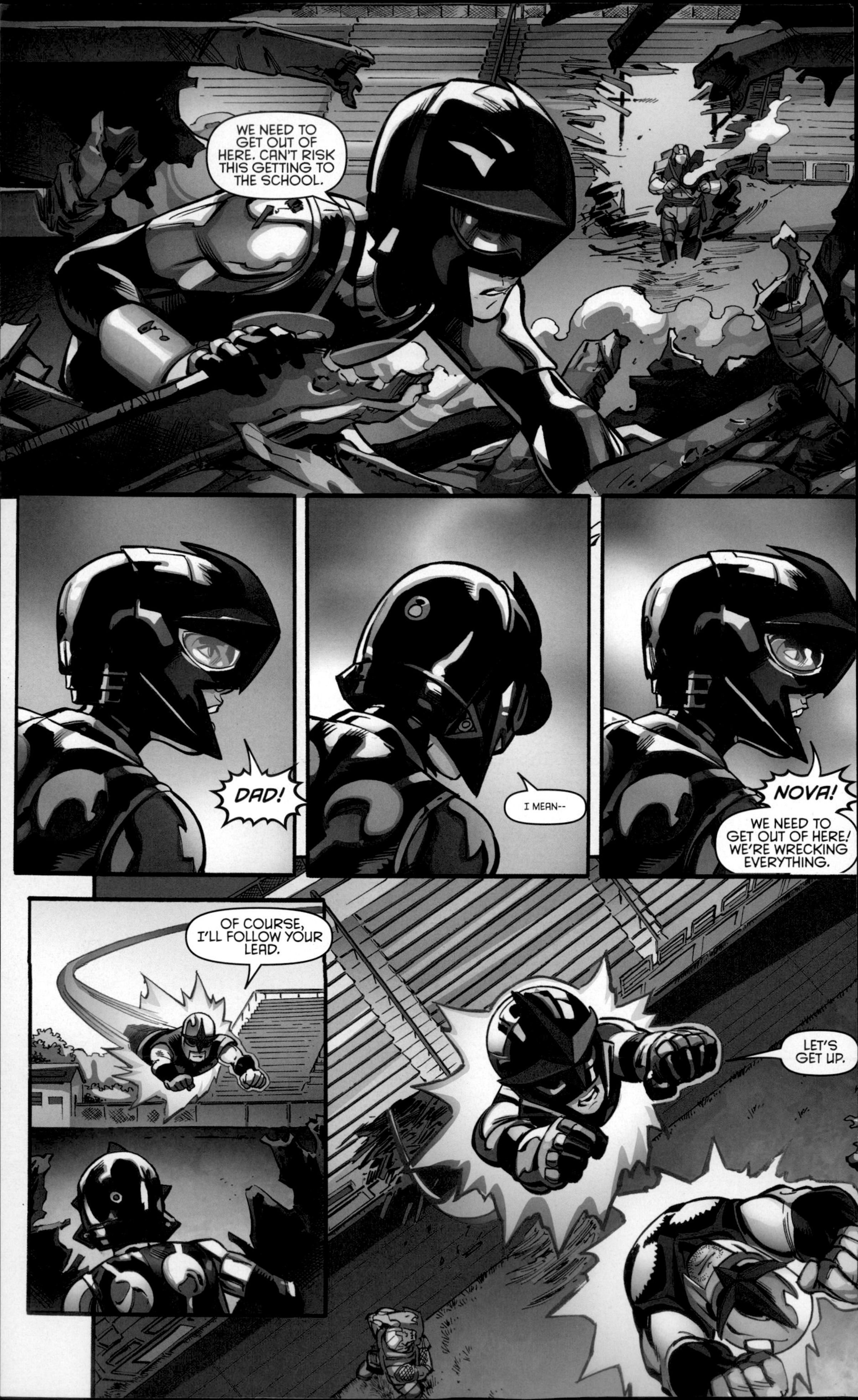
WE NEED TO GET OUT OF HERE. CAN'T RISK THIS GETTING TO THE SCHOOL.
DAD!
I MEAN--
NOVA!
WE NEED TO GET OUT OF HERE! WE'RE WRECKING EVERYTHING.
OF COURSE, I'LL FOLLOW YOUR LEAD.
LET'S GET UP.

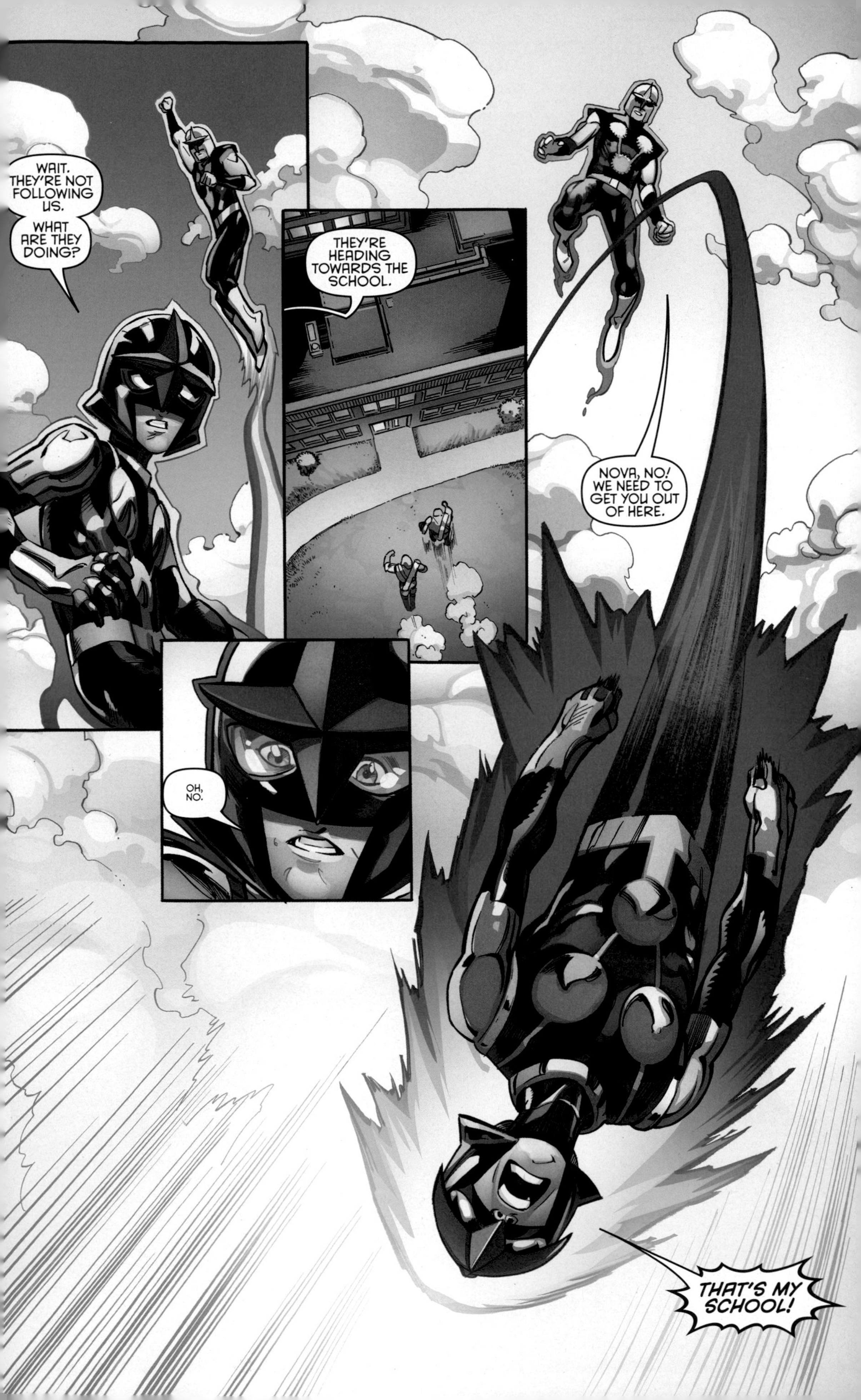
WAIT. THEY'RE NOT FOLLOWING US.
WHAT ARE THEY DOING?
THEY'RE HEADING TOWARDS THE SCHOOL.
NOVA, NO! WE NEED TO GET YOU OUT OF HERE.
OH, NO.
THAT'S MY SCHOOL!

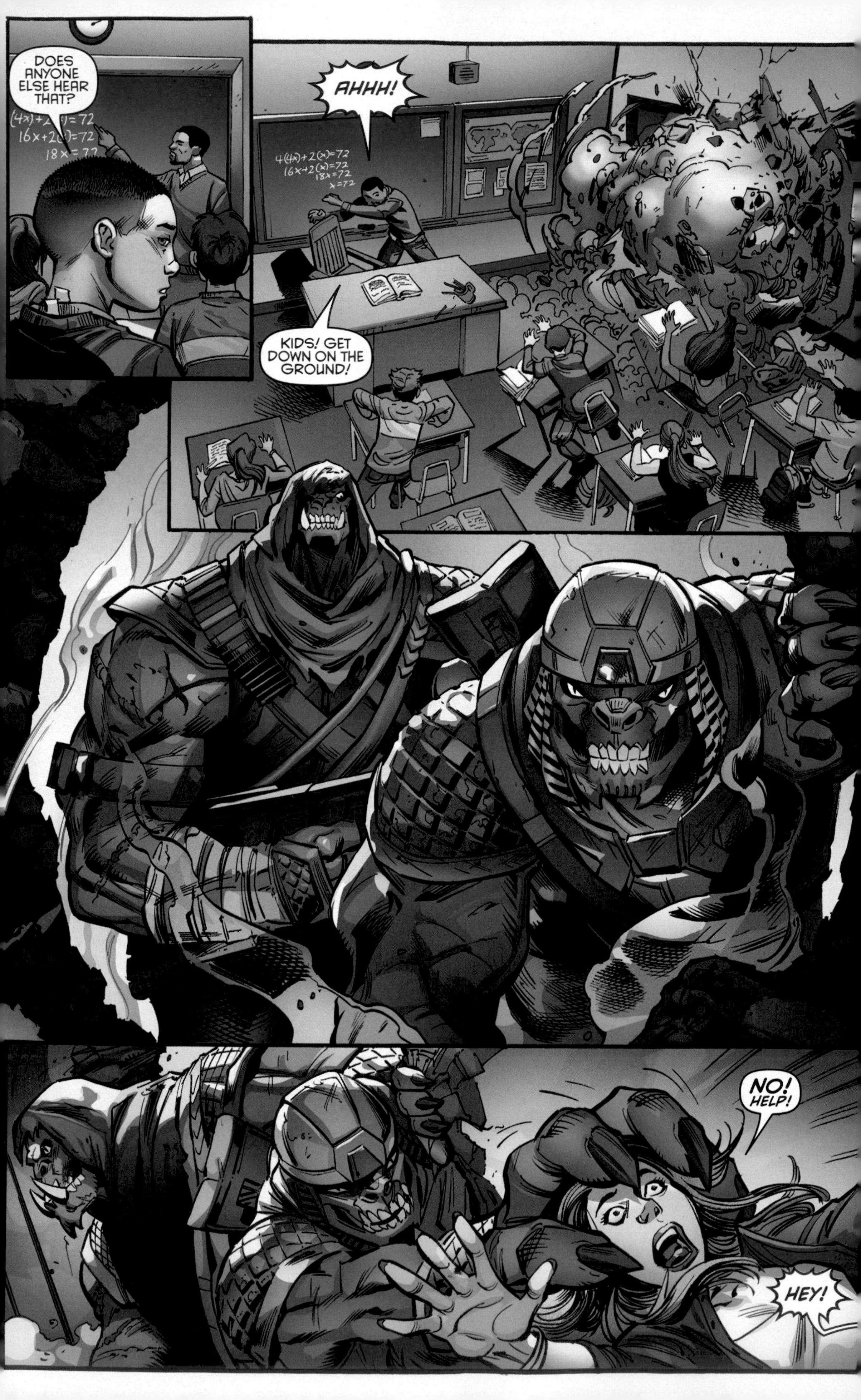
DOES ANYONE ELSE HEAR THAT?
AHHH!
4(4x)+2(x)=72
16x+2(x)=72
18x=72
x=72
KIDS! GET DOWN ON THE GROUND!
NO! HELP!
HEY!

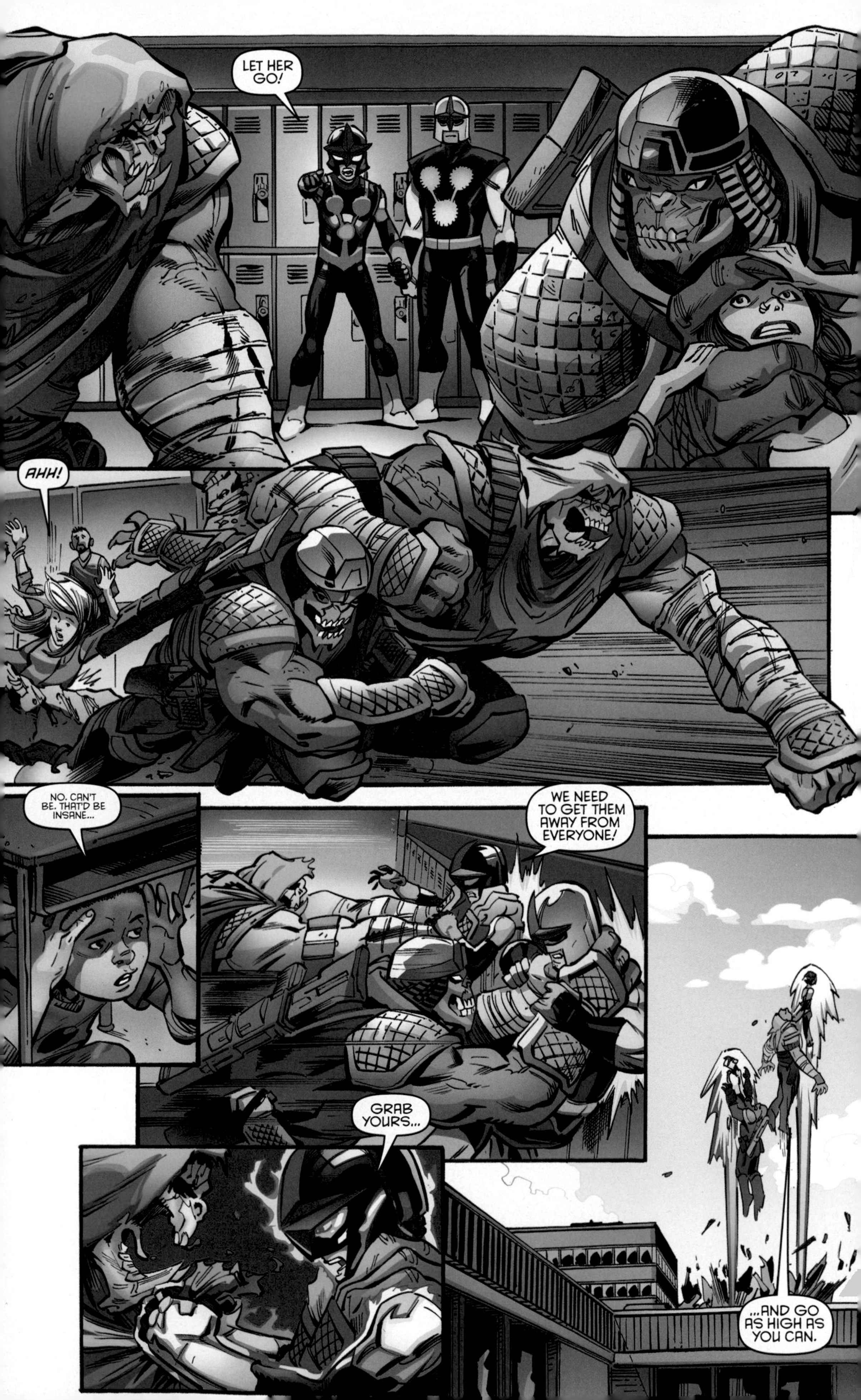
LET HER GO!
AHH!
NO. CAN'T BE. THAT'D BE INSANE...
WE NEED TO GET THEM AWAY FROM EVERYONE!
GRAB YOURS...
...AND GO AS HIGH AS YOU CAN.

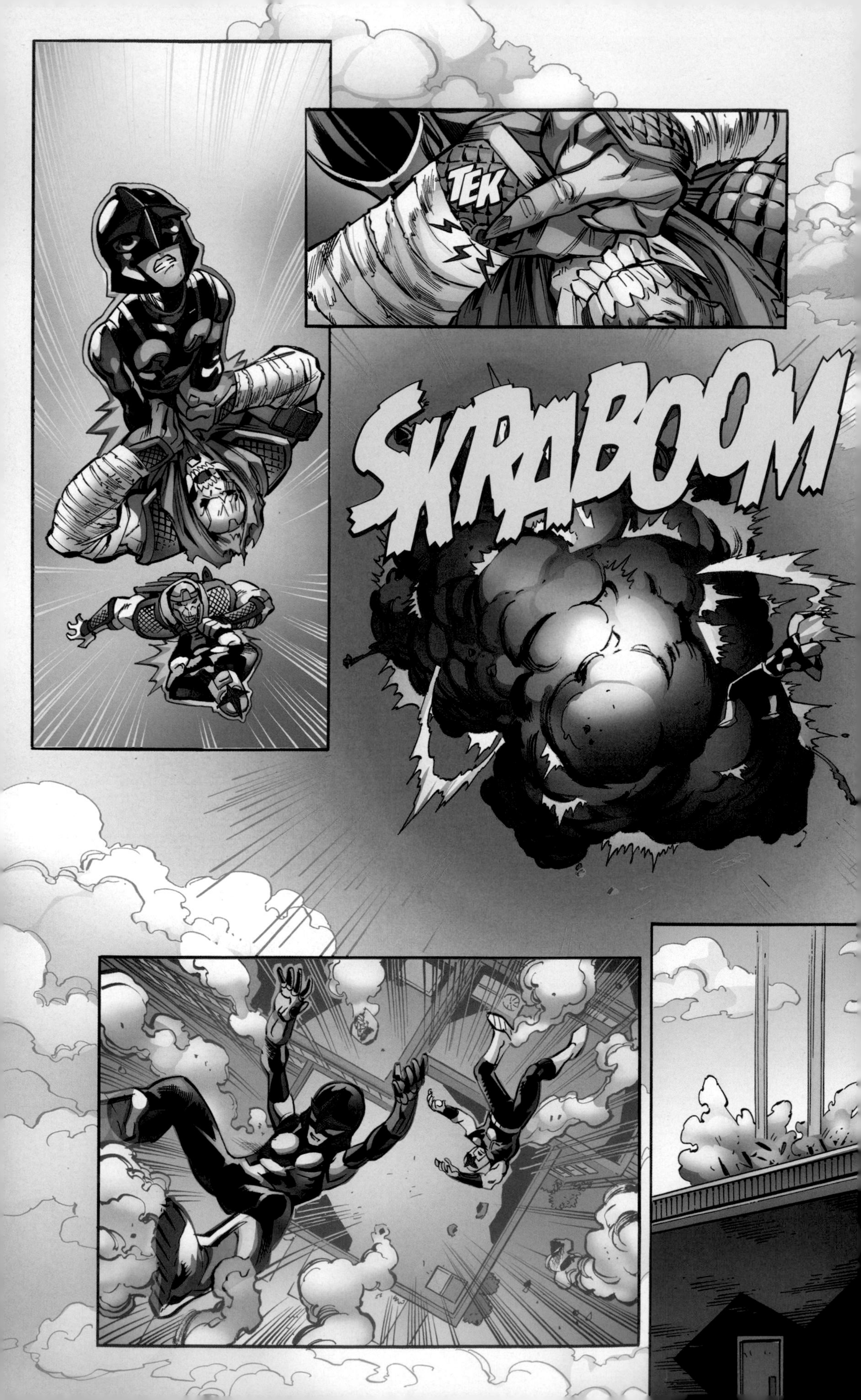
TEK
SKRABOOM

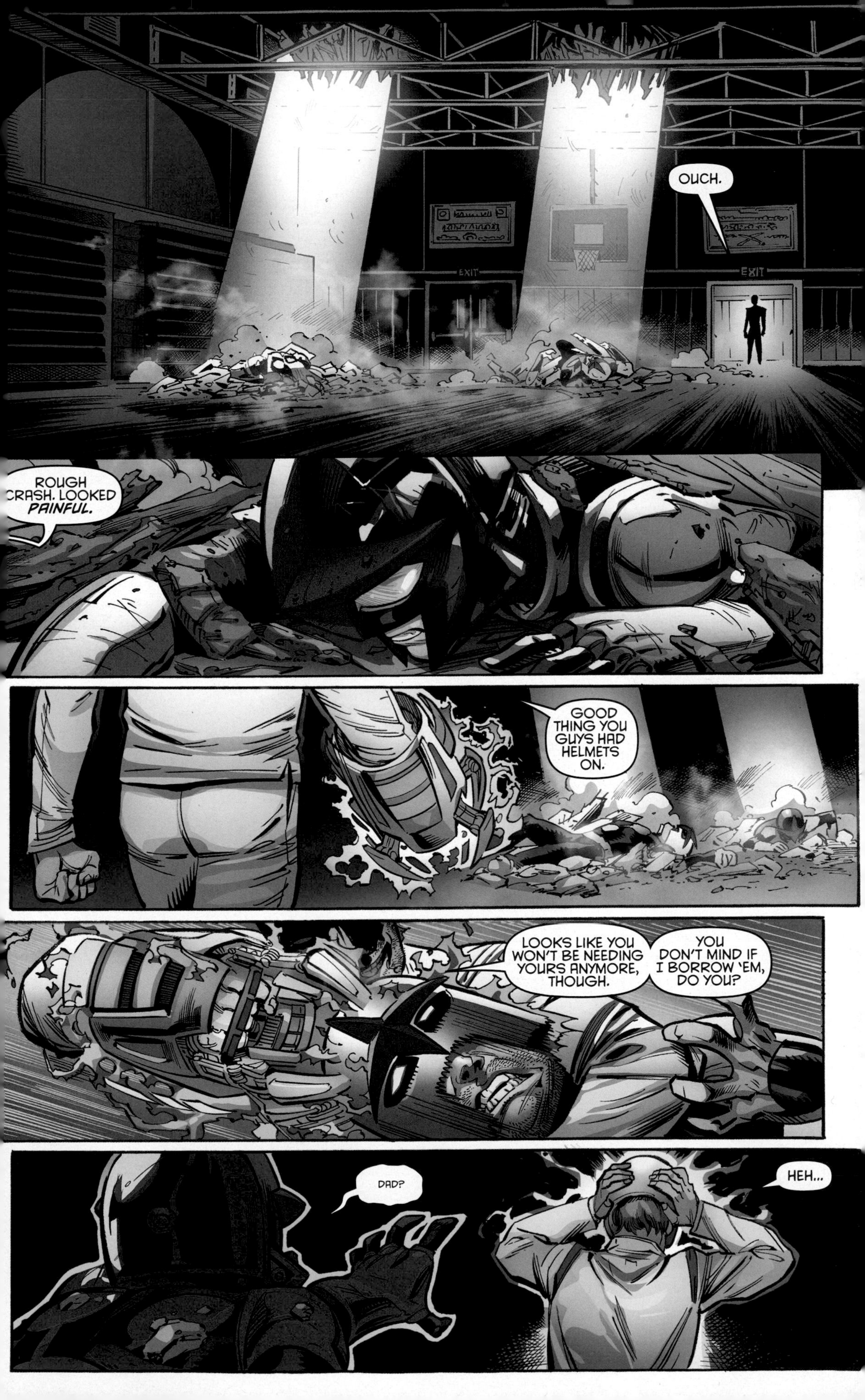
OUCH.
ROUGH CRASH. LOOKED *PAINFUL.*
GOOD THING YOU GUYS HAD HELMETS ON.
LOOKS LIKE YOU WON'T BE NEEDING YOURS ANYMORE, THOUGH.
YOU DON'T MIND IF I BORROW 'EM, DO YOU?
DAD?
HEH...

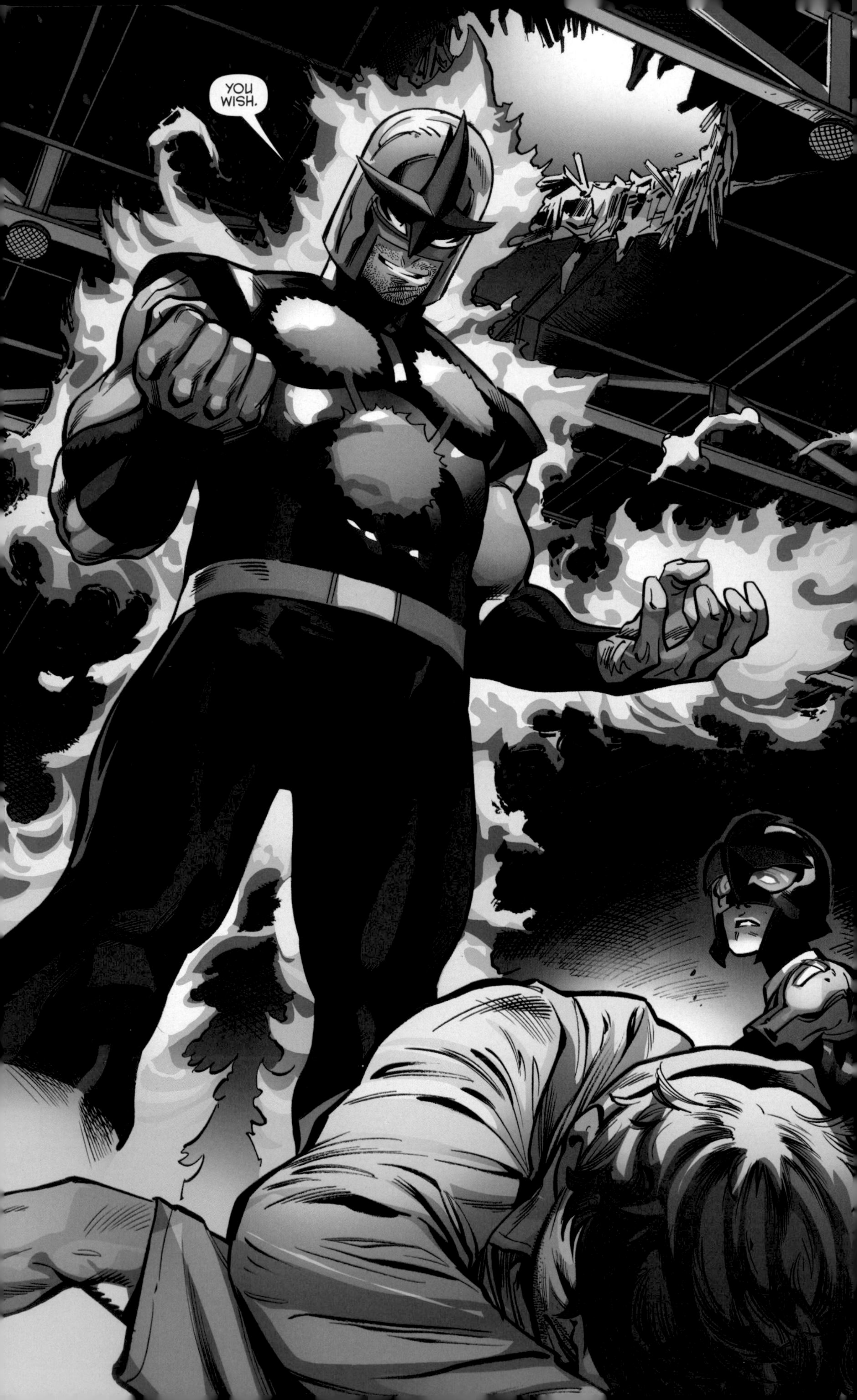
YOU WISH.

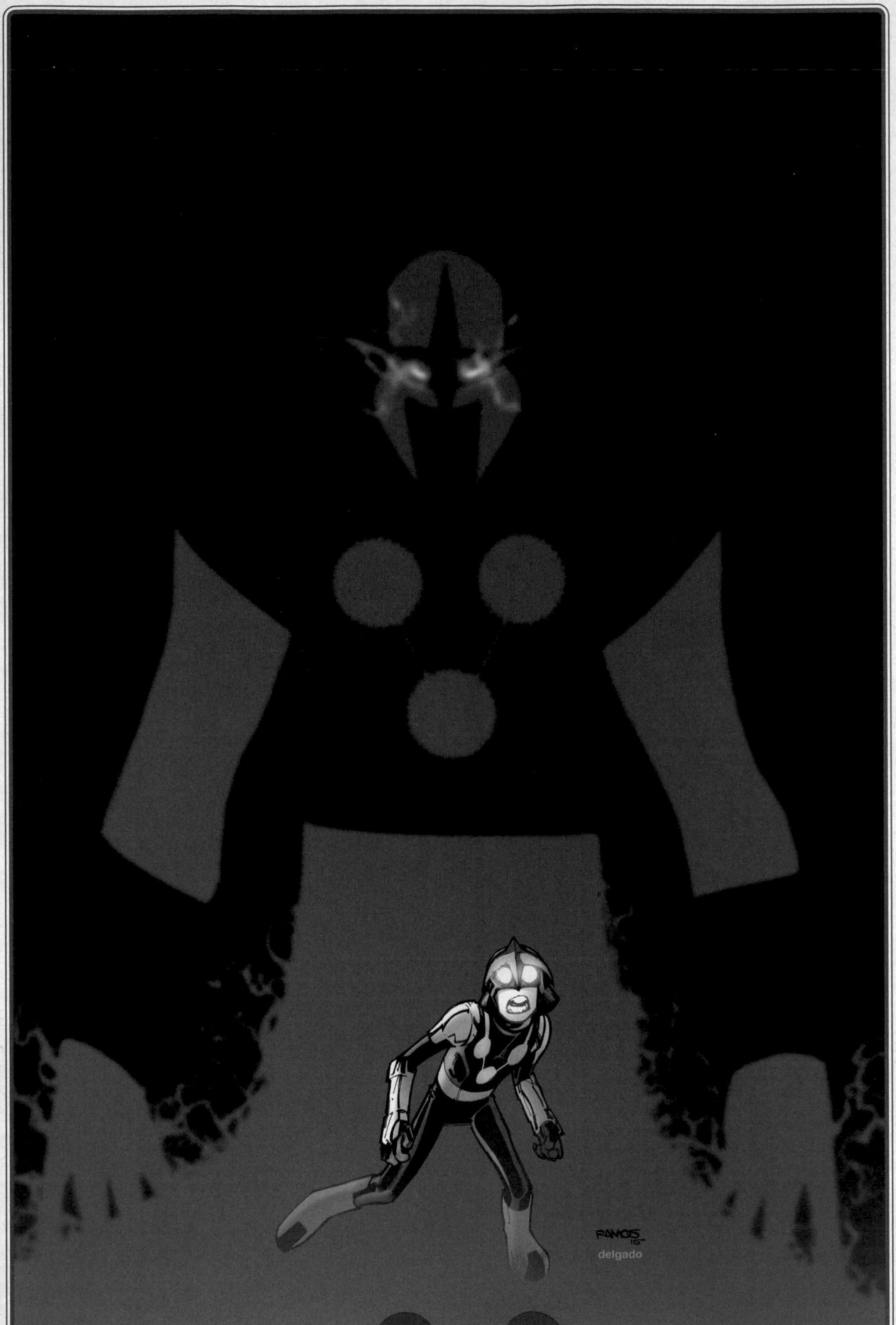
RAMOS 15
delgado

6

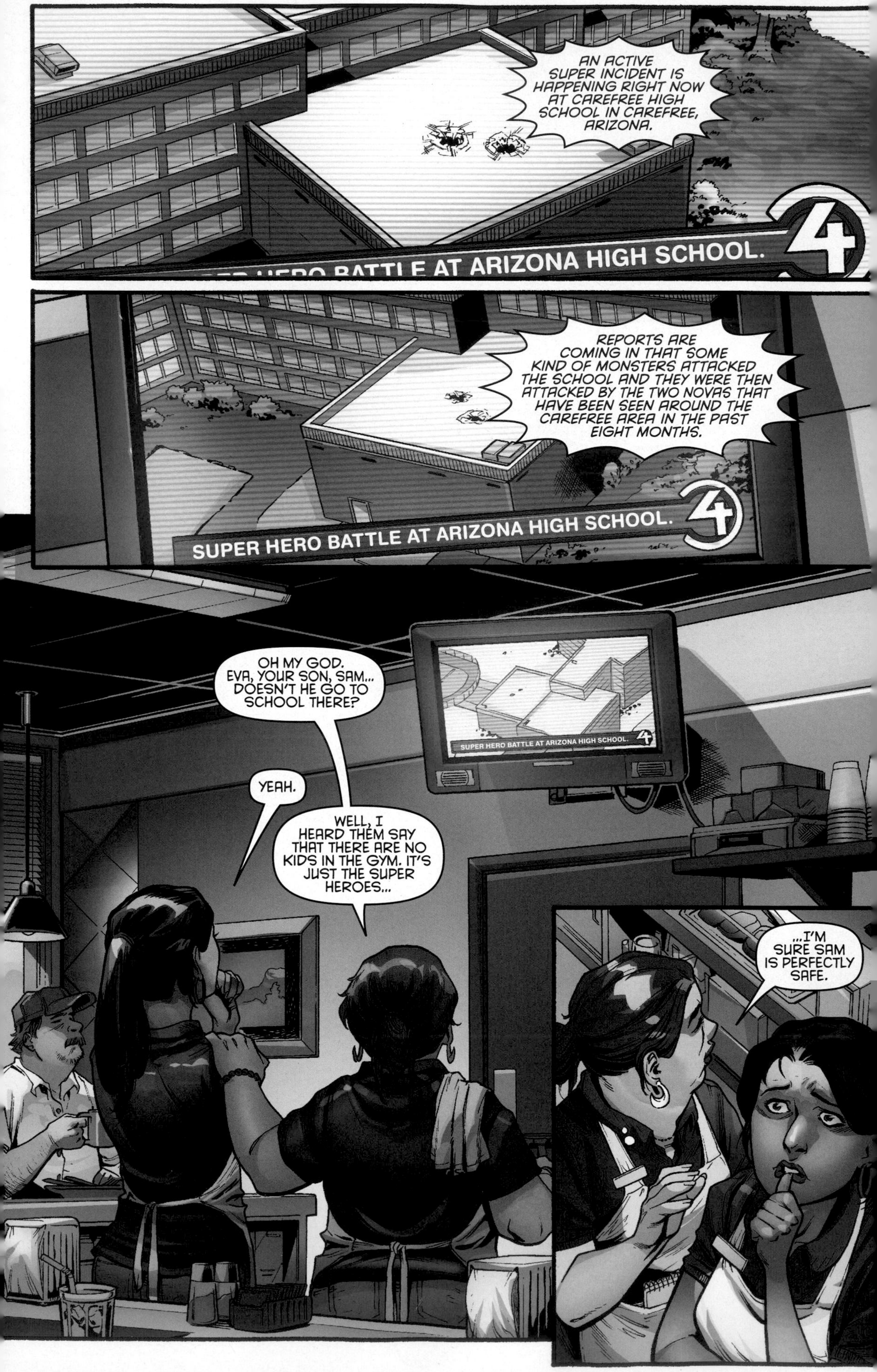
AN ACTIVE SUPER INCIDENT IS HAPPENING RIGHT NOW AT CAREFREE HIGH SCHOOL IN CAREFREE, ARIZONA.
SUPER HERO BATTLE AT ARIZONA HIGH SCHOOL.
REPORTS ARE COMING IN THAT SOME KIND OF MONSTERS ATTACKED THE SCHOOL AND THEY WERE THEN ATTACKED BY THE TWO NOVAS THAT HAVE BEEN SEEN AROUND THE CAREFREE AREA IN THE PAST EIGHT MONTHS.
SUPER HERO BATTLE AT ARIZONA HIGH SCHOOL.
OH MY GOD. EVA, YOUR SON, SAM... DOESN'T HE GO TO SCHOOL THERE?
SUPER HERO BATTLE AT ARIZONA HIGH SCHOOL.
YEAH.
WELL, I HEARD THEM SAY THAT THERE ARE NO KIDS IN THE GYM. IT'S JUST THE SUPER HEROES...
...I'M SURE SAM IS PERFECTLY SAFE.

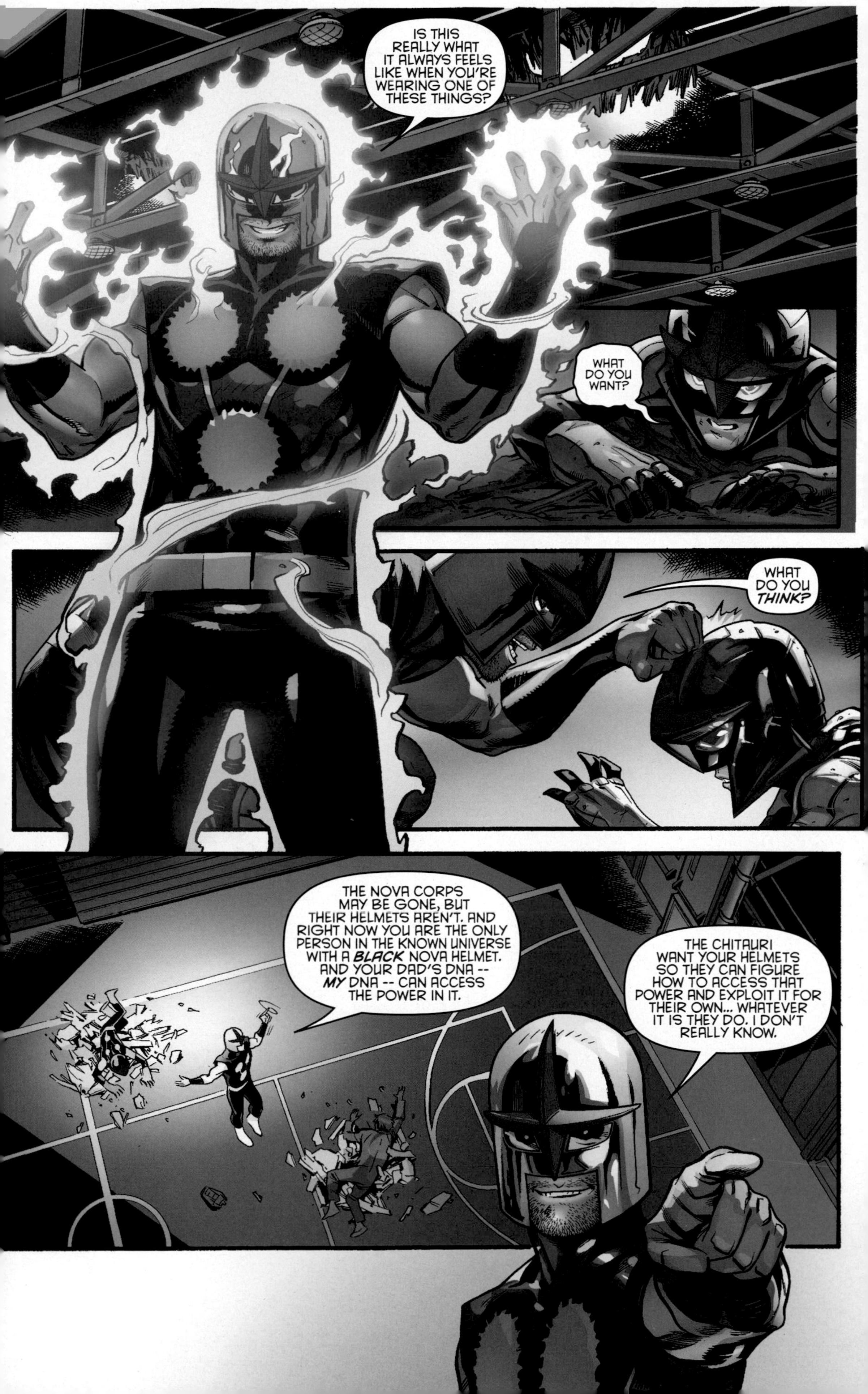
IS THIS REALLY WHAT IT ALWAYS FEELS LIKE WHEN YOU'RE WEARING ONE OF THESE THINGS?
WHAT DO YOU WANT?
WHAT DO YOU *THINK?*
THE NOVA CORPS MAY BE GONE, BUT THEIR HELMETS AREN'T. AND RIGHT NOW YOU ARE THE ONLY PERSON IN THE KNOWN UNIVERSE WITH A *BLACK* NOVA HELMET. AND YOUR DAD'S DNA -- *MY* DNA -- CAN ACCESS THE POWER IN IT.
THE CHITAURI WANT YOUR HELMETS SO THEY CAN FIGURE HOW TO ACCESS THAT POWER AND EXPLOIT IT FOR THEIR OWN... WHATEVER IT IS THEY DO. I DON'T REALLY KNOW.

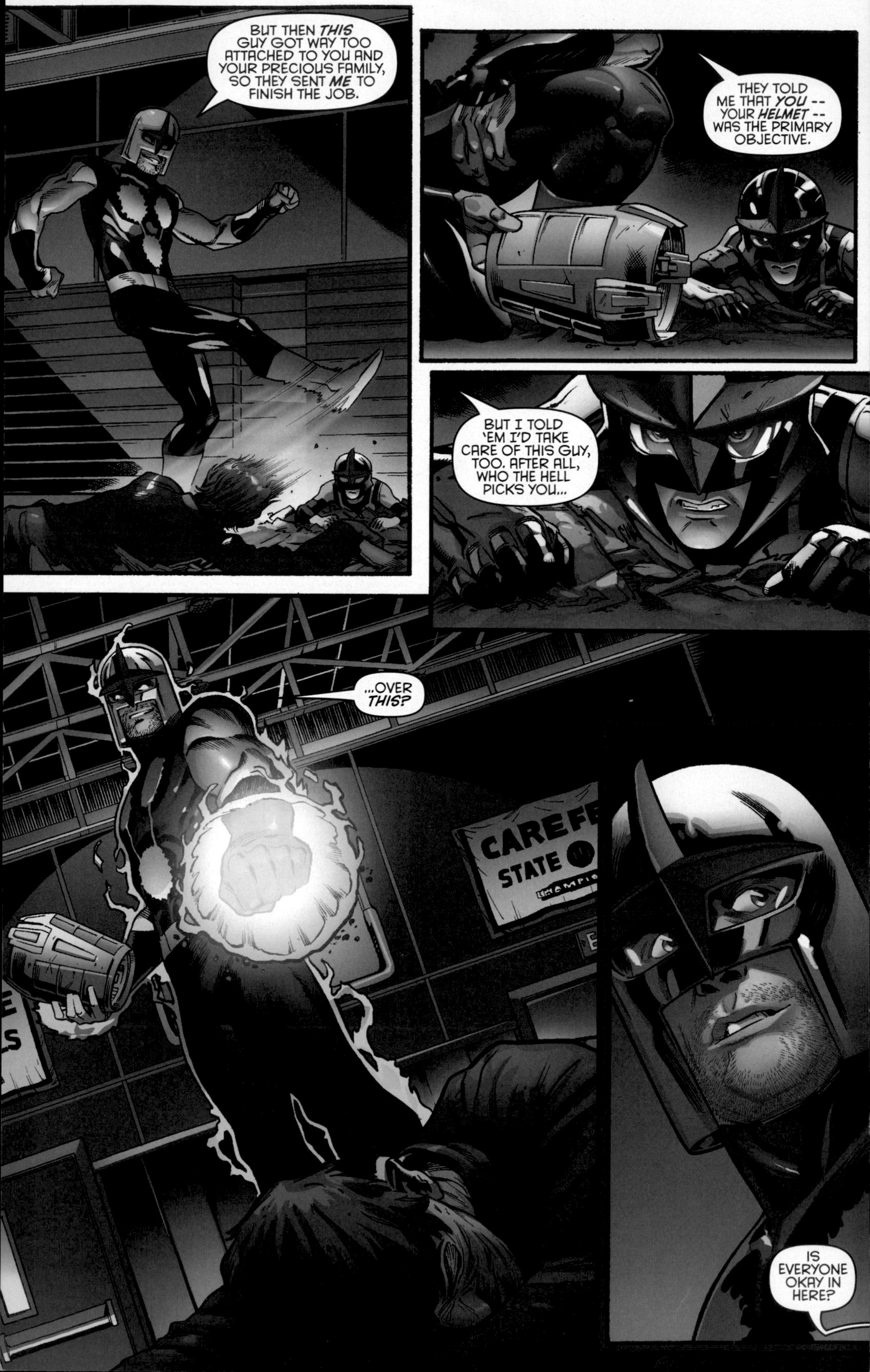
BUT THEN THIS GUY GOT WAY TOO ATTACHED TO YOU AND YOUR PRECIOUS FAMILY, SO THEY SENT ME TO FINISH THE JOB.
THEY TOLD ME THAT YOU -- YOUR HELMET -- WAS THE PRIMARY OBJECTIVE.
BUT I TOLD 'EM I'D TAKE CARE OF THIS GUY, TOO. AFTER ALL, WHO THE HELL PICKS YOU...
...OVER THIS?
CARE
STATE
IS EVERYONE OKAY IN HERE?

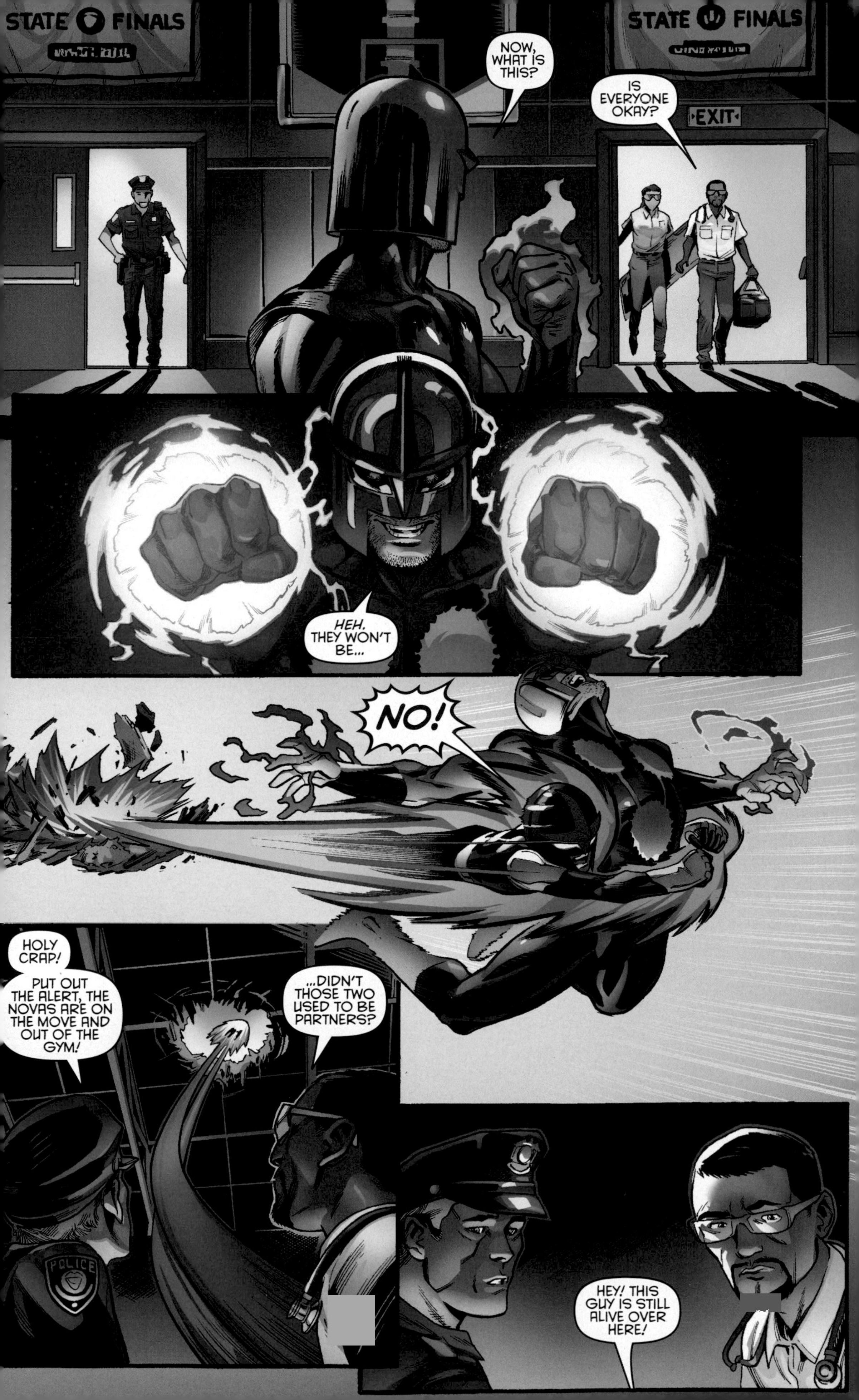
STATE FINALS
STATE FINALS
NOW, WHAT IS THIS?
IS EVERYONE OKAY?
EXIT
HEH. THEY WON'T BE...
NO!
HOLY CRAP!
PUT OUT THE ALERT, THE NOVAS ARE ON THE MOVE AND OUT OF THE GYM!
...DIDN'T THOSE TWO USED TO BE PARTNERS?
POLICE
HEY! THIS GUY IS STILL ALIVE OVER HERE!

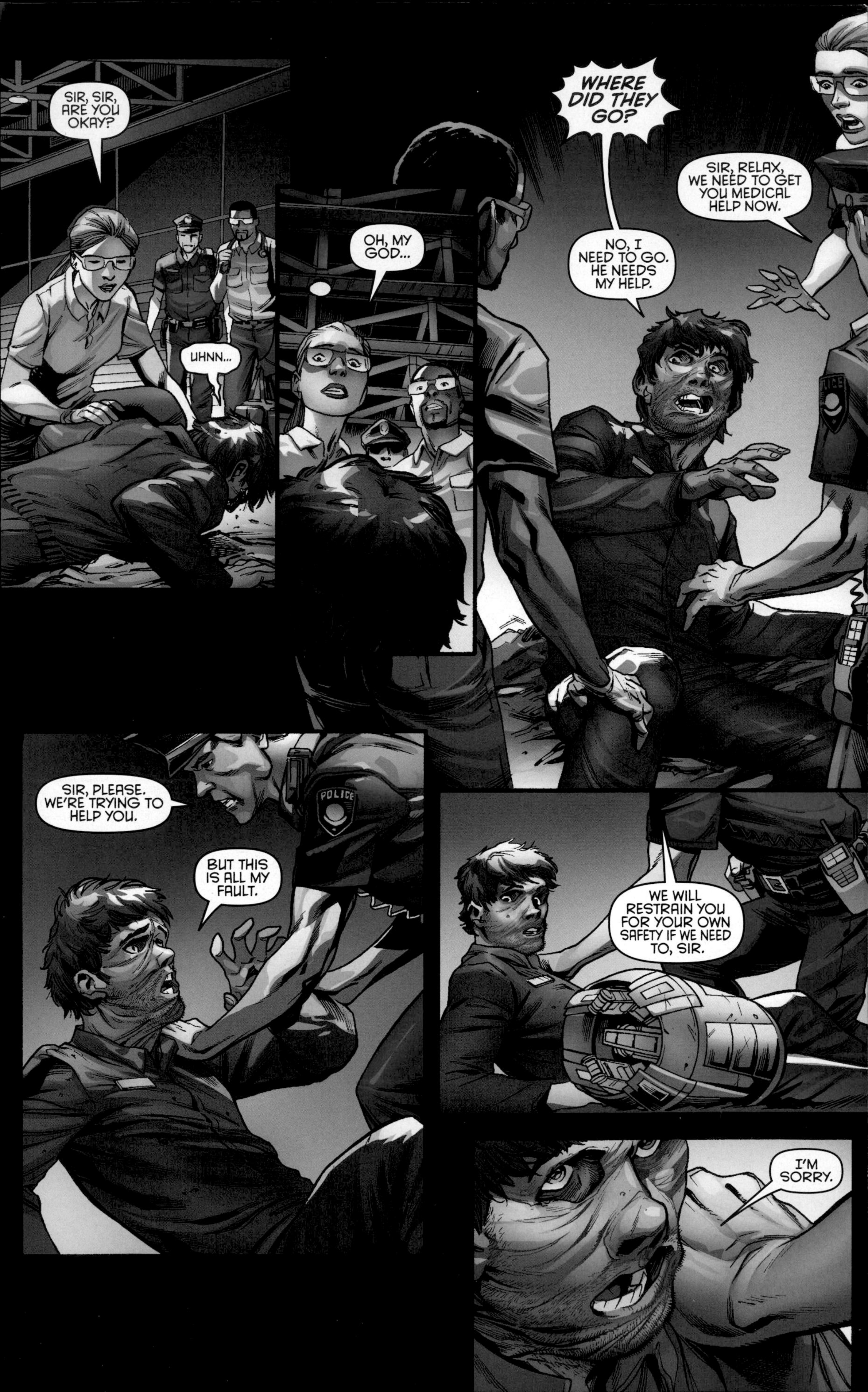
SIR, SIR, ARE YOU OKAY?
UHNN...
OH, MY GOD...
WHERE DID THEY GO?
NO, I NEED TO GO. HE NEEDS MY HELP.
SIR, RELAX, WE NEED TO GET YOU MEDICAL HELP NOW.
SIR, PLEASE. WE'RE TRYING TO HELP YOU.
POLICE
BUT THIS IS ALL MY FAULT.
WE WILL RESTRAIN YOU FOR YOUR OWN SAFETY IF WE NEED TO, SIR.
I'M SORRY.

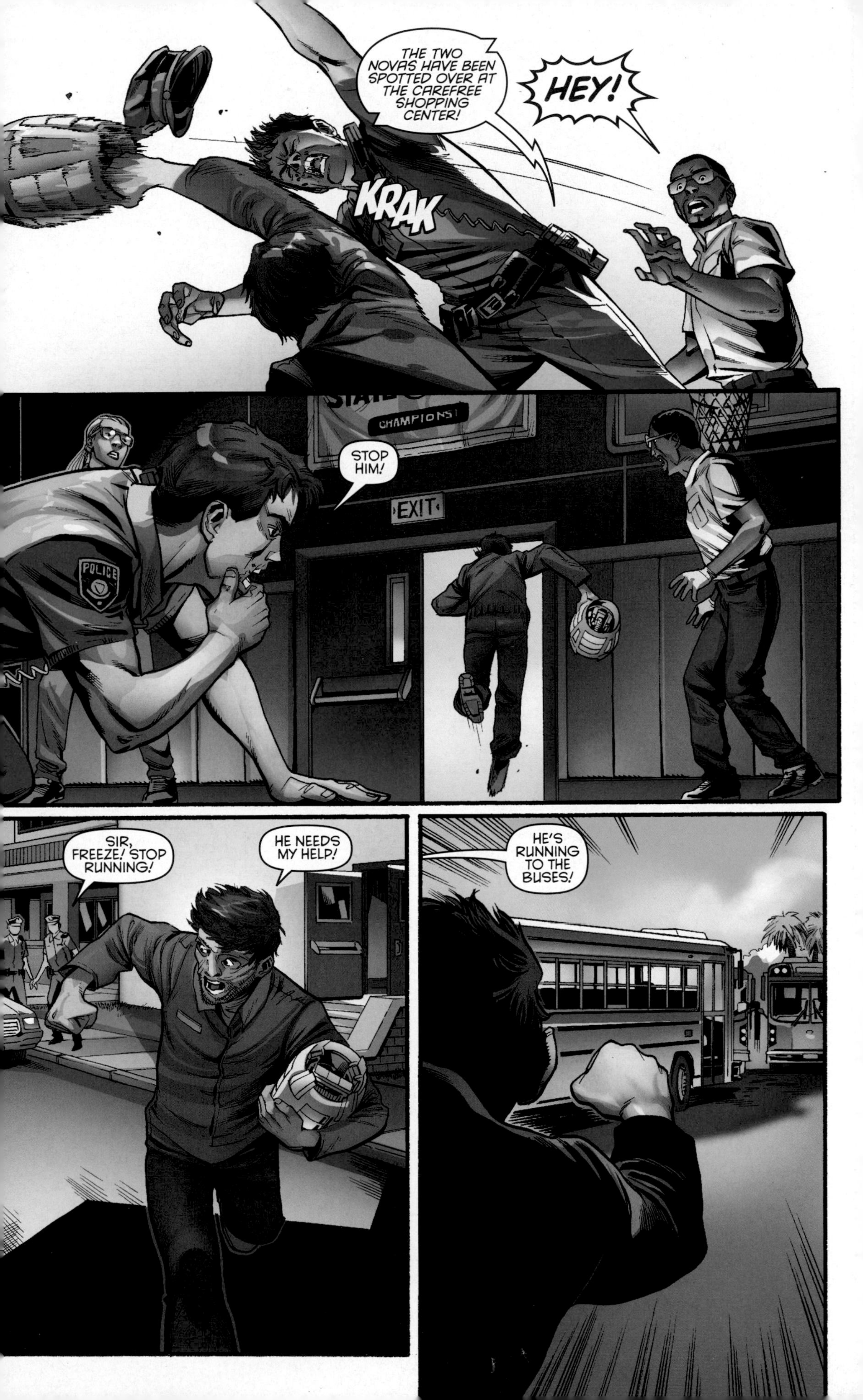
THE TWO NOVAS HAVE BEEN SPOTTED OVER AT THE CAREFREE SHOPPING CENTER!
HEY!
KRAK
CHAMPIONS!
STOP HIM!
EXIT
POLICE
SIR, FREEZE! STOP RUNNING!
HE NEEDS MY HELP!
HE'S RUNNING TO THE BUSES!

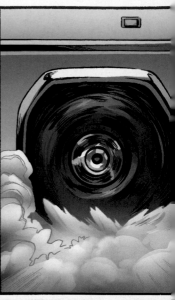

THE CAREFREE SHOPPING CENTER... TRAFFIC IS GOING TO BE BRUTAL.

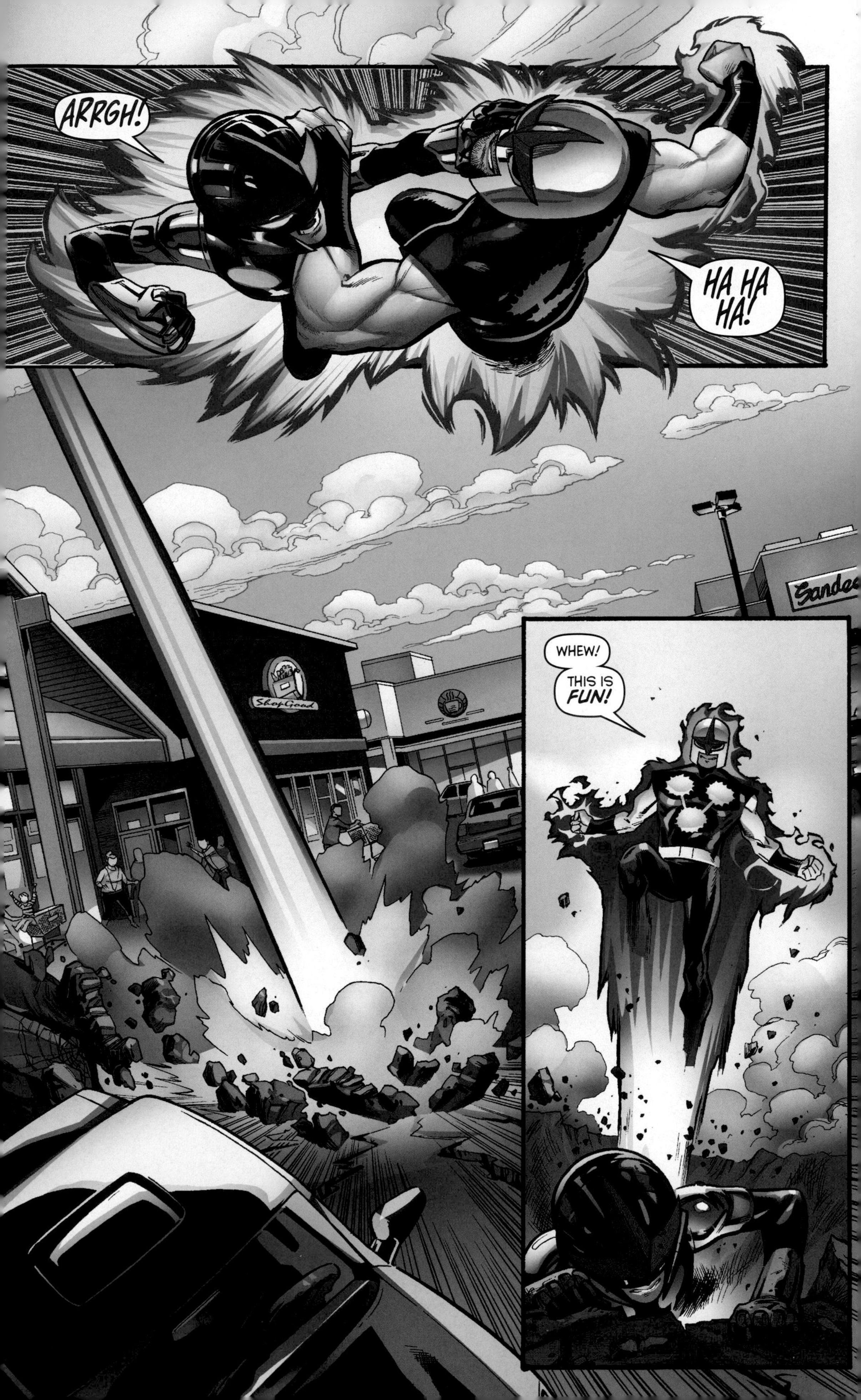
ARRGH!
HA HA HA!
ShopGood
Sandee
WHEW!
THIS IS FUN!

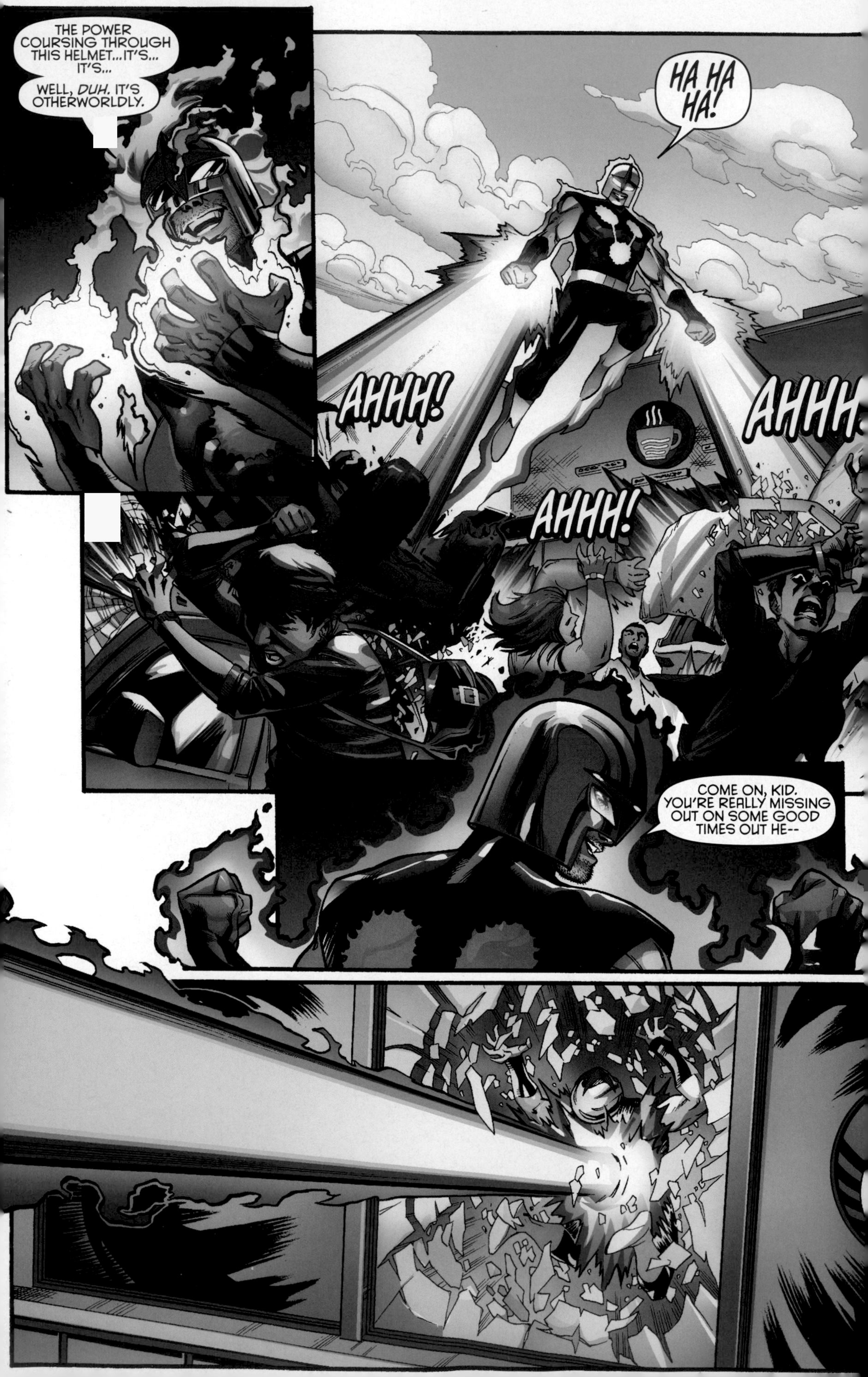
THE POWER COURSING THROUGH THIS HELMET...IT'S... IT'S...
WELL, DUH. IT'S OTHERWORLDLY.
HA HA HA!
AHHH!
AHHH!
AHHH!
COME ON, KID. YOU'RE REALLY MISSING OUT ON SOME GOOD TIMES OUT HE--

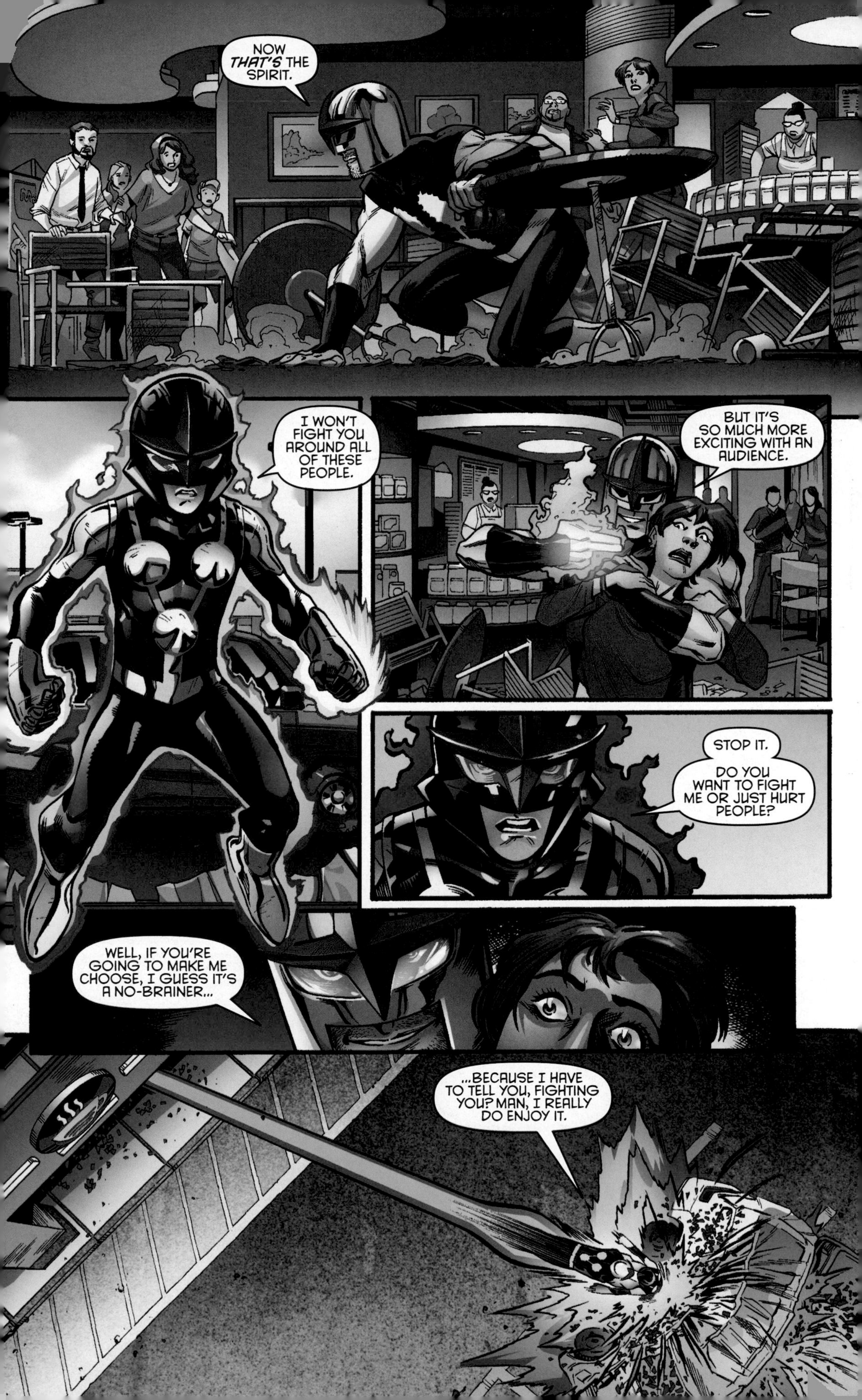
NOW *THAT'S* THE SPIRIT.
I WON'T FIGHT YOU AROUND ALL OF THESE PEOPLE.
BUT IT'S SO MUCH MORE EXCITING WITH AN AUDIENCE.
STOP IT.
DO YOU WANT TO FIGHT ME OR JUST HURT PEOPLE?
WELL, IF YOU'RE GOING TO MAKE ME CHOOSE, I GUESS IT'S A NO-BRAINER...
...BECAUSE I HAVE TO TELL YOU, FIGHTING YOU? MAN, I REALLY DO ENJOY IT.

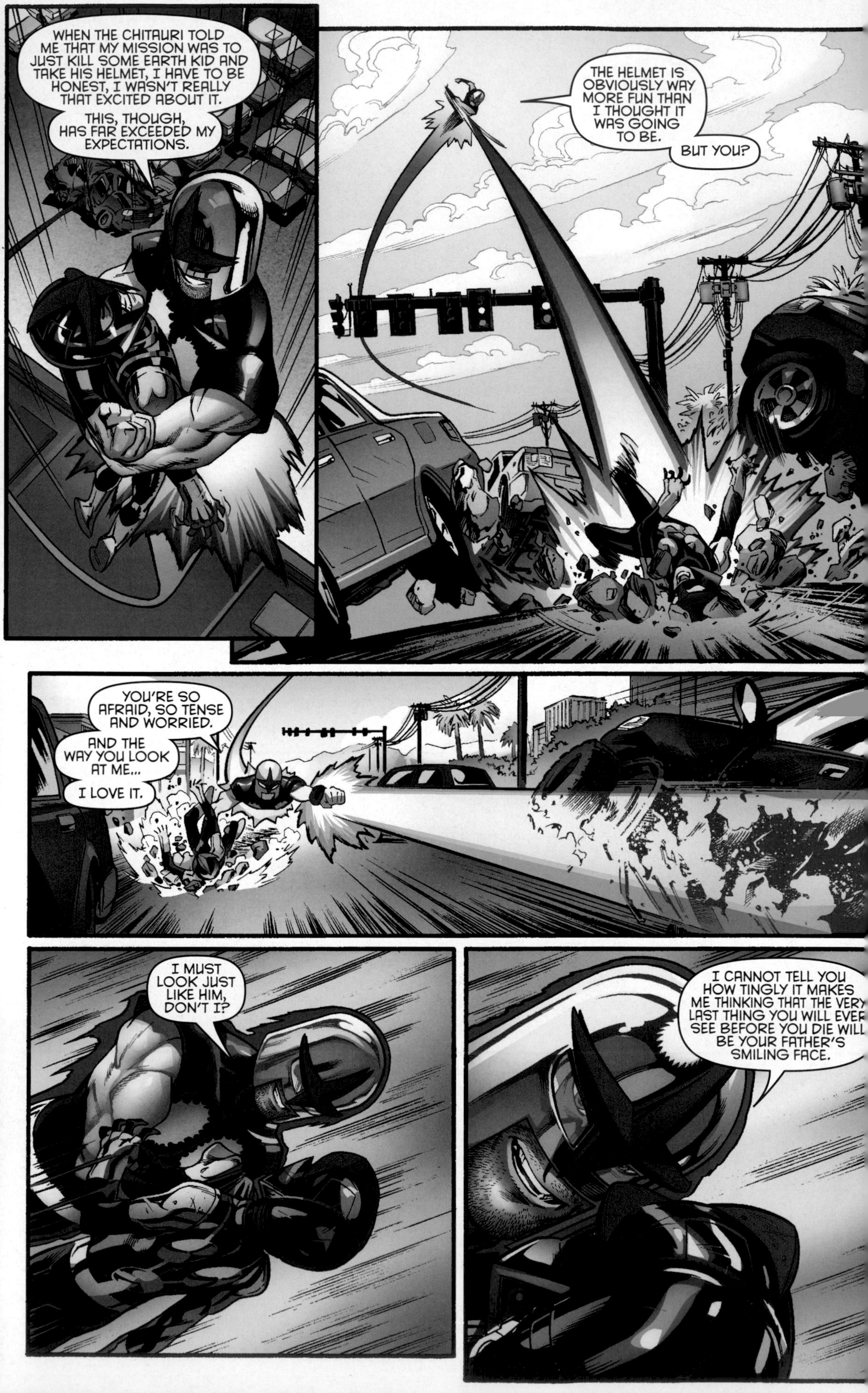
WHEN THE CHITAURI TOLD ME THAT MY MISSION WAS TO JUST KILL SOME EARTH KID AND TAKE HIS HELMET, I HAVE TO BE HONEST, I WASN'T REALLY THAT EXCITED ABOUT IT.
THIS, THOUGH, HAS FAR EXCEEDED MY EXPECTATIONS.
THE HELMET IS OBVIOUSLY WAY MORE FUN THAN I THOUGHT IT WAS GOING TO BE.
BUT YOU?
YOU'RE SO AFRAID, SO TENSE AND WORRIED.
AND THE WAY YOU LOOK AT ME...
I LOVE IT.
I MUST LOOK JUST LIKE HIM, DON'T I?
I CANNOT TELL YOU HOW TINGLY IT MAKES ME THINKING THAT THE VERY LAST THING YOU WILL EVER SEE BEFORE YOU DIE WILL BE YOUR FATHER'S SMILING FACE.

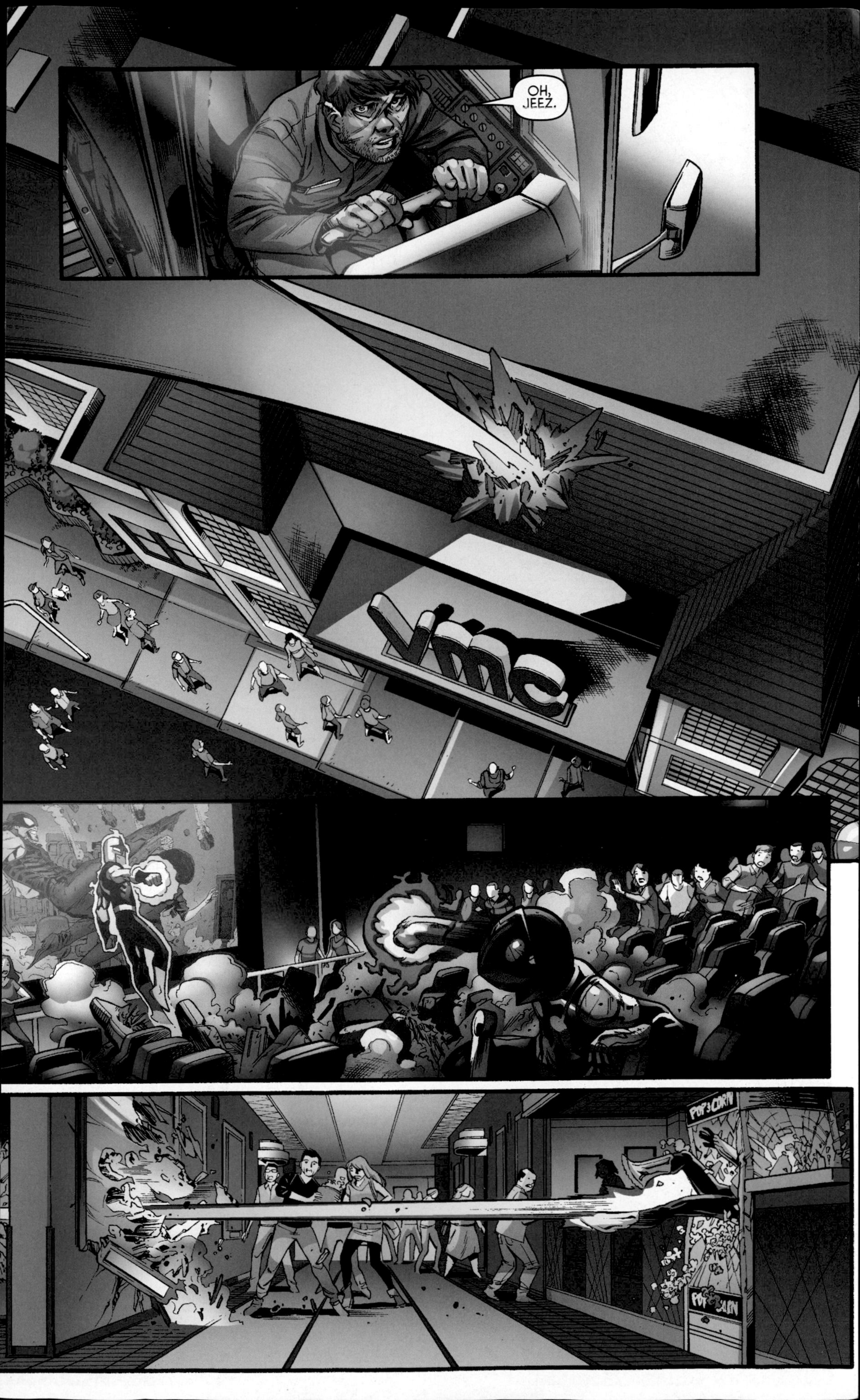

OH, JEEZ.
VMC
POP'S CORN
POP & CORN

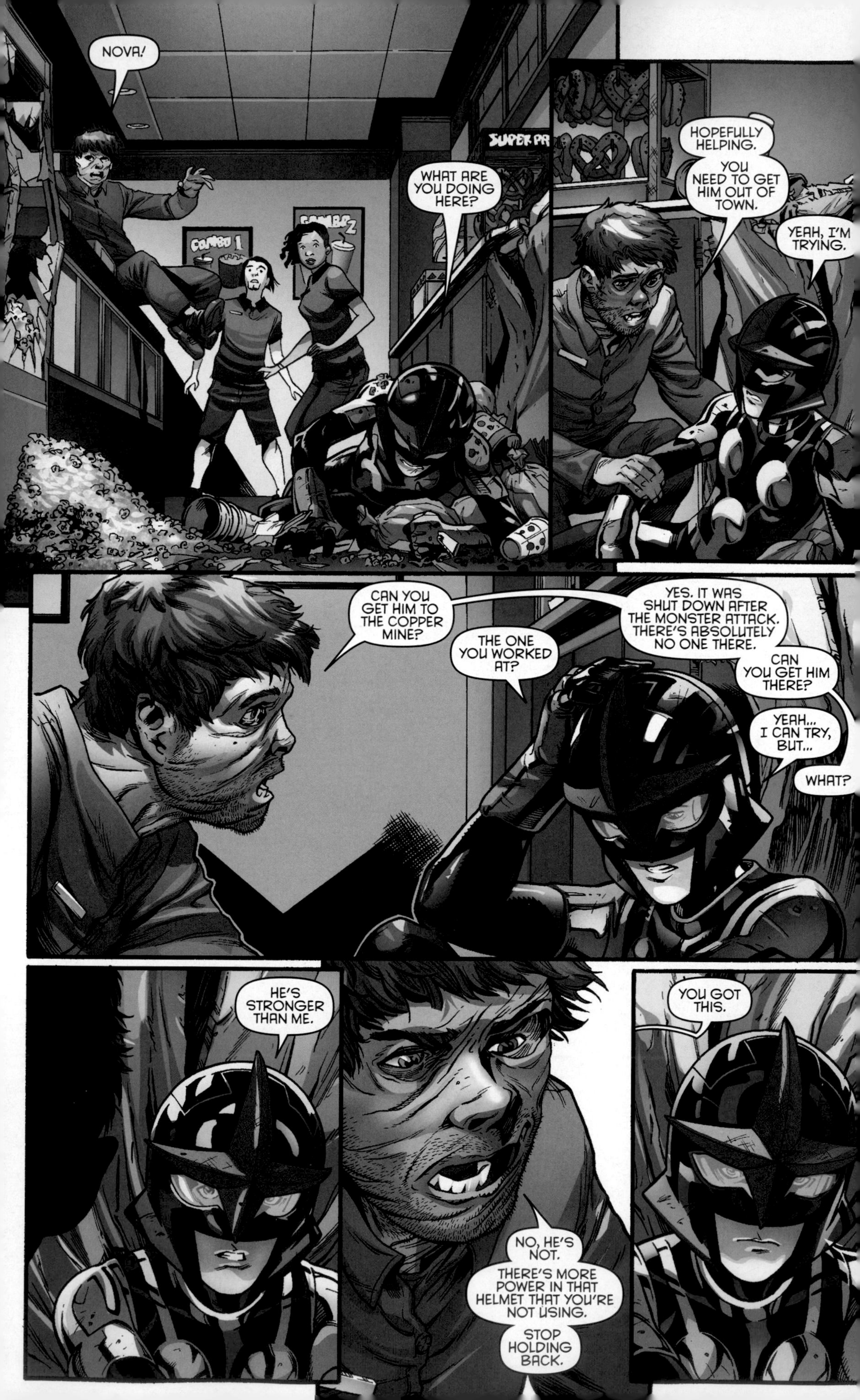
NOVA!
WHAT ARE YOU DOING HERE?
HOPEFULLY HELPING.
YOU NEED TO GET HIM OUT OF TOWN.
YEAH, I'M TRYING.
CAN YOU GET HIM TO THE COPPER MINE?
THE ONE YOU WORKED AT?
YES. IT WAS SHUT DOWN AFTER THE MONSTER ATTACK. THERE'S ABSOLUTELY NO ONE THERE.
CAN YOU GET HIM THERE?
YEAH... I CAN TRY, BUT...
WHAT?
HE'S STRONGER THAN ME.
NO, HE'S NOT.
THERE'S MORE POWER IN THAT HELMET THAT YOU'RE NOT USING.
STOP HOLDING BACK.
YOU GOT THIS.

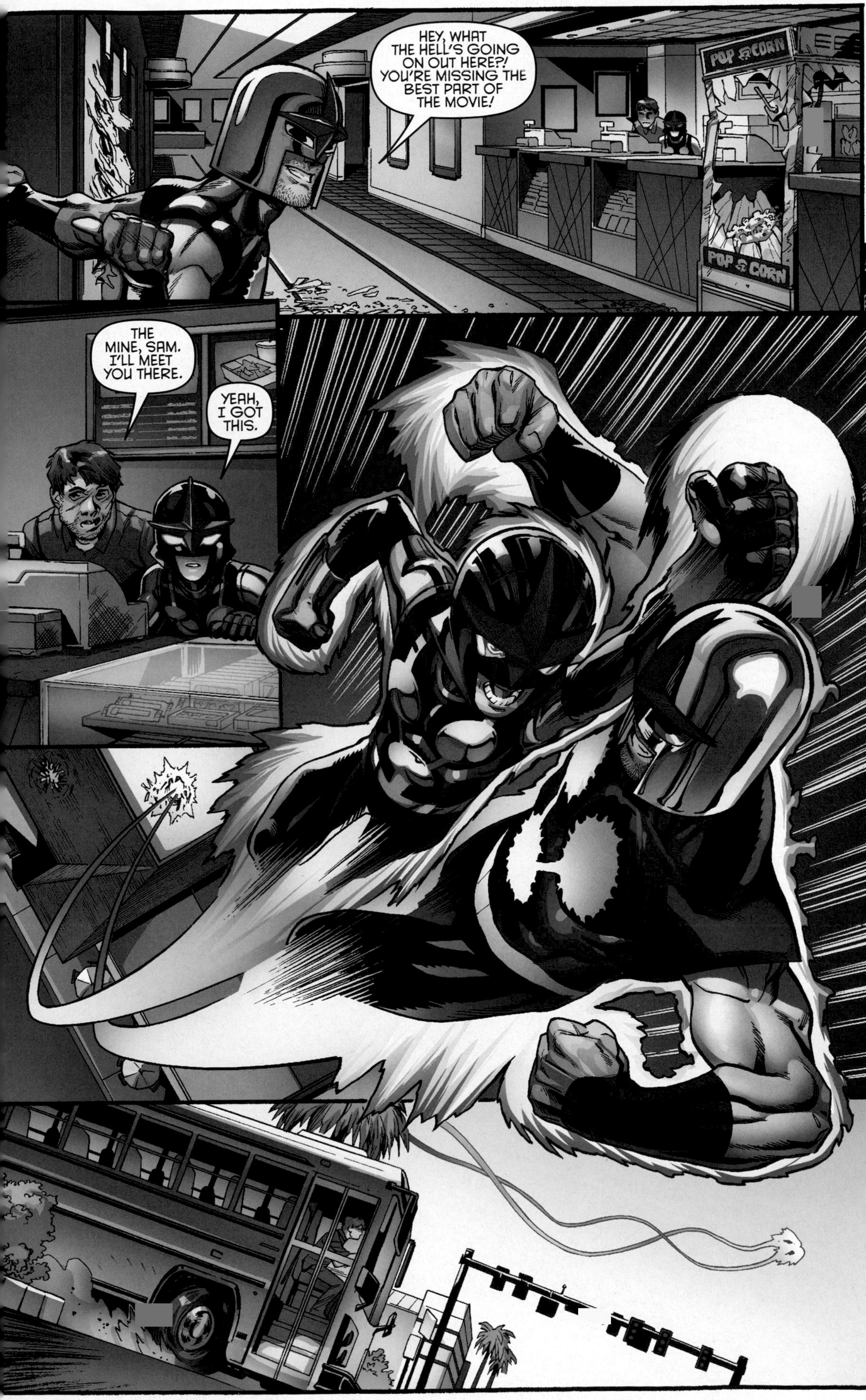
HEY, WHAT THE HELL'S GOING ON OUT HERE?! YOU'RE MISSING THE BEST PART OF THE MOVIE!
POP CORN
THE MINE, SAM. I'LL MEET YOU THERE.
YEAH, I GOT THIS.
POP CORN

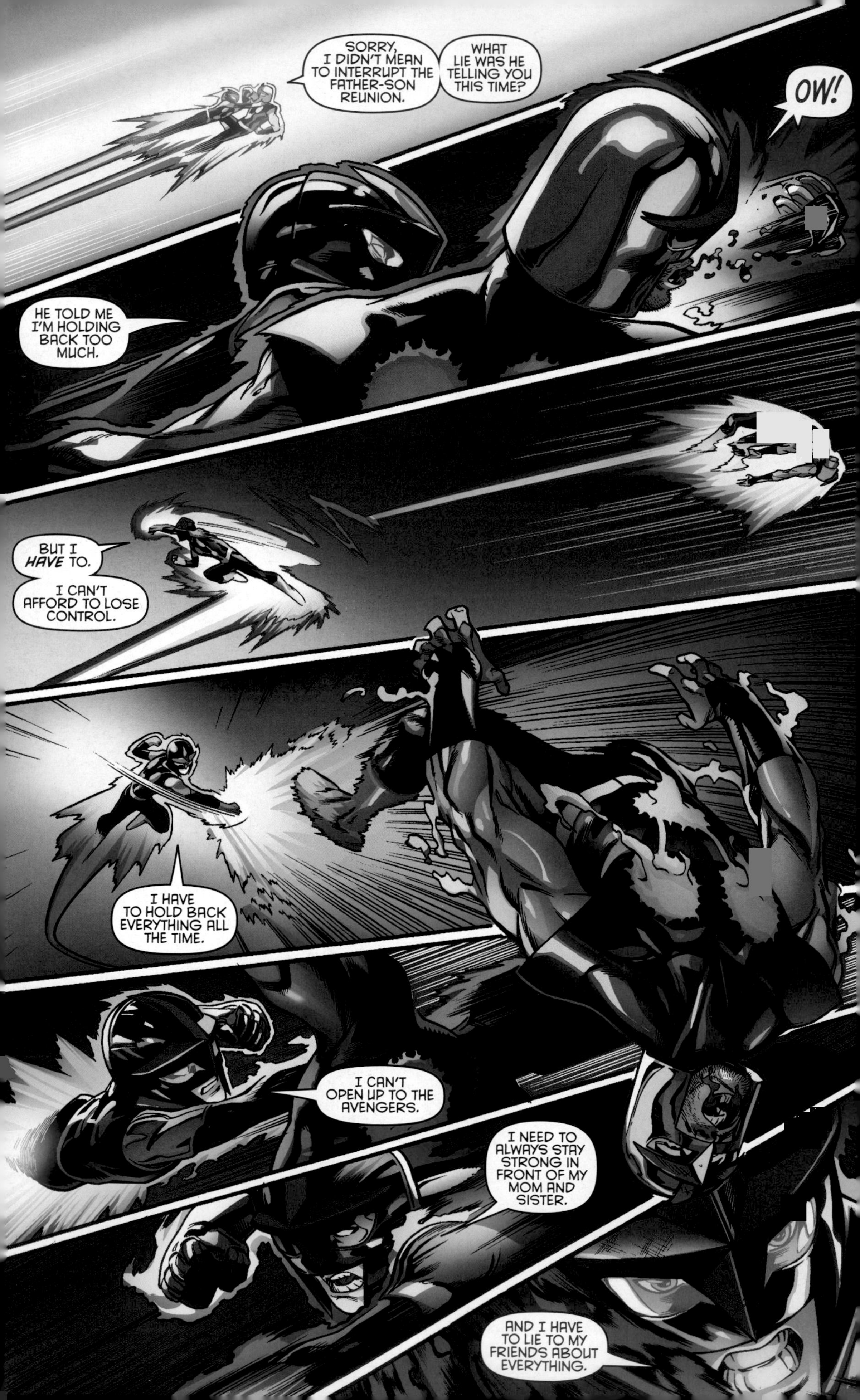
SORRY, I DIDN'T MEAN TO INTERRUPT THE FATHER-SON REUNION.
WHAT LIE WAS HE TELLING YOU THIS TIME?
OW!
HE TOLD ME I'M HOLDING BACK TOO MUCH.
BUT I *HAVE* TO.
I CAN'T AFFORD TO LOSE CONTROL.
I HAVE TO HOLD BACK EVERYTHING ALL THE TIME.
I CAN'T OPEN UP TO THE AVENGERS.
I NEED TO ALWAYS STAY STRONG IN FRONT OF MY MOM AND SISTER.
AND I HAVE TO LIE TO MY FRIENDS ABOUT EVERYTHING.

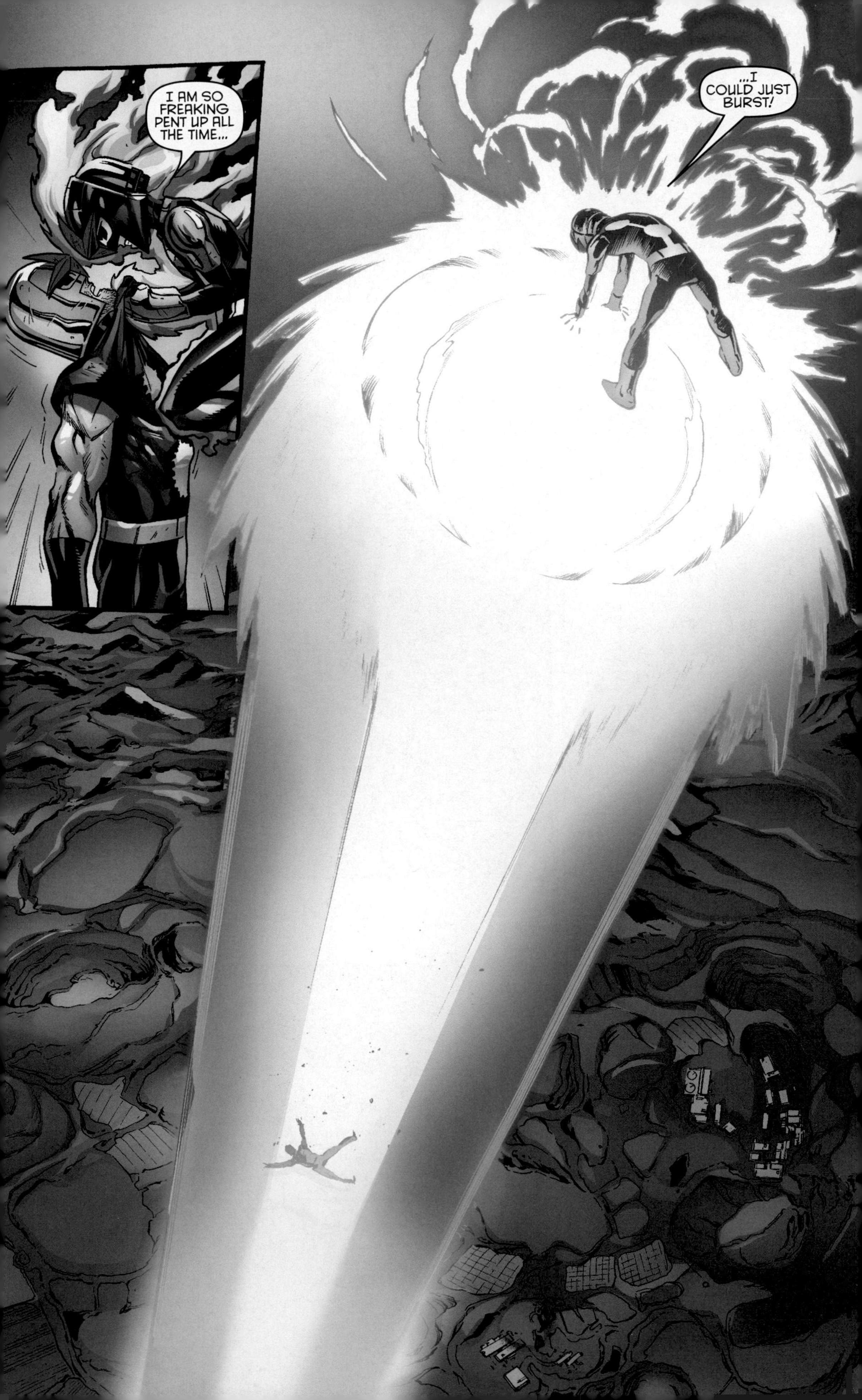
I AM SO FREAKING PENT UP ALL THE TIME...
...I COULD JUST BURST!

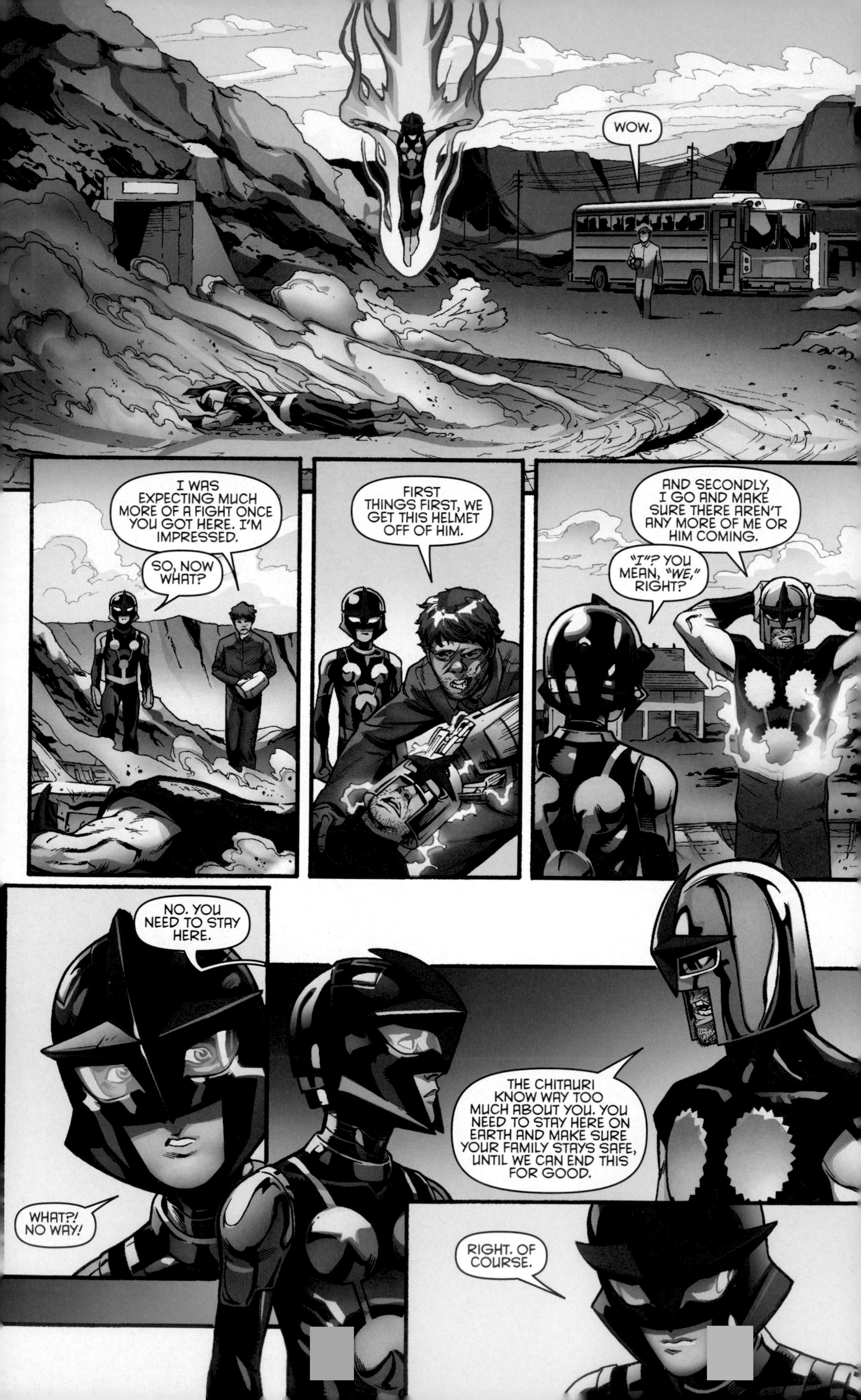
WOW.
I WAS EXPECTING MUCH MORE OF A FIGHT ONCE YOU GOT HERE. I'M IMPRESSED.
SO, NOW WHAT?
FIRST THINGS FIRST, WE GET THIS HELMET OFF OF HIM.
AND SECONDLY, I GO AND MAKE SURE THERE AREN'T ANY MORE OF ME OR HIM COMING.
"I"? YOU MEAN, "WE," RIGHT?
NO. YOU NEED TO STAY HERE.
WHAT?! NO WAY!
THE CHITAURI KNOW WAY TOO MUCH ABOUT YOU. YOU NEED TO STAY HERE ON EARTH AND MAKE SURE YOUR FAMILY STAYS SAFE, UNTIL WE CAN END THIS FOR GOOD.
RIGHT. OF COURSE.

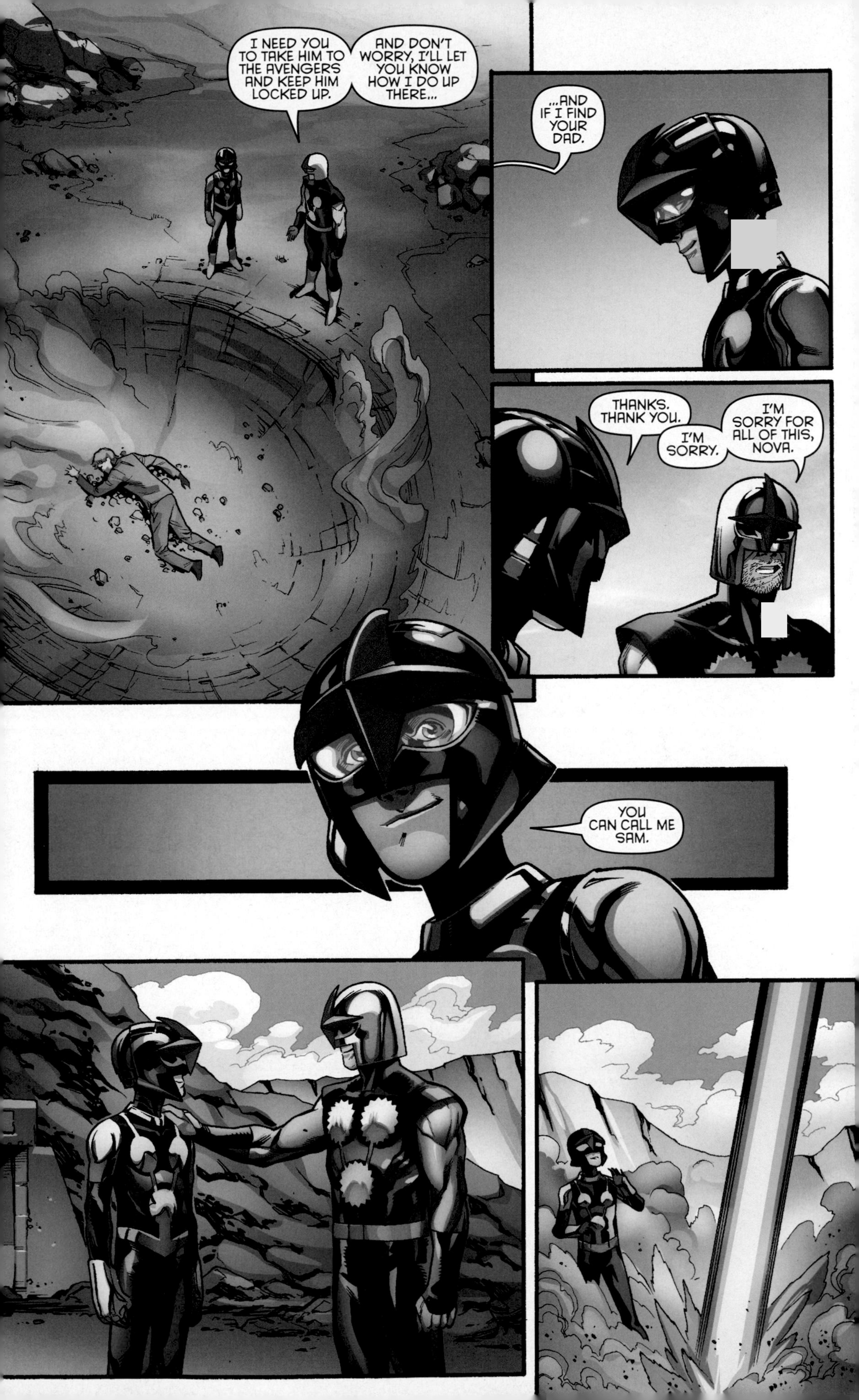
I NEED YOU TO TAKE HIM TO THE AVENGERS AND KEEP HIM LOCKED UP.
AND DON'T WORRY, I'LL LET YOU KNOW HOW I DO UP THERE...
...AND IF I FIND YOUR DAD.
THANKS. THANK YOU.
I'M SORRY.
I'M SORRY FOR ALL OF THIS, NOVA.
YOU CAN CALL ME SAM.

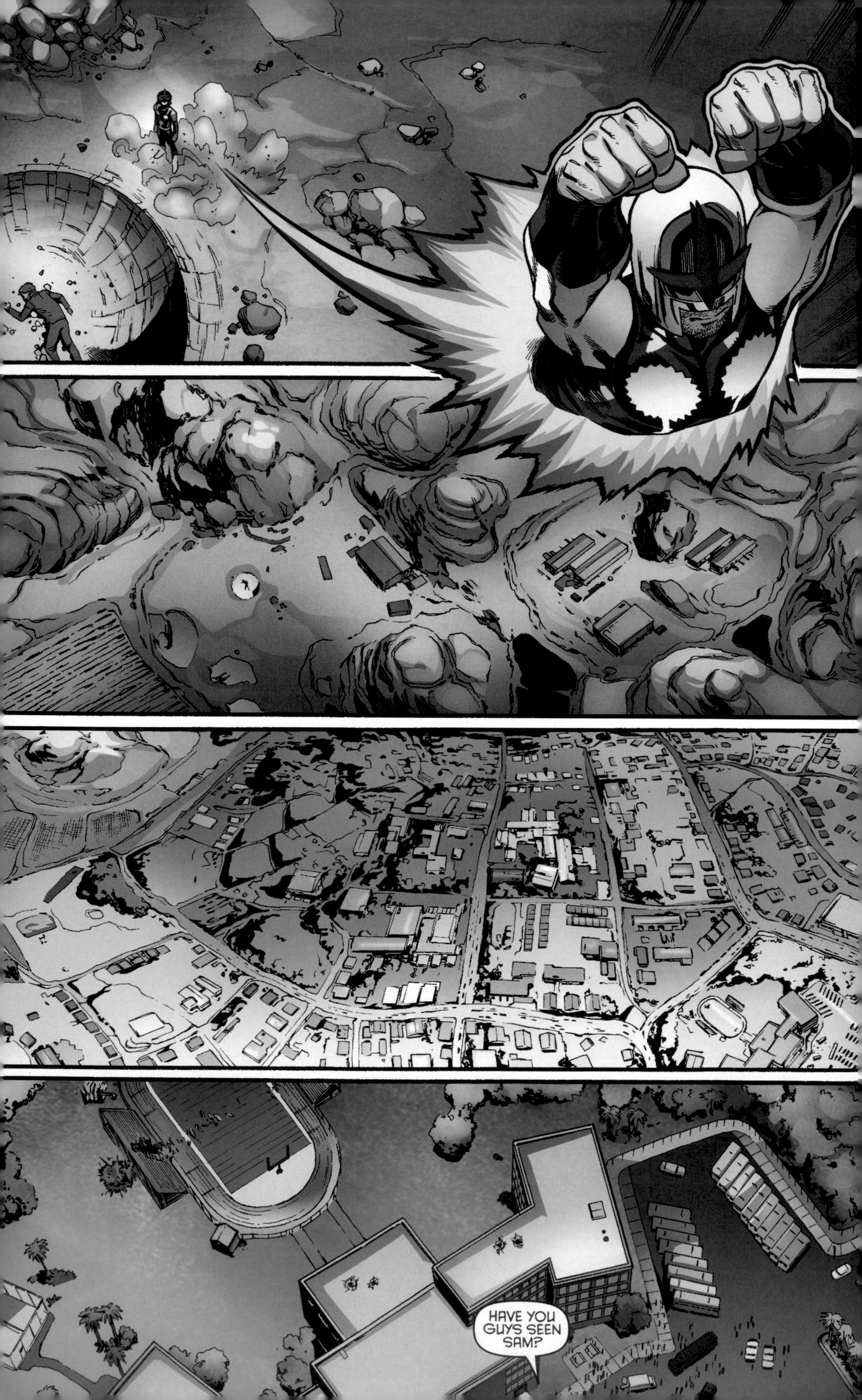
HAVE YOU
GUYS SEEN
SAM?

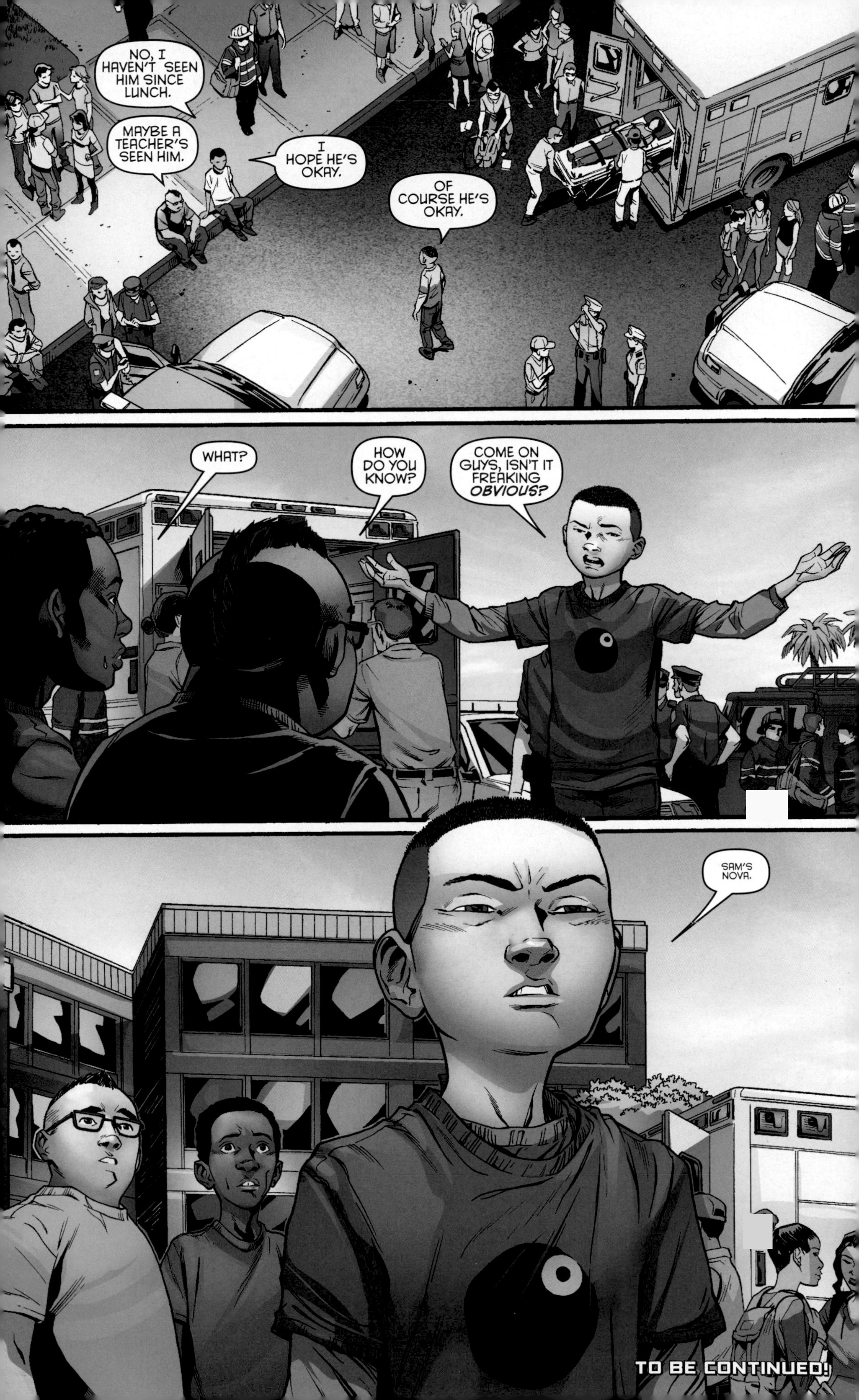
NO, I HAVEN'T SEEN HIM SINCE LUNCH.
MAYBE A TEACHER'S SEEN HIM.
I HOPE HE'S OKAY.
OF COURSE HE'S OKAY.
WHAT?
HOW DO YOU KNOW?
COME ON GUYS, ISN'T IT FREAKING *OBVIOUS?*
SAM'S NOVA.
TO BE CONTINUED!

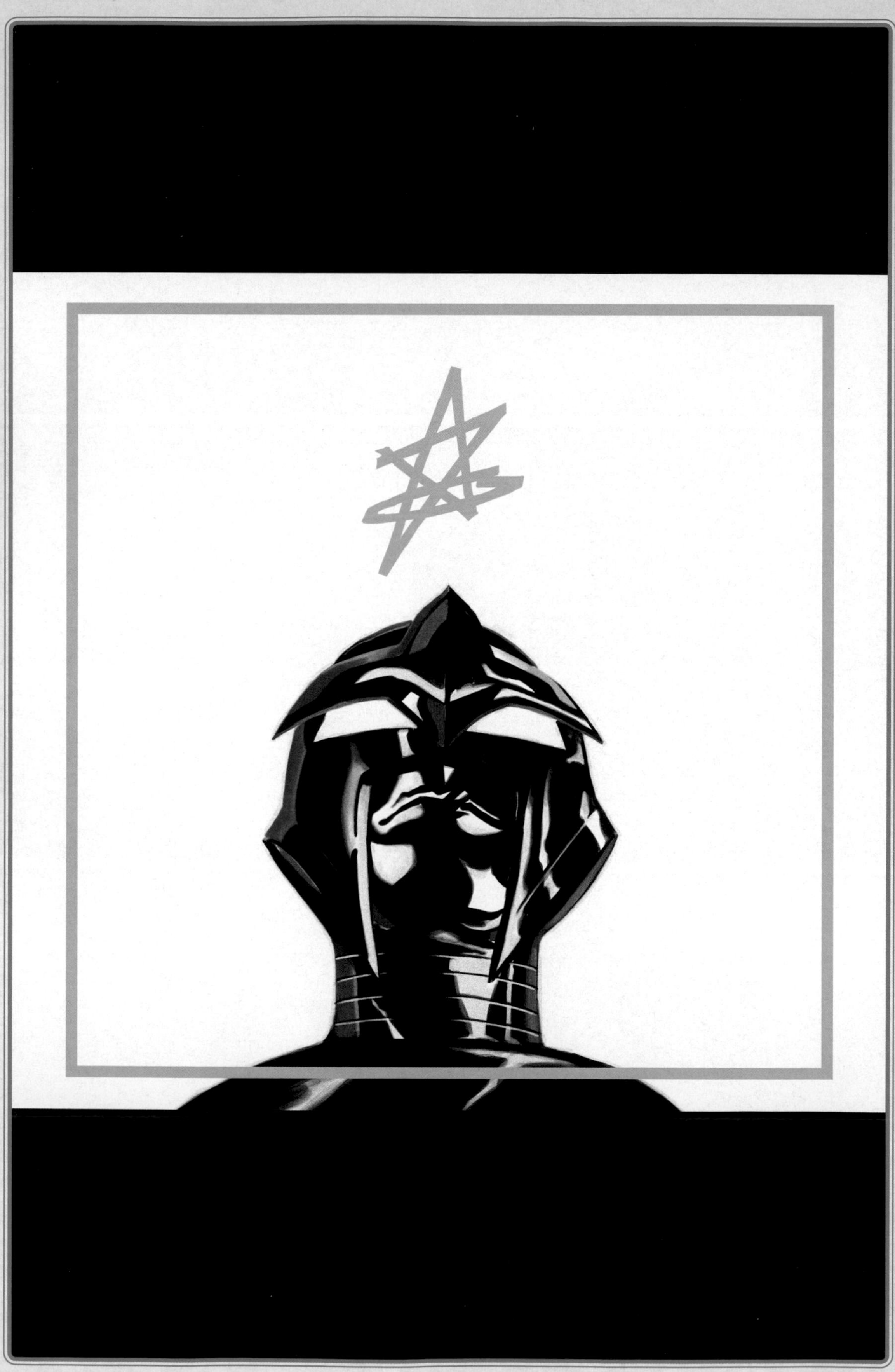

ERIC CANETE
No. 1 HIP-HOP VARIANT

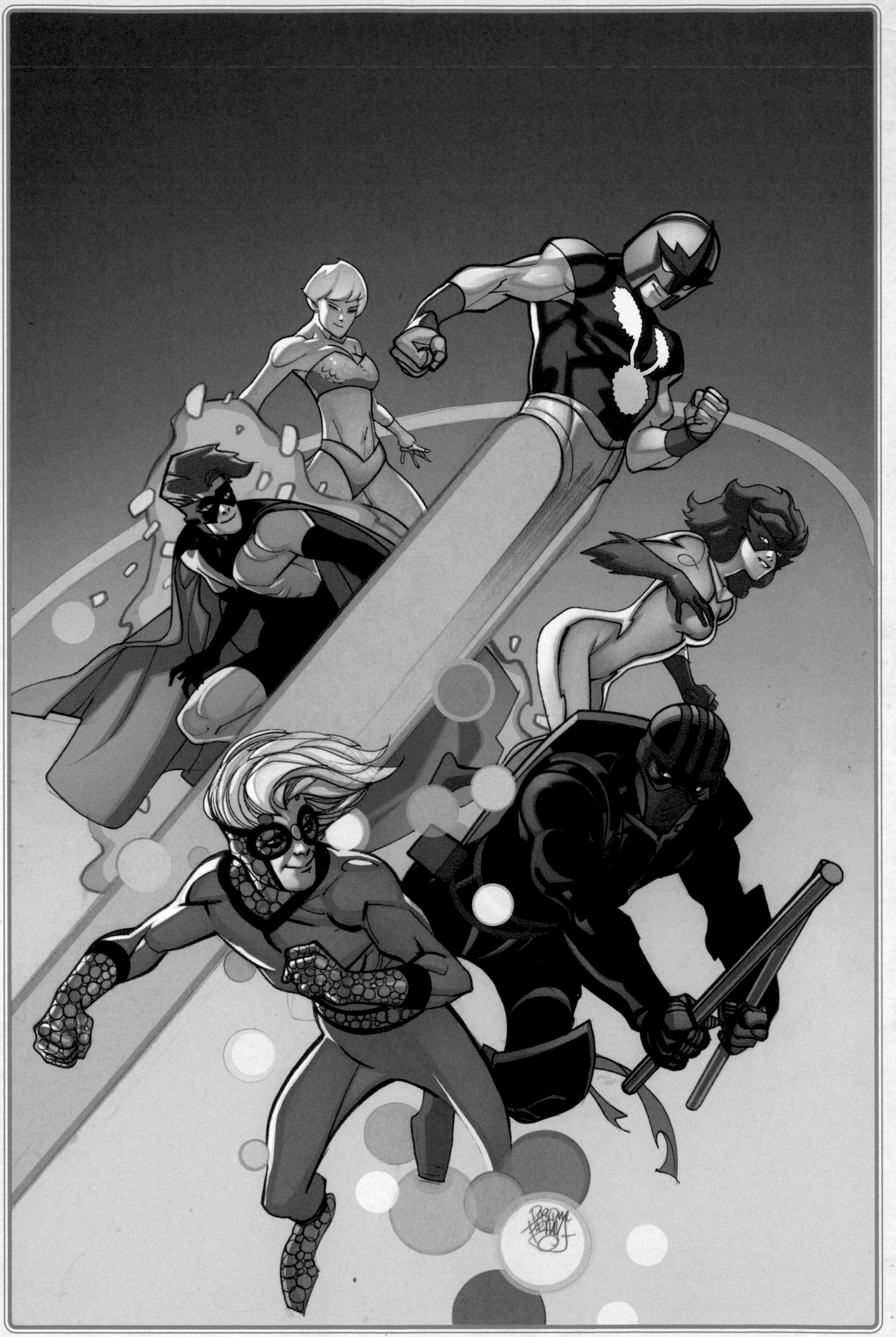

PASQUAL FERRY
No. 2 MARVEL '92 VARIANT

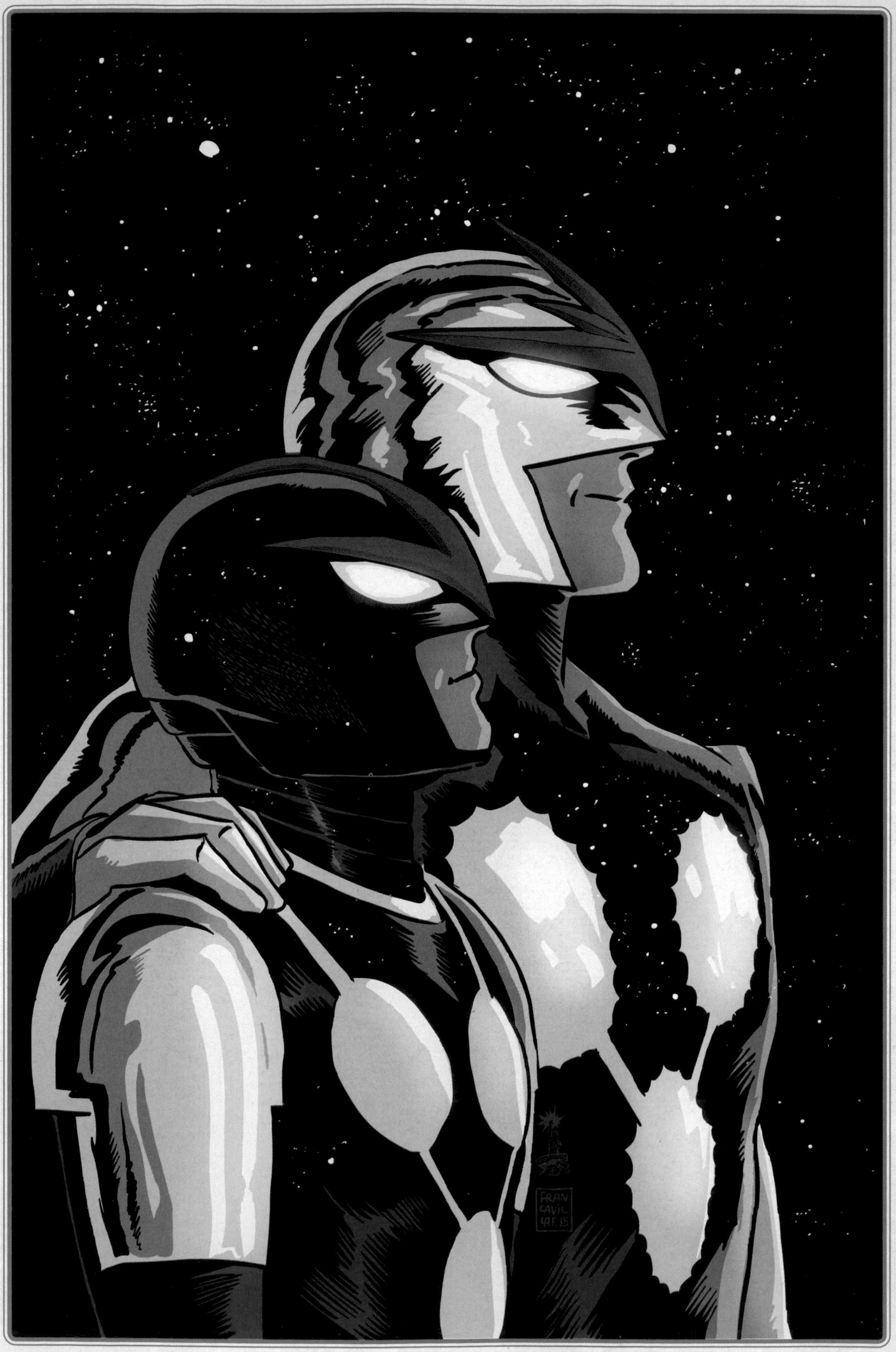

FRANCESCO FRANCAVILLA
No. 2 VARIANT

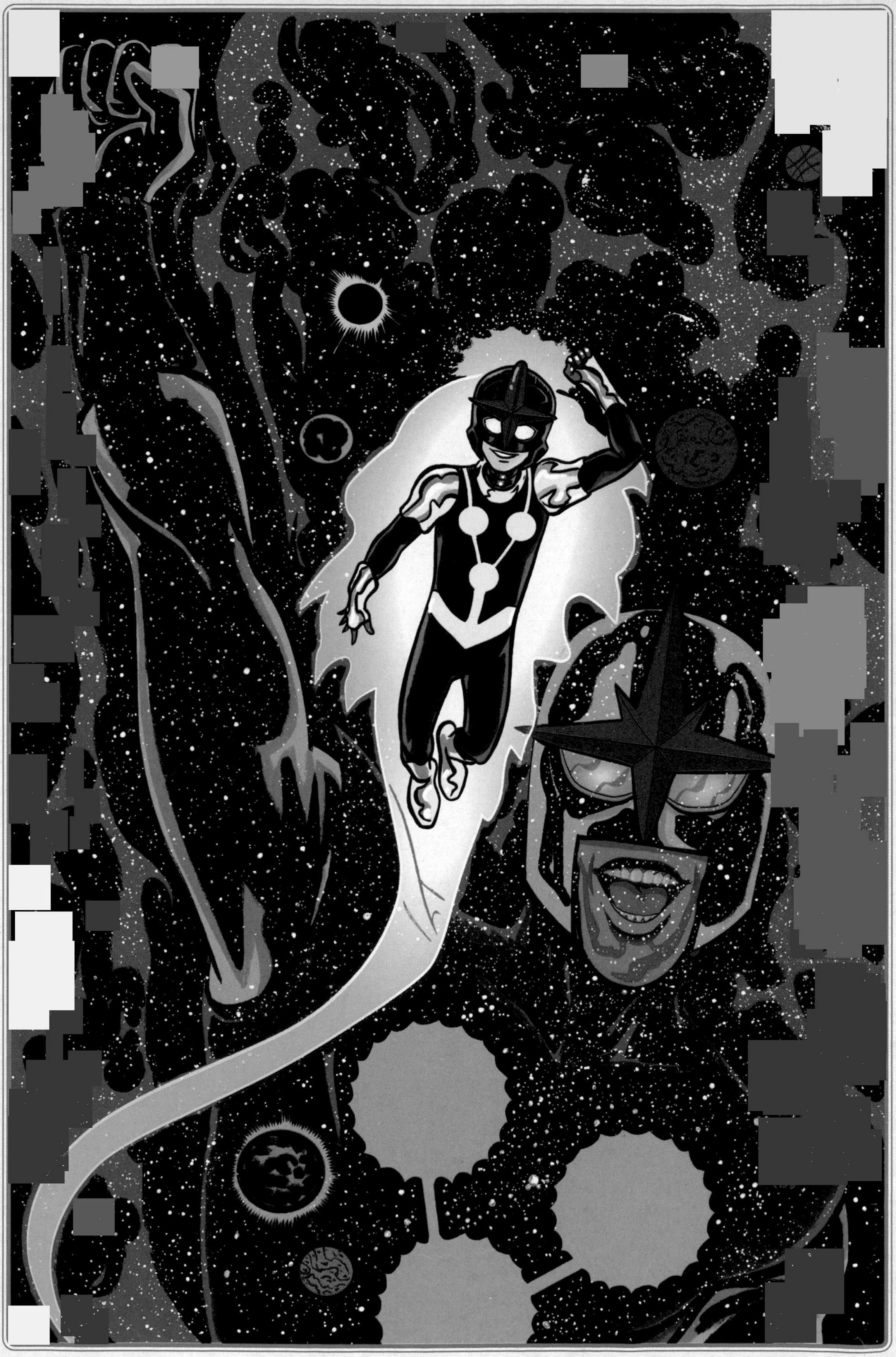

MICHAEL ALLRED & LAURA ALLRED

No. 3 VARIANT

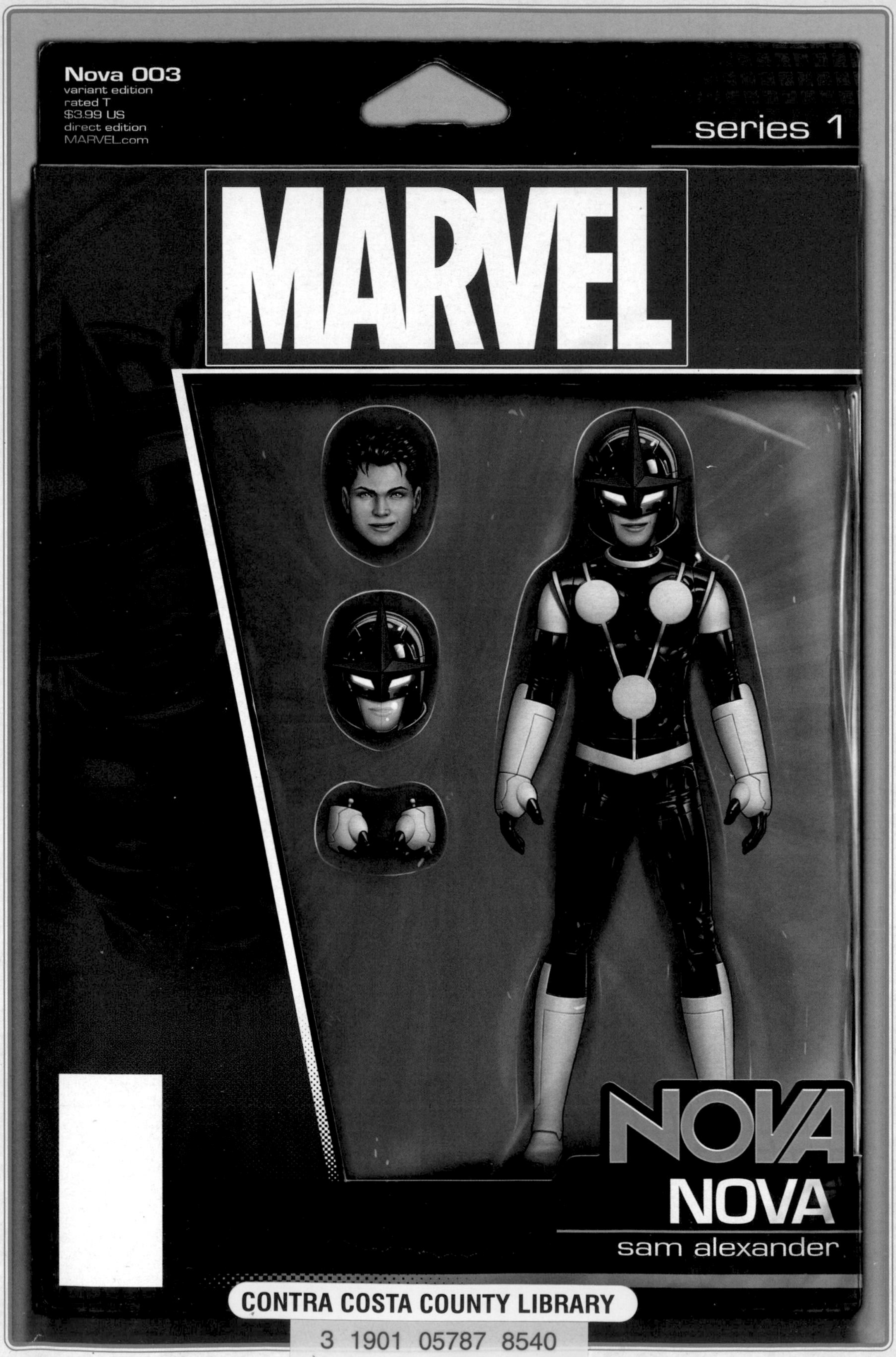
Nova 003
variant edition
rated T
$3.99 US
direct edition
MARVEL.com
series 1
MARVEL
NOVA
NOVA
sam alexander

JOHN TYLER CHRISTOPHER
No. 3 ACTION FIGURE VARIANT